What some are saying...

In a time when the knowledge of Scripture ___ the world, we desperately need a book like this to encourage people to re-engage with God's Word. Russ Resnik has done a commendable job of joining scholarly insights with warm-hearted application. His extensive interaction with rabbinic sources may be challenging to some but will open up a whole new world to those interested in the Jewish roots of the Messianic faith.

—David Brickner
Executive Director, Jews for Jesus

This new book offers an illuminating pathway through the riches of the Jewish heritage.

—Dan Cohn-Sherbock, Ph.D
Reform Rabbi and Professor of Judaism, University of Wales

Russ Resnik has done it again. His earlier work on the Five Books of Moses, *Gateways to Torah*, showed us the Law as the blessing it is, not the burden many people see it as. In this work, he has taken another step, showing us more clearly our role with God in bringing his Creation to it's completion. You will be encouraged reading that we all have a concrete, daily part to play in God's Master plan for our world.

—John Fischer, Ph.D., Th.D.
Executive Director, Menorah Ministries
Academic Vice President, St. Petersburg Theological Seminary
Rabbi, Congregation Ohr Chadash
Palm Harbor, Fla.

Once, again, Russ Resnik has used his understanding of Scripture and rabbinic interpretation to uncover buried treasure in the Parashot. I appreciate both the spiritual depth and everyday practicality of Rabbi Resnik's observations. He weaves a wonderful story through the weekly portions that are

Messiah-centered and will strengthen and inspire all who read and meditate on his comments. I highly recommend Creation to Completion to anyone who loves the Lord and appreciates the Hebrew Scriptures.

—Mitch Glaser, Th.D.
Executive Director, Chosen People Ministries

This new book of reflections applies Torah with a depth of understanding from a Yeshua-centered perspective. It is a book that provides elevated inspiration and excellent information.

—Daniel Juster, Th.D.
Executive Director, Tikkun Ministries

Rabbi Russell Resnik has written a warm, devotional commentary that will help you understand and apply the Law of Moses to your life in a practical way."

—Coach Bill McCartney
Founder and Chairman, Road to Jerusalem
Founder and former President, Promise Keepers

Resnik seriously engages the *parashot-hashavua*, the weekly synagogue portions. He speaks from heart to heart but also from mind to mind and spirit to spirit. He molds Jewish, Christian and academic into a creative and stimulating interpretation that moves seamlessly from analytical to devotional. I recommend this important Messianic Jewish book.

—David H. Stern, Ph.D.
Translator of the Complete Jewish Bible and
the Jewish New Testament
Author of Restoring the Jewishness of
the Gospel and Messianic Jewish Manifesto

CREATION TO COMPLETION

CREATION TO COMPLETION

A Guide to Life's Journey
from
The Five Books of Moses

Rabbi Russell Resnik
With a Foreword by Coach Bill McCartney

Lederer Books
a division of
Messianic Jewish Publishers
Clarksville, Maryland

Cover Design by
John Huhn, Design Point, Inc.

11 10 09 08 07 06   6 5 4 3 2 1

ISBN-13: 978-1-880226-32-2
ISBN 10: 1-880226-32-4

Library of Congress Control Number: 2006927984
Printed in the United States of America

Lederer Books
A division of
Messianic Jewish Publishers
P.O. Box 615
Clarksville, Maryland 21029

Distributed by
Messianic Jewish Resources International
Order line: (800) 410-7367
E-mail: lederer@messianicjewish.net
Website: www.messianicjewish.net

To Jane

עזר כנגדו

Gift of God—A sustainer beside me
Genesis 2:18[1]

Other Books by Author

*Gateways to Torah: Joining the Ancient
Conversation on the Weekly Portion*

Lederer Books/Messianic Jewish Pub., ©2000

CONTENTS

Foreword xi

Introduction xiii

The Book of Genesis 1
   Creation and It's Goal: B'resheet   3
   He Who Covers the Naked: Noach   7
   Obedience and Beyond: Lekh L'kha   11
   Sacrifice of the Son: Vayera   15
   Sarah's Life: Hayyei-Sarah   18
   The Living Water: Tol'dot   22
   At Rachel's Well: Vayetze   25
   Turned Into Another Man: Vayishlach   29
   Contest for Continuity: Vayehsev   33
   Election and Envy: Mikketz   36
   And He Drew Near…: Vayigash   40
   A Coffin in Egypt: Vayechi   44

The Book of Exodus 49
   God Rediscovered: Shemot   52
   You Gotta Serve Somebody: Va'era   56
   The Heart of Pharaoh: Bo   60
   Splitting the Sea: B'shallach   64
   Huppah of Glory: Yitro   67
   Your Enemy's Donkey: Mishpatim   71
   Creation and Rest: T'rumah   74
   Stones of Remembrance: Tetzaveh   78
   The Test of Intercession: Ki Tissa   81
   Bezalel: VaYakhel   84
   The Cloud Fills the Tabernacle: P'kudei   87

The Book of Leviticus 90
   Fearsome Nearness: Vayikra   93
   Continual Worship: Tsav   96
   Misrepresenting God: Sh'mini   99

Eighth Day, First Day: Tazria   103
The Leper Priest: M'tzora   106
To Azazel…And Back: Acharei Mot   110
Justice and Beyond: K'doshim   114
Times of Encounter: Emor   118
Jubilee is Coming: B'har   121
Possession and Dispossession: B'chukkotai   124

The Book of Numbers 129
Wilderness of Revelation: B'midbar   133
A Merciful Curse: Naso   136
Guide and Glory-Cloud: B'a'alotkha   139
Clothes Make the Man: Shlach L'kha   143
Land of Milk and Honey: Korach   146
Water From the Rock: Hukkat   149
The Meek and The Mighty: Balak   153
A Word for the Wise: Pinchas   157
Pathway to Promise: Mattot   160
Courage is Contagious: Masa'ei   163

The Book of Deuteronomy 167
God Carries Israel: D'varim   171
The Great Commandment: Va'etchanan   175
The Reward of Righteousness: 'Ekev   179
The Gods of Others: Re'eh   183
The Prophet Like Moses: Shof'tim   186
Remember Amalek: Ki Tetse   190
All Things New: Ki Tavo   194
Two Returnees: Nitzavim   198
The Hidden God: Vayelekh   203
Torah and Spirit: Ha'azinu   206
"This is the Blessing…": V'zot HaBrachah   210

Epilogue 213
Notes 215
Glossary 221
Bibliography 227
Other Related Books 231

FOREWORD

If ever there has been a time for Christians to understand their Jewish roots, it's now. For centuries, anti-Law teaching has influenced the Church to cut itself off from its rich roots, found in the Old Testament. Yet, these were the same Scriptures that Paul encouraged Timothy to live by (2 Timothy 3:16). Fortunately, though, the Messianic Jewish movement has come to our rescue. This movement of God is helping us reconnect with our roots.

I have had the privilege of working with many of the leaders in this revival of the Jewish people. While maintaining their identity and practice as Jews, they are dedicated to following Yeshua (the Hebrew name for Jesus). And, they have generously shared what they know with interested Christians, enriching our lives.

Even before leaving Promise Keepers, I had a heart to help the Messianic Jews regain their initial influence in the Body. After all, all the first followers of the Messiah were Jews, and it was *those* chosen people who brought the Gospel to us Gentiles. They were ordained as a people to bring the whole Truth to the entire world. That's the main reason Dr. Raleigh Washington and I began a new organization, The Road to Jerusalem. We've worked with many Messianic Jews who have been a tremendous blessing to us.

Now, it's my privilege to commend this most needed book by my friend, Russ Resnik. Russ is the executive director of the Union of Messianic Jewish Congregations, one of the two largest groups of such congregations in the world. With Messianic congregations in nearly every state of the U.S., as well as many nations outside America, Russ serves believers around the world, both Jewish and Gentile. He's been a great encouragement to me, personally, too. In a sense, he's been my rabbi.

Here, in *Creation to Completion: A Guide to Life's Journey from the Five Books of Moses*, Rabbi Resnik, in true rabbinic fashion, gently and warmly instructs people about each of the Torah portions studied in synagogues around the world each week. Digging into the original meaning of each section, our rabbi interacts with other commentators, many of them also rabbis, to elucidate the word of God to us. Each week's devotional material guides us about living in the world today. Based on the concept that since the Creation, God has wanted people to "partner" with him to bring the world to its completion, I was motivated to take an even more active role in this process.

I'm sure that you will find each devotional commentary to be fascinating, enjoyable, and valuable as you journey through life.

—COACH BILL MCCARTNEY

Founder and Chairman, The Road to Jerusalem
Founder and former President, Promise Keepers

INTRODUCTION

Everyone loves a story, and some stories can change your life. Stories have the power to touch us deeply when mere information or admonition leaves us cold. From generation to generation, Jewish families have repeated the story of the Exodus from Egypt, and Christian families have cherished the stories of the birth and resurrection of Jesus.

Many readers, however, approach the Bible without recognizing the big story that it tells. Rather, they see a collection of unrelated, smaller stories tossed together with laws, genealogies, and theological instructions. In this book, we will explore the earliest portion of the Bible—the Five Books of Moses, or *Torah*, as it is known in Judaism—as one continuous and compelling story. Even more important, we will read it as a story that involves you, the reader, in a transforming way.

What is this story about, and how does it include readers born centuries after it was written down? One clue is in the calendar that the Lord gave to Israel.

> Three times you shall keep a feast to Me in the year: You shall keep the Feast of Unleavened Bread (you shall eat unleavened bread seven days, as I commanded you, at the time appointed in the month of Abib, for in it you came out of Egypt; none shall appear before Me empty); and the Feast of Harvest, the firstfruits of your labors which you have sown in the field; and the Feast of Ingathering at the end of the year, when you have gathered in the fruit of your labors from the field. Three times in the year all your males shall appear before the Lord God. (Exod. 23:14–17)

These three festivals kept by the Jewish people since ancient times hold a universal message for all people in all times. During these festivals, the Israelites were required to make a pilgrimage to the Temple in Jerusalem. Therefore, they are termed in Jewish tradition *shalosh regalim*, the three pilgrim-festivals. Each one is tied to the *agricultural* cycle of the Land of Israel, to the *history* of the people of

Israel, and to the *prophetic* overview of human history, which is fulfilled in Jesus—Yeshua—the Messiah.

Agriculturally, the Feast of Unleavened Bread, celebrated today as Passover, or *Pesach*, occurs in the springtime, when the ewes give birth to lambs, and the early grain harvest begins. The Feast of Harvest, or *Shavuot* (Weeks) comes seven weeks later, at the height of the growing season, when the full grain harvest is underway. The Feast of Ingathering, or *Sukkot* (Tabernacles), exactly six months after Passover, marks the end of summer and the completion of the harvest. It is followed by six dormant months in which there is no pilgrimage, and then the cycle begins again.

This cycle reflects the grand narrative of the entire Bible, which can be summarized in three words—Creation, Revelation, Completion.

Passover is a reminder of Creation. It is the time of renewal after the dormancy of winter. The earth brings forth green herbs and livestock brings forth new life. Historically, it was at this season that Israel was created as representative of a new, redeemed humanity through its deliverance from Egypt. Shavuot arrives when the fullness of nature's vitality and glory is revealed. Likewise, historically, it marks the self-revelation of God at Mount Sinai, when all Israel beheld his glory and he gave the Torah, the foundational document of the revealed Scriptures. Sukkot comes at the "end of the year," when the natural cycle of growth and abundance reaches its conclusion and all is gathered in. This festival parallels the consummation, or more simply, completion of Creation.

Creation-Revelation-Completion provides the grid for understanding the theme of the Five Books of Moses and, hence, of the entire Bible—and of the plan for humanity revealed in it. God creates all things in six days and sees that his Creation is "very good" (Gen. 1:31). But the Creation does not yet reach its completion. Rather, on the sixth day, God tells Adam to "be fruitful and multiply, fill the earth and subdue it" (Gen. 1:28). There is still work to be done. Humankind has a task to fulfill in cooperation with God, a task that will bring Creation to fulfillment. Between Creation and completion is a continuing process of Revelation, unfolding through the lives of the patriarchs, the calling of Israel, the Exodus and giving of Torah on Mount Sinai, the words of the prophets, and most fully in the coming of Yeshua the Messiah.

This entire plan is set in place in Torah. We will see how this theme of Creation to completion is developed throughout the Torah and unifies its stories and teachings.

Yeshua said, "Scripture cannot be broken" (John 10:35). If his Messianic claim required a radical break from Torah and the rest of the *Tanakh*—which Christians call the Old Testament—then it would be questionable at best. But the appearance of a Messiah, who will fulfill the process of Revelation and lead the way into the Consummation of all things, is not just predicted in a few places in the Torah; it is the inescapable climax of the entire narrative. This is the big story.

The Importance of Torah

The story of Creation-Revelation-Completion is fulfilled in Yeshua the Messiah, but it begins in the Torah, the foundational document for all expressions of Judaism. To this day Jewish worshipers carry scrolls of the Torah through the congregation, as described in this contemporary synagogue service:

> Why do they take the Torahs out for a walk? Because everyone is equally entitled to honor the handwritten sacred scrolls by touching them. This is never done directly, but by reaching out with a prayer book or tallis, touching the Torah with it, and then kissing the place where it made contact. In Judaism, belief in God is optional, something you may wrestle with your entire life. But respect for and fascination with the Torah, the first record of men and women's struggles with belief in God, is not optional. And the Torahs themselves are both holy and wholly accessible. There are endless rules about how to dress, undress, unroll and read them, but they are meant to be read and studied, not worshipped. A Torah is meant to be honored as a living presence, not an icon.[2]

Eighteen centuries earlier, the Jewish sages (who certainly did not consider belief in God to be optional!) described the Torah as foundational to all human existence. "The world stands on three things—the Torah, the [Temple] service, and loving acts of kindness."[3] Building upon this conviction, pious Jews for centuries have devoted themselves to the study and application of Torah, including the highly developed body of law that is derived from this highly esteemed document. Indeed, it is hard to imagine Jewish life apart from the active engagement with the text of Torah and its teachings.

Christianity, in contrast, has tended to emphasize the transitional aspect of Torah as "as a custodian until the Messiah came" (Gal. 3:24, CJB). Indeed, Christian rhetoric sometimes portrays law, or Torah, the Hebrew term, in entirely negative terms, as a source of bondage and condemnation. But, of course, this is not the language of Yeshua, who said, "Don't think that I have come to abolish the Torah or the Prophets. I have come not to abolish but to complete. Yes indeed! I tell you that until heaven and earth pass away, not so much as a *yud* or a stroke will pass from the Torah—not until everything that must happen has happened" (Matt. 5:17–18, CJB). Nor is it the language of Paul in Romans 7:12, "So the Torah is holy; that is, the commandment is holy, just and good" (CJB).

If you are already a Bible reader, this book will change the way that you study and understand the Scriptures from Genesis to Revelation. If the Bible has been a closed book to you until now, this book will serve as an introduction. When we read the Torah as a living and relevant document for Christians, as well as Jews, we will gain new insights into the life and ministry of Messiah, and into our own lives as well. But just how are we to go about reading the Torah in this way?

Our Approach to Torah

We will take a canonical approach to the Torah, which means that we accept the text as we have it today as the God-given text. Centuries ago, the great rabbinic sage Maimonides, or Rambam, put forth thirteen principles of the Jewish faith, including this one: "I believe in perfect faith that the whole Torah which is now in our hands is the one given to Moses our teacher, may he ascend in peace" (from the *Siddur*, the traditional Jewish prayer book).

As with most things Jewish, there is a lively discussion on the exact meaning of Rambam's precept, but it clearly defines Torah as canon, a sacred, complete, God-given text. Translator Everett Fox points out that the concept of canon is rooted in Scripture itself, as in Deut. 13:1:

> Everything that I command you,
> that you are to take-care to observe,
> you are not to add to it, you are not to diminish from it!

Fox says that this verse "forms a fitting superscript for the bulk of the laws, and hints that Deuteronomy is a kind of final, closed, 'canonical' dispensation."[4]

Since the text we possess is given by God, it is filled with meaning. Every word and letter has significance that can be mined by the interpreter and applied to the community. Reading the Torah in this way has led to interpretive creativity that has fueled Jewish life for millennia. Such creativity will allow us to remain grounded in the text, and in touch with traditional Jewish readings, even as we discover distinctly New Covenant meanings.

Another great Jewish sage, Nachmanides, or Ramban, writes, "Whatever has happened to the patriarchs is a sign to the children."[5] He sees the sacred text as packed with God-given meaning that reverent and informed readers must discover. Nothing is accidental or superfluous; every deed of our forefathers has unlimited significance. Hence, Yeshua-believers may read the story of Abraham's near-sacrifice of Isaac as a sign of the death and resurrection of the Son of God, or the story of Joseph and his brothers as a sign of the rejected son who becomes deliverer of the nations, as well as Israel.

Such readings are creative, but they depend directly on the authority of the very words of the text itself. In this book, we will see how the text of Torah itself carries us beyond traditional Jewish readings, as much as we respect them, to see our messianic hope in Yeshua.

Another implication of a canonical approach is that the place of a given text within the larger canon contributes to its meaning.

Through its long history of honoring Torah, the synagogue has developed the tradition of reading through the entire Five Books of Moses every year, or in three years, in weekly installments. Because of the complexity of the Hebrew calendar, the Torah is divided into 54 units, each called a *parashah*. Each parashah has a title, usually based on one of the first words in that section. Thus the first is entitled *B'resheet*, "In the beginning," from the first word in Genesis. Just as readers today generally refer to the chapter and verse of a text, in Jewish tradition we often refer to the name of the parashah in discussing Scripture.

A canonical approach sees each parashah and book as building on what came before, and interprets accordingly. Furthermore, it sees the Torah as foundational for the rest of the canon of Scripture. We fully accept the B'rit Hadashah, commonly called the New Testament, as part of the Word of God. Still, we will not read the Torah through the lens of the B'rit Hadashah, but as far as we are able, on its own terms. We will not use the term "Old Testament," because we believe the Hebrew Scriptures remain living and powerful today, just as they were described long ago in the Letter to the Hebrews (4:12). Rather, we will refer to these Scriptures by their Jewish name, the *Tanakh*, an acronym for the Hebrew words Torah, *Neviim* (Prophets), and *Ketubim* (Holy Writings). We read all Scripture from the perspective of Torah, and we seek to understand Torah in light of the revelation of Yeshua as Lord and Messiah.

Narrative as the vehicle of theology

We accept the extensive narrative portions of the Torah, and the rest of the Bible, as fully part of the Word of God, able to reveal profound theological and moral truth. This view is in contrast with a modern, Western approach that often favors abstract truth over concrete facts, and thus tends to favor the letters of the B'rit Hadashah and read the rest of the Scriptures through their lens. But the Torah employs narrative to convey truth. It retells and expands the story of Creation to completion as the way of advancing its theology. Theological meaning and ethical application often arise out of the context of the unfolding story. We will pay attention to such development and let the story be our teacher.

Interaction with Jewish sources

Since the synagogue community has been reading through the Torah portions every year for millennia, it has developed a vast and fruitful interpretive tradition. Unlike some schools of interpretation, Jewish commentators do not necessarily seek the one true meaning, or even the best interpretation, of a given text. Rather, Jewish scholars speak of several levels of meaning, each one capable of teaching us inspiring truths.

One formulation of this multi-faceted approach is the acronym *pardes*, which means "garden" in Hebrew. Pardes stands for four layers of understanding:

P. *P'shat*—the plain sense. Even though Jewish interpretations are creative and can be rather imaginative, they generally respect the plain and simple meaning of the text as the starting point. The medieval commentators, some of whom we've already mentioned and whose names will appear regularly throughout this book, were the first to insist upon an understanding of p'shat as the beginning point. And they applied a sophisticated and insightful understanding of Hebrew grammar and syntax to unfold the p'shat meaning.

R. *Remez*—a hint within the text itself. Since every word and letter is given by divine inspiration, even a single letter can be a key to profound meaning. For example, in Genesis 2:7 we read, "And the Lord God formed man . . ." The Hebrew for "and he formed" is וייצר or *vayyetzer*, which is spelled with two *yuds*, the Hebrew equivalent of Y. In Genesis 2:19, we read that "God formed every beast . . ." Here, the Hebrew word ויצר or *vayetzer* has only one yud, even though the plain meaning is identical. This is a remez, or hint, that man, in contrast with the beasts, has two natures, an animal nature and a divine nature.

D. *D'rash*—a deeper reflection based on the text. This term is the basis for *midrash*, the creative explication of Scripture that underlies so much Jewish interpretation, and appears in the B'rit Hadashah, as well. For example, Paul employs midrash in 1 Corinthians 10:1–4.

> For, brothers, I don't want you to miss the significance of what happened to our fathers. All of them were guided by the pillar of cloud, and they all passed through the sea, and in connection with the cloud and with the sea they all immersed themselves into Moshe, also they all ate the same food from the Spirit, and they all drank the same drink from the Spirit—for they drank from a Spirit-sent Rock which followed them, and that Rock was the Messiah (CJB).

The idea that a Rock followed the Israelites throughout their wanderings is not based on a literal reading of Exodus. Rather, it is an imaginative expansion of the story that unfolds an important truth. Messiah was with our forefathers in their wanderings, and he is with us.

The use of midrash is explained in the following description:

> The Rabbis were not concerned to elucidate the meaning of the Biblical text according to the strictly scientific canons of scholarship, but rather to find in it teachings and messages needed by the problems which they encountered in their own days.[6]

S. *Sod*—the mysterious or secret meaning. This level of interpretation is often based on *gematria*, the numerical value of Hebrew letters.

Thus, one reading of Numbers 7:19 combines midrash and sod to argue for the type of biblical interpretation that we have been discussing. It pictures the offering of "one silver bowl of seventy shekels" presented by the tribe of Issachar as representing the Torah, because Issachar was considered the tribe of great Torah scholars. Furthermore, the midrash claims, Torah is like wine and it is customary to drink wine in a bowl, like the silver bowl of the offering. But why is the bowl seventy shekels in weight? "As the numerical value of *yayin* (wine) is seventy, so there are seventy modes of expounding the Torah."[7]

The point of this rather imaginative interpretation is that Torah has multiple meanings and applications. Moreover, it is to the Torah's glory that it has such a wealth of meanings. Seventy is a number of completion and perfection, ten times seven. It intimates that every verse of Torah is filled with meaning. Further, seventy is equivalent to yayin, wine, according to the Hebrew numbering system. Torah yields sweet and even intoxicating meanings as we drink of it deeply. The best Jewish minds throughout the ages have spent their best energies exploring its meaning and never come to the end of it.

Reading the text as multi-dimensional leads to a conversational approach to study, since there is always something new to learn and consider. Thus, the great medieval commentator, Rashi, savored the views of his predecessors, explained them to his contemporaries, and expanded upon them for future generations. He kept an ancient conversation going for generations to come, and is still considered the definitive commentator by many traditional Jews to this day.

Of course, this approach to Scripture has its limitations. Some of us may balk at the more imaginative interpretations. We need to always seek the p'shat, the plain sense of Scripture, and accept its message as authoritative. Still, a more conversational approach is not foreign to Scripture itself, which seems to allow at times for the possibility of multiple meanings. Let's consider three examples.

- Yeshua portrays John the Baptist as Elijah to come, as promised in Malachi 4:5–6 (3:23–24). (Occasionally, as here, the numbering of verses will differ between Jewish and Christian Bibles. In such cases, the Christian numbering appears first, followed by the Jewish numbering in parentheses.) Yeshua hints that this prophecy will have multiple fulfillments when he says. "And *if you are willing to receive it,* he is Elijah who is to come" (Matthew 11:14, italics added). This sense of multiple fulfillment underlies Mark 9:11–13:

  > They also asked him, "Why do the Torah-teachers say that Eliyahu has to come first?" "Eliyahu will indeed come first," he answered, "and he will restore everything. Nevertheless, why is it written in the Tanakh that the Son of Man must suffer much and be rejected? There's more to it: I tell you that Elijah has come, and they did whatever they pleased to him, just as the Tanakh says about him" (CJB).

- In the Olivet Discourse, Yeshua mentions "the abomination that causes desolation spoken about through the prophet Daniel" (Matthew 24:15, CJB). Yeshua undoubtedly was aware of the fulfillment of this prophecy two hundred years before, when Hellenistic empire under Antiochus defiled the Temple in Jerusalem, setting the stage for the victory of the Maccabees and the story of Hanukkah. Yet, here Yeshua seems to apply the prophecy both to the Roman destruction of the Temple, which occurred about forty years later, and to a final catastrophe at the end of the age. It is one original prophecy spoken by Daniel, with multiple meanings revealed throughout history.

- When Yeshua disputes with the Sadducees concerning the resurrection, he says, "But concerning the dead, that they rise, have you not read in the book of Moses, in the Burning Bush passage, how God spoke to him, saying, 'I am the God of Abraham, the God of Isaac, and the God of Jacob'? He is not the God of the dead, but the God of the living. You are therefore greatly mistaken" (Mark 12:26–27). This is midrash, an imaginative use of Scripture that discovers new and unexpected meaning in a familiar passage, without depriving it of its more obvious meaning. Hence, Mark records that "one of the scribes," an expert in the Jewish conversation concerning Torah, overheard Yeshua and "saw that he had answered them well" (12:28). Yeshua's way of interpreting the Torah was highly credible in the eyes of his Jewish contemporaries. It may be an approach that would further Jewish appreciation of Yeshua's teachings today.

A Messianic perspective

As we go through the Five Books of Moses, we will not just seek isolated predictions of a coming Messiah, types and shadows, or proof-texts for Yeshua. Rather, we will explore the Messianic promise as essential to the story of Creation-Revelation-Completion that provides the underlying theme for the whole of Torah. We will demonstrate that Torah is not just an accessory to faith in Yeshua, but provides the broad theological framework for his appearance and work. Without Torah, the rest of the Scriptures, including the New Testament, would make little sense.

Unless noted, Bible references are from the New King James Version, but many references in the New Testament, or B'rit Hadashah, are from the *Complete Jewish Bible* (CJB), a translation by my friend Dr. David Stern. This translation employs Hebrew names and terms to capture the Jewish flavor and context of the B'rit Hadashah. I thank David Stern for permission to change most of the Hebrew names back to their more familiar English versions, and to change to regular font the boldface used in the CJB to identify quotations from the Tanakh.Tanakh, Hebrew terms that appear in the CJB are included in the Glossary.

Torah as instruction for life's journey

The Hebrew word Torah is derived from the root vrh *yarah*, which can be translated as "instruction" or "teaching." Torah, even in its legal aspects, is not just a list of rules, but a teaching on how to live. In Jewish thought, this aspect of Torah is called *halakhah*, which means literally, "the walk." Through its stories, examples, precepts, and rituals, Torah teaches us how to walk. Just as we avoid making a dichotomy between narrative and theology, we will avoid the dichotomies of law and narrative, ritual law and moral law, and so forth. Torah teaches a way of life throughout, even if many of the particulars of that way of life have changed dramatically since it was first written.

At the same time, our emphasis in reading the Torah will not be on halakhah as much as on *aggadah*, which means "telling" or "story." Judaism recognizes both aspects of Torah and sees them as interrelated. Often halakhah, legal or ethical instruction, is revealed through aggadah, the narrative of Torah. As we focus on aggadah, we will discuss how to apply Torah to our walk as followers of Messiah, but we will not discuss all the details of halakhah. To explore the specific instructions of Torah from a Messianic Jewish perspective merits a book of its own, which would still only scratch the surface. In this book, we will not avoid such instructions, but our focus will be on the overarching narrative and its ethical and theological implications. Above all, we will see how Torah, the foundational document for all forms of Judaism, remains foundational for Messianic Judaism as well, thereby strengthening our claim that Yeshua is the Messiah of Israel.

The big story of the Torah is Creation to completion, a completion called the Age to Come, the Kingdom of God, the restoration of all things, *Tikkun Olam* (Repair of the World), and other terms throughout this book. Beyond tracing this big story, these studies do not claim to be systematic. They do not seek to cover the entire content of the Torah, or even to provide an outline for it. Indeed, some studies depart from the dominant theme to explore other aspects of the Torah's teaching. In all of this, I take a conversational tone, engaging with the words of other readers and students far more qualified than I, including the writers of the New Testament, as well as later rabbinic authorities.

Even though I explore some important theological points, my tone will be devotional rather than academic. I hope to speak from the heart and to the heart. Each chapter is a study on the parashah of the week and can be read on its own, apart from the context of the entire book. I imagine some readers will use the book as a weekly devotional guide to take them through a year of reading the traditional Torah portions.

Finally, I will introduce aspects of Jewish life and tradition throughout the book, not in a pedantic way, but to invite you to sample the riches of this culture. Here again I am not systematic, but I give glimpses of a way of life, and especially a way of reading Scripture, that have helped to sustain the richness and strength of Jewish life for many centuries.

I read and write as a Jew who believes that Jesus (I prefer calling him by his Hebrew name, Yeshua) is the Messiah promised to Israel in the writings of Moses and the prophets. Along with numerous other Jewish believers in Yeshua, I seek to express this faith in a way that maintains solidarity with the whole house of Israel. This Jewish faith in Yeshua has much in common with other expressions of Judaism, including our common emphasis upon Torah. For Messianic Jews, the thoughts on Torah that I share in these pages are particularly significant. They show that our faith in Yeshua is not only compatible with the Torah, the document that defines us as Jews, but inherent to it.

At the same time, this book is written for Jewish people who do not recognize Yeshua as Messiah, and for Christians with little background in Judaism. The text of Scripture itself unites us. Torah is the particular treasure of the Jewish people, but it is filled with lessons and insights for all peoples. I believe some precepts, such as circumcision on the eighth day, or the ritual fringes described in Numbers 15, are specifically for the Jewish people. But the principles of Torah apply to all. Anyone seeking a spiritual pathway through the wilderness of our times will find direction and inspiration in its words.

This book, then, is one step on a journey of exploration. If it provides new insights, they will merely be the starting-points for further discussions. As one of the ancient rabbis said, "It is not up to you to finish the work, yet you are not free to avoid it."[7] The work of Torah continues and great are the rewards to those who pursue it, including you. May this volume serve as an inspiration to all!

בְּרֵאשִׁית

THE BOOK OF GENESIS

Genesis records the beginnings of all things, things vast and things intimate, things holy and things ordinary. Hence, its Hebrew name, בְּרֵאשִׁית (*B'resheet*), meaning "In the Beginning."

Genesis also looks ahead to the distant future, to the culmination of all things. God creates the first man and woman in the book's first chapter and charges them to "subdue the earth," launching a process that is still to reach completion. Just before the book's conclusion, Jacob gathers his sons to tell them what shall befall them "in the last days." Genesis reveals that from the beginning, the divine goal of Creation—its consummation or completion—is clearly in sight, and will prevail over all obstacles.

We also encounter in Genesis the profound wisdom of the ancient Jewish division of Torah into weekly reading portions, or *parashiyot*. The parashiyot are longer than chapters and verses, which tend to interrupt the narrative flow. Instead, the parashiyot respond to that flow, and echo the larger patterns of biblical revelation.

The weekly readings of Genesis reflect the narrative structure of the entire book, which comprises twelve portions in the traditional reading cycle. The first two portions (chapters 1–11) cover the first twenty generations of humankind—ten generations from Adam to Noah, and ten from Noah to Abraham. They constitute Part One of Genesis, recounting the origins of the cosmos and of the human race, and the early history of all humankind. The final ten parashiyot (chapters 12–50) constitute Part Two, and cover only four more generations. The story shifts from a universal focus to

one specific human family, from epochal stories of Creation, innocence, sin, and judgment, to domestic stories of marriage, children,
and inheritance. Still, this one specific and very real family will
carry God's initial purpose of blessing to the whole human race.

Translator and commentator Robert Alter summarizes this shift
in Genesis:

> The human creature is now to be represented not against the
> background of the heavens and the earth and civilization as
> such but rather within the tense and constricted theater of the
> paternal domain, in tent and wheatfield and sheepfold . . .
> working out all hopes of grand destiny in the coil of familial
> relationships. . . . In keeping with this major shift in focus from
> the Primeval History to the Patriarchal Tales, style and narra-
> tive mode shift as well. The studied formality of the first eleven
> chapters . . . gives way to a more flexible and varied prose.[1]

From a Messianic perspective, we note two major continuities
in Genesis despite this shift.

First is the theme of *redemption*. The human race, created in the
image of God, has a destiny, which will be fulfilled despite failure
and opposition. Early in the story, when the sin of Adam and Eve
seems to have sidetracked God's purpose, God promises a seed, an
offspring of the woman who will defeat the opposition. The theme
of the promised seed carries throughout the book.

Second is the theme of *covenant*. After the Flood, God makes a
covenant with the whole Creation through Noah. Then, when God
raises up a restored humanity through Abraham, he establishes a
covenant with him as well, which God will preserve and pass on to
each succeeding generation.

These themes of redemption and covenant are foundational to
the whole Torah, and to all of the Scriptures built upon it, the Bible
that we possess and read today. These themes will enable us to read
Torah, not just as an ancient history or rulebook, but as the story of
Creation to completion, a story filled with hope for our world.

CREATION AND ITS GOAL
Parashat B'resheet, Genesis 1:1–6:8

A classic Jewish story tells of two men who fell into a dispute and agreed to bring the matter to their rabbi for judgment. The first one told his story and ended with the claim that the other owed him twenty pieces of silver. The rabbi said, "You know . . . you're right!" When the second told his story, he claimed that the first one owed *him* twenty pieces of silver. The rabbi responded, "You know . . . you're right!" The rabbi's assistant called out, "Rabbi, they can't both be right!" And the rabbi replied, "You know . . . you're right too!"

We begin our study of Torah with its very first word—*B'resheet* or "In the beginning"—which has been the subject of debate among Jewish interpreters for centuries. The great medieval commentator Rashi says of Genesis 1:1, "This verse says nothing but 'Expound me!'" The medieval Jewish commentators were experts in Hebrew grammar, and Rashi begins his exposition with a grammatical look at the first word, B'resheet. Other commentators over the following centuries will either agree or disagree with Rashi.

Let's listen in on this discussion. It will be worth the effort, because it reveals a unique aspect of Jewish interpretation that will expand our understanding of Scripture. Two different viewpoints may both have something vital to teach us.

The word b'resheet is in the construct form, used when one noun combines with another. It combines *b'* or "in" with *resheet*, meaning "first" or "beginning," so that it would normally mean "in the beginning of. . . ." Rashi says, "You have no instance of the word *resheet* in Scripture that is not attached to the word that follows it." Accepting this argument, one traditionally-oriented Jewish version translates the opening lines of Genesis:

> In the beginning of God's creating the heavens and the earth—when the earth was astonishingly empty, with dark-

ness upon the surface of the deep, and the Divine Presence hovered upon the surface of the waters—God said, "Let there be light, and there was light."[2]

In contrast with Rashi, however, another leading medieval commentator, Ramban, points out two instances of resheet that are not in the construct form: Isaiah 46:10, "Declaring the end from *resheet*—the beginning," and Deuteronomy 33:21, "He provided *resheet*—the first part—for himself." Furthermore, Ramban says that the construct form is always used to connect one noun with another, but in Genesis 1, b'resheet connects with a verb. Therefore, he translates the opening words, "In the beginning, God created the heavens and the earth," signifying the Creation of all things out of nothing. He explains,

> The Holy One, blessed be he, created all things from absolute non-existence. Now we have no expression in the sacred language for bringing forth something from nothing other than the word *Bara* [translated 'created' here].[3]

This discussion of b'resheet may seem a bit technical, but it shows that two opposing views can both teach us something. We might even end up like the rabbi in the story, saying "You're right" to two interpretations that seemed at first to oppose each other.

In this case, Genesis is telling us *both* that God created all things out of nothing, simply by his word, *and* that this creative process was a matter of bringing order to the original chaos. Creation is the miraculous coming-into-being of all things through the divine utterance, and also a battle with the disorder that was present almost from the first.

In this understanding, Creation is not an end in itself, but is moving toward a goal—the completion of God's order and *shalom* (peace, wholeness). Indeed, the theme of Creation and its consummation underlies the entire Torah.

This theme also unlocks the meaning of our own lives. When God created humankind, he gave them a role in improving his Creation: "Then God blessed them, and God said to them, 'Be fruitful and multiply; fill the earth and subdue it; have dominion over the fish of the sea, over the birds of the air, and over every living thing that moves on the earth'" (Genesis 1:28). Humans are to fill the earth that God has created, to subdue and rule it in a divine-human partnership.

Thus, when God places Adam and Eve in the Garden, they are not to remain in innocent passivity. Rather, the Lord gives them real responsibility: "Then the LORD God took the man and put him in the Garden of Eden to tend and keep it" (Gen. 2:15). Human tending and keeping of the Garden will increase it, until the whole earth becomes a garden, and Creation reaches the fulfillment for which it was designed.

God gives us humans a vital role in his ultimate plan for the Creation, but before our first ancestors begin to fulfill this role, disorder breaks out again. God had placed Adam and Eve in the Garden as his representatives, and had commanded them not to eat of the Tree of the Knowledge of Good and Evil in its midst. The disorder, vanquished during the week of Creation, enters the Garden in the form of a serpent that entices the humans to eat. Because of their disobedience, God expels Adam and Eve and cuts them off from the Tree of Life.

Exile from the Garden sets the stage for the human quest throughout the rest of Torah, and into our own times, the quest for the Tree of Life. Traditional Judaism sees Torah as the Tree of Life. In the synagogue service, after reading from the Torah scroll, one of the men will grasp its handles and lift it high for the whole congregation to see, calling out, "This is the Torah which Moses placed before the children of Israel at the command of the Lord. A Tree of Life it is to those who take hold of it." Cleaving to Torah, then, will open the way back to the Tree of Life.

Genesis suggests another way back. The expulsion from the Garden is the first of many exiles and warnings of exile, which will culminate in the Babylonian exile centuries later. "So from the very beginning we are introduced to the theme of exile, exile that comes as the result of violating God's commands."[4]

One of the earliest of all commentaries on Genesis makes the same connection. The Lord says,

> [J]ust as I led Adam into the garden of Eden and commanded him, and he transgressed My commandment, whereupon I punished him by dismissal and expulsion . . . so also did I bring

> his descendants into the Land of Israel and command them, and they transgressed My commandment, and I punished them by sending them away and expelling them.[5]

Before God drives Adam and Eve into exile, however, he curses the serpent, saying, "I will put enmity between you and the woman, and between your seed and her seed; he shall bruise your head, and you shall bruise his heel" (Gen. 3:15). An offspring of the woman—a Son born "in the fullness of time" (Gal. 4:4) will destroy the deceiver. As the first exile, the expulsion from the Garden contains the promise of restoration from all exile.

In the end, we will not be restored to the Garden of Eden, but to a place of far greater order and holiness, "a city built by God." And there we will regain access to the Tree of Life. "In the middle of its street, and on either side of the river, was the tree of life, which bore twelve fruits, each tree yielding its fruit every month. The leaves of the tree were for the healing of the nations" (Rev. 22:2). Out of this city, with the Tree of Life in its midst, will come the fulfillment of God's original plan for all humanity. Genesis reveals that we have a genuine part to play—a part that will become clearer as we continue our study of Torah—in reaching the city.

For the journey: As I trust in God's instructions and obey them, I discover the part that I am to play in fulfilling his purposes. I have an assignment here on earth that God planned from the very beginning, which is revealed in Scripture. How do I go about fulfilling this assignment today?

HE WHO COVERS THE NAKED
Parashat Noach, Genesis 6:9–11:32

Rabbi Hama said: What does it mean, "You shall walk after the Lord your God" [Deut. 13:5]? Is it possible for a person to walk and follow in God's presence? Does not the Torah also say "For the Lord your God is a consuming fire" [Deut. 4:24]? But it means to walk after the attributes of the Holy One, Blessed be He. Just as He clothed the naked, so you too clothe the naked, as it says "And the Lord made the man and his wife leather coverings and clothed them" [Gen. 3:21].[6]

Genesis, the book of Creation, portrays Noah's Flood and its aftermath as a new Creation. As at the beginning, waters cover the earth. Eventually, as in Genesis 1, a wind from God goes forth (8:1) and the dry land appears. The earth is renewed and the divine order is re-established. When Noah and his family go forth from the ark, God repeats to them the mandate of Genesis 1:28: "Be fruitful and multiply, and fill the earth. And the fear of you and the dread of you shall be upon every beast of the earth, and upon every fowl of the air, and upon all wherewith the ground teems, and upon all the fish of the sea: into your hand are they delivered" (9:1–2).

Now we understand why the Lord decrees that a flood will never again destroy the earth. There may indeed be divine judgment in the future, but not this degree of judgment. He will never again return the earth to the primal chaos of the first day, as he did at the Flood.

As in the original Creation, however, not long after the divine order is established, it is disrupted. After the flood waters recede, Noah plants a vineyard, drinks of its wine, gets drunk, and lies down uncovered in his tent.

And Ham, the father of Canaan, saw the nakedness of his father, and told his two brothers outside. But Shem and Japheth took a garment, laid it on both their shoulders, and

7

went backward and covered the nakedness of their father. Their faces were turned away, and they did not see their father's nakedness. So Noah awoke from his wine, and knew what his younger son had done to him. Then he said: "Cursed be Canaan . . ." (Genesis 9:22–25a)

The nature of Ham's offense is unclear, but its effect is devastating. The earth has just come through judgment and renewal to receive God's blessing. Now the curse becomes lodged in it again. In the original Creation story, the curse is introduced through the agency of the serpent in the Garden of Eden; here, through the agency of a vine in the garden of Noah.

Rabbi Judah and Rabbi Jose differed as to the origin of this vine. One said that it came from the Garden of Eden and Noah now planted it here. The other said that it had been on the earth before the Flood and Noah had plucked it and now replanted it. On the same day it blossomed, ripened, and brought forth grapes. Noah then pressed out from them wine, drank of it and became drunken.[7]

A startling midrash: the vine came from the Garden of Eden! Perhaps Noah is seeking to regain the original bounty and innocence of the human condition. In the recreated earth, he desires to drink of such fruits as Adam and Eve enjoyed before their transgression and exile. But the Garden has not been restored and its produce is too much for Noah. It overpowers him and leaves him vulnerable, so that sin and disorder reenter the scene. God has spared the human race through the family of Noah, but he has not yet restored them to the primal bliss of Eden. The message for us is clear: We have a long journey ahead of us before our exile is over.

The real problem is not the vine, but man's continuing folly in pursuing divine knowledge or bliss in his own way. Even after the purification of the Flood and the renewal of God's blessing upon humankind, humans continue to follow their own ways. The action of Shem and Japheth, however, leaves us with a note of hope. Noah's sons take pains to cover his nakedness.

Here is another reminder of the Creation story, in which the Lord covered the nakedness of Adam and Eve in the Garden after their transgression. They are sent into exile, but their human dignity is affirmed and protected. This act of God is an example of what Jewish writings call *g'milut hasadim*, deeds of kindness, which God performs as an example for us.

Noah's two sons follow God's example. In contrast with Ham, they refuse to even look upon Noah's nakedness, but they cover it, hoping to restore his dignity and maintain the wholeness of the family.

Transgression may be inevitable within our families and communities, but here is a lesson in how we are to respond. When someone offends us, we can magnify their offense by uncovering it for all to see, or we can counter it by preserving the dignity of the offender.

Accordingly, the Messiah teaches us, "If your brother sins against you, go and tell him his fault between you and him alone. If he hears you, you have gained your brother" (Matt. 18:15). We are tempted, when someone has offended us, to imitate Ham and expose the offense, at least to a few sympathetic friends. We couch our act of exposing someone else as a request for prayer, or a need for advice. But somehow we enjoy exposing the fault of the other person. The example of Shem and Japheth, however, leads us to cover the offense by handling it directly with the offender, so that he can turn from the offense, make amends, and regain his dignity.

Rav Shaul, the apostle Paul, writes, "Brothers, suppose someone is caught doing something wrong. You who have the Spirit should set him right, but in a spirit of humility, keeping an eye on yourselves so that you won't be tempted too. Bear one another's burdens—in this way you will be fulfilling the Torah's true meaning, which the Messiah upholds" (Gal. 6:1–2, CJB).

> A respected woman once came to ask advice of the rabbi of Apt. The instant he set eyes on her he shouted: "Adulteress! You sinned only a short while ago, and yet now you have the insolence to step into this pure house!" Then from the depths of her heart the woman replied: "The Lord of the world has patience with the wicked. He is in no hurry to make them pay their debts and he does not disclose their secret to any creature, lest they be ashamed to turn to him. Nor does he hide his face from them. But the rabbi of Apt sits there in his chair and cannot resist revealing at once what the Creator has covered."

> From that time on the rabbi of Apt used to say: "No one ever got the better of me except once—and then it was a woman."[8]

Until Messiah returns, we remain in exile, on the way toward Creation completed, but still far from it. In this exile we inevitably become tainted by sin and vulnerable to shame. The issue is how we handle our vulnerability and that of our brothers and sisters. Will we heighten it, as Ham did, and turn it into a curse, or will we cover it as the brothers did, restoring dignity and peace to the whole family?

For the journey: How do I apply the principle of covering the naked without letting people get away with wrongdoing, or falling into religious denial? As I recall how God has covered my sins and misdeeds, I will look for opportunities to practice this act of loving kindness toward others.

OBEDIENCE AND BEYOND
Parashat Lekh L'kha, Genesis 12:1–17:27

"The brave things in the old tales and songs, Mr. Frodo: adventures, as I used to call them. I used to think that they were things the wonderful folk of the stories went out and looked for. . . . But that's not the way of it with the tales that really mattered, or the ones that stay in the mind. Folk seem to have just landed in them, usually—their paths were led that way, as you put it. But I expect they had lots of chances, like us, of turning back, only they didn't."
—(Sam Gamgee in *The Lord of the Rings: The Two Towers*)

The call of faith is often—perhaps always—demanding. To respond, we must leave behind all that is comfortable and follow the Lord into unknown territory. And the journey of faith does not end with this initial call. We must walk by faith, not only at the beginning of the journey, but throughout. We will have to resist lots of chances of turning back, as Sam said to Frodo. Abraham, our great example of faith, had to persevere and not turn back many times. "With ten trials was Abraham our father tried before the Holy One, blessed be he, and in all of them he was found steadfast, to wit: Twice when ordered to move on . . ."[9]

Abraham undergoes trials, not just in his early years, but throughout his whole life. Like Sam and Frodo, and most of us, Abraham didn't look for these trials, but "landed in them." This landing, however, is no accident; rather Abraham's path is "led that way" by God himself. In the same way, when we encounter trials, that doesn't mean we have lost our way. Often we too are "led that way" by God, and Abraham's story may help us to understand why.

Abraham's first and last trials both begin with the same command, *Lekh l'kha*, literally "Go for yourself" or "Go-you-forth."[10] These commands involve an unusual combination of words that appears in Scripture only one other time outside of the story of

11

Abraham. The two commands frame Abraham's entire story and especially the issue of obedience, which it exemplifies.

In the first command the Lord says, "Lekh l'kha—Go for yourself from your land, from your family, and from your father's house, to a land that I will show you" (Gen. 12:1). Only as he obeys this difficult command does Abraham begin to fulfill the divine purpose for his life.

The second Lekh l'kha comes in the land that God showed him, the land of promise. Abraham hears the words again, "Lekh l'kha— Go for yourself to the land of Moriah, and present Isaac there as an offering to me" (Gen. 22:2). This second command is even tougher than the first. Abraham has already begun to dwell in the land of promise, and to receive some elements of the promise, including an heir born to him in his old age. Now he must renounce this heir, his son Isaac, who is more precious to him than life itself, and continue down the path of rigorous obedience.

When Abraham responds in faith to the second Lekh l'kha, the Lord responds to him as well. At the climax of the story, Abraham stretches out his hand and takes the knife to slay his beloved Isaac. At that instant, the angel of the Lord calls out from heaven to stop him, saying, "Now I know that you fear God, since you have not withheld your son, your only son, from me" (Gen. 22:12). If the story were not so stark, this statement would sound funny. *Now* you know!? After Abraham has walked for more than a century in obedience to God?

Abraham has indeed proven his faithfulness through many trials, but the second Lekh l'kha establishes a new level of faithfulness.

The Hebrew term for commandment, *mitzvah*, also denotes the great blessing that the commandment brings with it. The first Lekh l'kha is a mitzvah; the second Lekh l'kha might be termed a "meta-mitzvah." It goes beyond ordinary obedience (which in reality is often quite extraordinary) to a rare level of devotion to God. The mitzvah is for this age; it lays out the way of obedience in this world. The meta-mitzvah points to the Age to Come, to "the restoration of all things" (Acts 3:21), when God will be all in all and his followers completely dedicated to him. Abraham has already shown his devotion to the Lord, "because [he] obeyed my voice and kept my charge, my commandments, my statutes, and my laws" (Gen. 26:5). Now he shows a level of devotion beyond the normal commandments, statutes, and laws.

The meta-mitzvah will reappear throughout Torah. Thus, Moses, who has seen the Lord "face to face" and spent forty days and forty nights atop Mount Sinai in his presence, says to the Lord, "I beseech you, show me your glory" (Exod. 33:18). In the experience of God, there is always something more, something beyond the commandments, holy as they are. The mitzvah of the Nazirite is another example (Num. 6). Torah recognizes that there will be those who desire a greater devotion to him, beyond the normal way of obedience outlined in the commandments. It therefore provides an additional, voluntary mitzvah of consecration to the Lord.

Abraham shows us that trials are opportunities to prove our faithfulness to the mitzvah. But the binding of Isaac points to the meta-mitzvah, to a greater level of devotion that will become the model for all who seek to follow the Lord in the footsteps of Abraham. The meta-mitzvah is displayed most fully in the life of Messiah, who "humbled Himself and became obedient to the point of death, even the death of the cross" (Phil. 2:8).

For those enduring trials, however, such considerations may sound too tidy. We must acknowledge that there is great mystery here. In the second Lekh l'kha, God appears cruel, toying with Abraham and Isaac, and he may appear cruel in our trials as well. Yet we must beware of worshiping a deity that is always safe and predictable; such a deity is not the God of Israel. Trials teach us to trust God despite our questions. We are responsible to maintain our faith without turning back, not to understand every aspect of God's character. Indeed, like Abraham, we may display our greatest faith when we walk in obedience without knowing where we are headed. "By faith Abraham obeyed when he was called to go out to the place which he would receive as an inheritance. And he went out, not knowing where he was going" (Heb. 11:8).

Abraham's trials begin and end with Lekh l'kha, "Get yourself up." He is our example because he never quite settles down, never allows his encounter with God to recede into the background. May we learn to emulate him, to embrace trials, even in the later stages of the journey, as opportunities to know God more fully.

> Rabbi Levi said: LECH L'CHA—'*Get thee*'—is written twice, and we do not know which was more precious [in the eyes of God], whether the first or the second.[11]

For the journey: Abraham demonstrates that trials are opportunities to show our commitment to God and his ways, opportunities for obedience. How do I demonstrate obedience to God in my life right now? What trials am I facing that may be opportunities to strengthen my commitment to him?

SACRIFICE OF THE SON
Parashat Vayera, Genesis 18:1–22:24

The Rock, perfect in all his deeds; who can say to him, 'What do you do?' The One who says and does, do undeserved grace upon us, and in the merit of him who was bound like a lamb, hear and act. (From the traditional Jewish burial service of the *Siddur*)

The Jews are a people bound together by stories. The story of our redemption from Egypt undergirds all our prayers and scriptures, and the cycle of the year itself, marked by the festivals of Passover, Weeks, and Tabernacles. The Exodus is a defining story, but there is an earlier story equally compelling, yet more ambiguous and troubling. This story is not part of the joyous festivals, but of the solemn holy days of *Rosh HaShanah* and *Yom Kippur*. It is the story of the *Akedah*, the Binding of Isaac.

The ambiguity of the story begins with God's initial command to Abraham to sacrifice Isaac, the same son whom God had recently identified as the promised heir. Mysteriously, Abraham remains silent. The same man who dared to argue with the Lord over the destruction of Sodom and over God's order to expel his son Ishmael now utters not a word.

The story also ends mysteriously as Isaac is spared, even though God had demanded him as a sacrifice. Or is he spared? When Abraham takes Isaac up toward Mount Moriah, the place of sacrifice, the text tells us twice (Gen. 22:6, 8), "the two of them went together." When Abraham descends the mount, however, there is no mention of Isaac: "So Abraham returned to his young men, and they rose and went together to Beersheba; and Abraham dwelt at Beersheba" (Gen. 22:19).

Now it is not Abraham and Isaac, but Abraham and his lads who "went together." A few verses later, Sarah dies and we are told, "Abraham set about to lament for Sarah and to weep over her" (Gen. 23:2). Again, no mention of Isaac, even at this most crucial moment.

Early readers saw in this absence a hint that the "offering-up" of Isaac was indeed a sacrifice, a killing. *Midrash Rabbah* compares it to

15

execution upon the stake, an all-too-familiar scene to the Jews of the first two centuries C.E., when the stories of this midrash originated:

> "And Abraham took the wood of the burnt-offering," like one who carries his stake on his shoulder. "And they went both of them together," one to bind and the other to be bound, one to slaughter and the other to be slaughtered.[12]

A later midrash says that when Abraham raised the knife to slay Isaac, Isaac's soul left him, but when the angel called out to Abraham to desist from harming Isaac, his soul returned to him. Abraham then untied Isaac, who rose up and began to recite, "Blessed are you O Lord, who raises the dead." To the Jewish mind, the Akedah had become a drama of death and resurrection.[13]

The original story, of course, concludes with the sacrifice of a ram, caught in a nearby thicket by his horns. God provides the substitute and Isaac lives. In remembrance of this great redemption, the Jewish people sound the ram's horn on Rosh HaShanah every year. The commentators, however, continue to see the symbolic death of Isaac. Rashi comments on the verse, "Abraham called the name of that place: The Lord Sees. As the saying is today: On the Lord's mountain it is seen" (Gen. 22:14):

> The Lord will see this binding and forgive Israel because of it every year [at Yom Kippur], and save them from punishment, so that it will be said on this day in all generations to come, "On the mountain of God there will be seen" the ashes of Isaac still piled up, as if he had actually been sacrificed for atonement on behalf of Israel.

The binding of Isaac—like the Exodus—binds the Jewish people together. The drama of death and resurrection gave hope to the generations of Israel that endured Roman domination, the destruction of the Temple, and the oppression that followed. It also provided a point of reference to understand a Messiah who took on the suffering and defeat of his people, endured execution at the hand of Rome, and arose from the dead. As the ram was offered in place of Isaac, the son of Abraham, so Messiah Yeshua was offered in the place of all the children of Abraham, "sacrificed for atonement on behalf of Israel," and on behalf of all humankind.

In the midst of such lofty considerations, however, we may miss the great shift in interpretation of the story. The Torah introduces its account with the words, "God tested Abraham" (Gen. 22:1). In the discussions in Midrash and gospel, however, the willingness of the son eclipses the testing of the father. The account of the testing and obedience of Abraham is now paired with the drama of the sacrifice and resurrection of Isaac. Father and son "go together," even, as "one to bind and the other to be bound, one to slaughter and the other to be slaughtered." Their wills are united and the son is ready to sacrifice himself.

This shift in telling the story speaks to us powerfully at the beginning of the twenty-first century, as many wonder if a new generation will continue in the heritage of their faith. We have grown to expect estrangement and misunderstanding between the generations, but here is the story of a son who embraces his father's will. Isaac, the sole representative of a new generation, makes the will of the father his own. Abraham and Isaac represent different generations but one response to God's call. Many of us long for just this sort of unity between the generations today.

The story of the Exodus from Egypt defines the Jewish people, but it does not tell us how we will keep the story alive. The Akedah provides a clue to our continuity. Surely, it was Abraham's lifelong faithfulness to God that so inspired Isaac, his willingness to leave what was safe and comfortable in order to serve God. When God demanded the best from Abraham, he was ready to give it, and Isaac became ready as well. In the same way, when we face difficulties and disappointment, we need to remember that a younger generation is watching, ready to learn from us either for good or ill.

Significantly, we read of the binding of Isaac at Rosh HaShanah, the Jewish New Year. As we mark the swift passage of another year, we remember that our time is limited, and our need for a new generation intense. This is the time to recount the story of the son who takes on fully the purpose of the father—even at the ultimate cost to himself. The story of the binding of Isaac has bound the Jewish people together for centuries; may it also serve to bind us all with our own younger generation as we "go together" to serve the God of Israel.

For the journey: How do I "go together" with members of an older generation of those who have followed the Lord? How do I encourage members of a younger generation to "go together" with me?

SARAH'S LIFE
Parashat Hayyei-Sarah, Genesis 23:1–25:18

> The world stands on three things—the Torah, the [Temple] service, and loving acts of kindness.[14]

The stories of Abraham and his descendants seem to be written from a patriarchal perspective, yet the first death recorded among them is that of a woman, Sarah. Torah records her life span in unusual detail, as befits the mother of Israel.

> Now Sara's life was one hundred years and twenty years and seven years, (thus) the years of Sara's life.
> Sara died in Arba-Town, that is now Hevron, in the land of Canaan.
> Avraham set about to lament for Sara and to weep over her . . . [15]

Before Sarah dies, however, Abraham learns of the birth of Rebekah, daughter of his kinsman Bethuel. Sforno notes this connection in his commentary: "After Rebecca—who is fit to replace Sarah—is born, and Abraham is notified, Sarah dies. As our sages tell us, 'One righteous person does not die before another is born, as it is written, *and the sun rises, and the sun sets*'" (Ecclesiastes 1:5).

After Sarah dies, Abraham seeks to restore the essential feminine element to his family by finding a bride for Isaac. Indeed, the title of this parashah, *Hayyei-Sarah*, means, "the life of Sarah." It begins with the sadness of a burial, but continues through the joy of a wedding. Sarah will live on through the wife of Isaac.

To find this woman, Abraham sends a servant back to his land and kindred. The entire story of the betrothal of Isaac hinges upon the actions of this servant, yet he remains nameless. He is called simply "the servant of Abraham." This servant takes on the role of best man, who helps bring the wedding party together and stands as attendant at the ceremony, but is never central to the event. His role is vital, and yet the attention is never on him. Instead, this story draws our attention to Isaac. With God's help, the servant finds Rebekah, arranges the marriage with her family, and gains her assent to return to his master. When they reach the land of Canaan at last, Rebekah sees Isaac in the distance and asks, "Who is this man walking in the field to meet us?" The servant says, "It is my master [*adoni*]." So she takes a veil and covers herself (24:65). In this story, the servant has called Abraham adoni, "my master," sixteen times. Only now, as he escorts the bride whom Abraham sent him to find, does he apply the term to Isaac. Isaac becomes complete when he encounters his bride.

The union of Isaac and Rebekah reminds us of an earlier wedding. In *Hayyei-Sarah*, the unnamed servant is the best man, but in that earlier wedding the best man was the Lord himself, who formed Eve from the side of Adam and brought her to him. Rabbi Abin said of this event, "Happy the citizen for whom the king is best man!"[16] Commenting on God's blessing of the man and woman that he created (Gen. 1:27–28), another rabbi says, "The Holy One, blessed be He, took a cup of blessing [essential to the traditional Jewish wedding] and blessed them."[17]

Arranging a wedding and attending to the bridal couple are acts of kindness, or g'milut hasadim, considered one of three things upon which the world stands, along with Torah and the divine worship. As we saw in the story of Noah, the Lord provides the example of such acts of kindness so that we can emulate him. "What does it mean, 'You shall walk after the Lord your God'? (Deut. 13:5) Is it possible for a person to walk and follow in God's presence? . . . But it means to walk after the attributes of the Holy One, Blessed be He."[18]

Acts of loving kindness form the fabric of community. Furthermore, they provide a foretaste of the Age to Come, the age of Creation consummated, which is the destination of our story. Then God will meet all our needs, and there will be none who are naked or lonely or abandoned. Therefore, Torah instructs us in this age to support others in joyous events, such as a wedding, and in sorrowful events, such as sickness or mourning: "Rejoice with those who rejoice, and weep with those who weep," writes Paul, the rabbi from Tarsus (Rom. 12:15).

By marrying Rebekah, Isaac receives comfort after the death of Sarah, takes on the legacy of his father Abraham, and ensures that the covenant will be passed on to another generation. This is a uniquely significant wedding, but it highlights the significance of every wedding. Every time we attend a wedding we agree with God that it is not good for the man (or woman) to be alone, that the couple is to bear a divine blessing, and that their marriage is to be fruitful in many ways. At such events, we are not a mere audience, but we are community, supporting the couple and adding our own blessing to the Lord's blessing.

It is no wonder then, that early in his account of the deeds of Messiah, John records Yeshua's attendance at a wedding:

> Yeshua told them, "Fill the jars with water," and they filled them to the brim. He said, "Now draw some out, and take it to the man in charge of the banquet"; and they took it. The man in charge tasted the water; it had now turned into wine! He did not know where it had come from, but the servants who had drawn the water knew. So he called the bridegroom and said to him, "Everyone else serves the good wine first and the poorer wine after people have drunk freely. But you have kept the good wine until now!" This, the first [or beginning] of Yeshua's miraculous signs, he did at Kanah in the Galil; he manifested his glory, and his *talmidim* came to trust in him. (Yochanan/ John 2:7–11, CJB)

The phrase "beginning of signs" brings us back to b'resheet, the beginning. There, "The Holy One, blessed be he, took a cup of blessing and blessed them." Here, Yeshua, Son of the Holy One, ensures an abundant supply of wine for a Galilean wedding. Wine is not just refreshment, but the emblem of the blessing and divine favor that will issue in fruitfulness for the new couple. To run out of wine is not just a social inconvenience for a family, but a threat to the peace of the new couple, and to the continuity of the community.

The God of Torah is not an impersonal "First Cause," but a God of compassion. He is not distant from the world he created and the human beings he has placed within it. Rather, it seems that he can hardly stay away from us. He is ready to enter our world, to feel our sorrows, and to share in our joys. And in Messiah, he steps fully into the community of men and women to embody the acts of kindness he has modeled since the beginning of Torah.

For the journey: In an age of consumerism and addiction to entertainment, God calls me to be part of community, rejoicing with those who rejoice, and weeping with those who weep. God has performed g'milut hasadim, acts of loving kindness, for me. How can I perform such deeds among those around me?

THE LIVING WATER
Parashat Tol'dot, Genesis 25:19–28:9

Come to these waters, there is a vast supply.
There is a river that never shall run dry.[19]

As the story of Genesis unfolds, Abraham, Isaac, and Jacob must struggle to establish themselves in the land God promised them. We have much to learn from these struggles, just as we do from their struggles in exile, for their story, like the entire Jewish story, takes place both within the Land and in exile. In both settings, the patriarchs must journey in faith on the way from Creation to completion.

The great medieval commentator Nachmanides, or Ramban, comments on Abraham's wanderings, "Whatever has happened to the patriarchs is a sign to the children."[20] Abraham's journey will anticipate Isaac's journey, and the journeys of their offspring, including the descent into Egypt of the twelve tribes, and their eventual deliverance by the mighty hand of God. Abraham goes before his descendants through this entire story.

Thus, after Isaac marries Rebekah and becomes father to Jacob and Esau, the LORD appears to him to renew the promise that he had originally made to Abraham:

> Dwell in this land, and I will be with you and bless you; for to you and your descendants I give all these lands, and I will perform the oath which I swore to Abraham your father. And I will make your descendants multiply as the stars of heaven; I will give to your descendants all these lands; and in your seed all the nations of the earth shall be blessed. (Gen. 26:3–4)

Isaac will live his whole life in the Promised Land, but he does sojourn for a time, as did Abraham, among the Philistines. There he, like Abraham, says that his wife is his sister, out of fear that the Philistines will kill him and take her for themselves. Both of our ancestors resort to a lie to protect themselves, but God in his mercy delivers Isaac, as he delivered Abraham. Isaac then continues in his father's footsteps:

> And Isaac dug again the wells of water which they had dug in the days of Abraham his father, for the Philistines had stopped them up after the death of Abraham. He called them by the names which his father had called them. (Gen. 26:18)

Isaac does not go into exile as Abraham and Jacob do, but he still must establish his own claim in the Land. Water is the heart of this claim, essential to fruitfulness and life itself in this barren place. To secure water, Isaac reopens the wells of Abraham, and calls them by the same names as did his father. Abraham's wells symbolize the proven resources of spiritual life, the legacy of Scripture and the traditions of life and community that have grown up around it. We will find that we must continually return to sources like these as we take our own journey.

Isaac, however, must go beyond returning to his father's legacy to create his own legacy, as it is written, "Also Isaac's servants dug in the valley, and found a well of living water there" (Gen. 26:19). The journey of faith is a journey of continuous renewal. It keeps open the proven resources and discovers new resources as well.

"Living water" in this verse is *mayim chaim* in Hebrew, a phrase that appears here for the first time in Scripture. When we find living water we do not need to draw it forth with a bucket, for it springs forth under pressure. It is a source of refreshment, blessing, and life in the arid land of promise.

The phrase mayim chaim will not appear again in the book of Genesis, but Jeremiah and Zechariah see it as a hint, or remez, of a deeper spiritual truth. In their writings, living waters are a symbol of divine blessing and life.

> For my people have committed two evils; they have forsaken me, the fountain of living waters, and hewed out for themselves cisterns, broken cisterns, that can hold no water. (Jer. 2:13)

> And it shall be in that day, that living waters shall go out from Jerusalem; half of them toward the former sea, and half of

them toward the hinder sea: in summer and in winter shall it be. (Zech. 14:8)

Yeshua takes up the same terminology when he requests a drink from a Samaritan woman whom he meets at Jacob's well. "If you knew the gift of God, and who it is that says to you, 'Give me to drink,' you would have asked him, and he would have given you living water" (John 4:10). Later he says, "He who believes in me, as the scripture has said, out of his belly shall flow rivers of living water" (John 7:38).

Yeshua reveals a truth that is as ancient as the Torah itself, yet ever new. The God of our fathers has a gift of endless and unlimited life to bestow on their children in every generation. Isaac has not only renewed the legacy of his father Abraham, but has uncovered a legacy of his own—the source of life that comes from God.

The lesson here is that we need to open and reopen continually the legacy given to us in Torah and the rest of Scripture, to drink deeply at our sources and not allow them to fall into neglect. We need to study, contemplate, and practice the teachings of the Bible, continually. But the Torah is also pointing to a source that is always new, immediate and irrepressible, an experience of the living Messiah himself, who is always near. The journey toward restoration passes through barren stretches, and we must not stray from the wells of renewal.

Isaac's story teaches us that all such renewal comes in the midst of struggle. The land of promise is an arid land. Isaac must reopen the wells of Abraham because the Philistines had plugged them up. He must dig new wells even as the herdsmen of Gerar strive with him. Where there is divine blessing, there will always be great opposition. This is the pattern throughout Scripture, from the call of Abraham, who must leave his home and family and all that is familiar, to the sacrifice of Messiah himself, who calls his followers to also deny themselves, take up the cross, and come after him. It is in the midst of opposition, however, that we find the living water.

For the journey: The journey of faith is a journey of continuous renewal. If we follow the journey of the fathers and of Messiah himself, it will bring us into struggle and opposition. Where will I find the wells of living water within my struggles?

AT RACHEL'S WELL
Parashat Vayetze, Genesis 28:10–32:3

Hillel and Shammai, two of the greatest rabbis of ancient Israel, lived at the same time and often disagreed on important aspects of Jewish law. One of these disagreements concerns the order of lighting the menorah for Hanukah. Hillel advocates lighting one light on the first night and adding one more light each night to reach the total of eight at the end of the holiday. Shammai takes the opposite approach: eight lights the first night and one less each night to conclude with one. Our custom follows the practice of Hillel, because in matters of holiness we seek to increase rather than decrease.[21]

The principle of increasing holiness is reflected not only in Hanukah, but also through the seven days of Sukkot, the Feast of Tabernacles. In ancient Israel, on each day of Sukkot, the people would gather young willow branches, bring them up to the altar of the Temple, and make one circuit around the altar crying out, "Save now, we beseech you O Lord!—*Ana Adonai Hoshia'na!*" But on the seventh day, they would make seven circuits around the altar, calling out the same words—*Ana Adonai Hoshia'na!*[22]

Likewise, on each of the seven days of Sukkot, a procession of worshipers went down to the pool of Shiloach. There a priest filled a golden flask with water, fulfilling the words, "With joy you shall draw water from the wells of salvation" (Isaiah 12:3). Then the people in the procession went up to the altar and poured the water out as an offering before the Lord in the midst of great rejoicing. The *Mishnah* comments on this ceremony: "Anyone who has not seen the rejoicing of *bet hashoebah* [the place of water drawing] in his life has never seen rejoicing."[23]

In accord with Hillel's principle, the rejoicing reached its peak on the seventh day, with song and dance, harps, cymbals, and trumpets sounding before the Lord.

The rejoicing of "the place of water drawing" became linked in the Jewish mind to the outpouring of the Holy Spirit promised for the Age to Come as part of Creation consummated. An old commentary on *Parashat Vayetze* makes the same connection. The Torah says, "So Jacob went on his journey and came to the land of the people of the East. And he looked, and saw a well in the field; and behold, three flocks of sheep lying by it; for out of that well they watered the flocks. A large stone was on the well's mouth" (Gen. 29:1–2).The Midrash comments:

> *And behold, three flocks of sheep*—the three festivals [Passover, Pentecost, and Tabernacles];
>
> *For out of that well they watered the flocks*—from there [the festivals] they imbibed the Divine spirit;
>
> *A large stone*—this alludes to the rejoicing of the place of water drawing.
>
> R. Hoshaya said, 'Why was it called the rejoicing of the place of water drawing? Because from there they imbibed the Divine spirit.'[24]

This is, of course, a highly imaginative interpretation, even by the standards of midrash. Isn't Jacob just a thirsty wanderer who is seeking water? He comes upon a well, sealed by a large stone, rolls away the stone, and drinks. But if we limit ourselves to this reading alone, we will miss a great deal that is in the text itself.

In the modern world, we don't often see wells of water, but they were a common sight to our ancestors. Isaac restored the wells of Abraham, and then dug new wells of living water (Gen. 26:19). Earlier, it was at a well that the servant of Abraham found Rebekah, who became Isaac's wife. And, now, at another well, Jacob will meet Rachel, who becomes his wife. Indeed, the wells of Rebekah and Rachel reveal much about the lives of Isaac and Jacob. At Rebekah's well, the servant arrives, sent by the father, loaded with gifts, on behalf of his son. At the end of the story, after Rebekah follows the servant home, Isaac is called *adoni*, my master. At Rachel's well, Jacob arrives himself, a vagabond without gifts or possessions at all. He will become a servant to Laban, rather than a master to anyone.

Despite such contrasts, the well is the source of life for both Isaac and Jacob. When Jacob rolls away the stone to water the flocks, he sets in motion events that will take us through the founding of Israel, the giving of Torah, the promise of renewal, and eventually the Age to Come, in which God pours out his spirit on all human-kind, as the Midrash notes.

Perhaps "three flocks of sheep" lying by the well is not an incidental detail after all. The Midrash makes a profound point in linking this number to the three festivals. Just as Jacob finds restoration at the well, and provides restoration for others by rolling away the stone, so Israel finds restoration at its annual festivals, and rehearses the restoration to come upon all nations.

Yeshua the Messiah once went up to Jerusalem against such a backdrop of expectancy to celebrate Sukkot. Yeshua's brothers had invited him to go up to "show yourself to the world" (Yochanan/ John 7:4, CJB), and he declined. But later "he too went up, not publicly but in secret. At the festival, the Judeans were looking for him. 'Where is he?' they asked" (vv. 10–11, CJB). All the festivals point to the day of Messiah and the prophetic fulfillment that only he can bring. In Yochanan's account, Yeshua finally shows himself to the world, as his brothers had suggested, "On the last day of the festival, *Hoshana Rabbah*" (7:37, CJB). The last day is great because in matters of holiness we seek to increase rather than decrease. The ritual of water drawing has just been completed, when Yeshua stands up and cries out: "If anyone is thirsty, let him keep coming to me and drinking! Whoever puts his trust in me, as the Scripture says, rivers of living water will flow from his inmost being!" (7:37–38, CJB). Yochanan comments: "Now he said this about the Spirit, whom those who trusted in him were to receive later—the Spirit had not yet been given, because Yeshua had not yet been glorified" (7:39, CJB).

Like our father Jacob, we are all thirsty. And as the Midrash suggests, we are thirsty for more than water, for we sense there is living water that comes directly from God, which will satisfy us with true and vibrant life.

Messiah offers this water to all who trust in him. He offers a profound transformation as well. We will have a supply of living water deep within ourselves, to sustain us *and* to refresh those whom we encounter in life. "If anyone is thirsty, let him keep coming to me and drinking! Whoever puts his trust in me, as the Scripture says, rivers of living water will flow from his inmost being!"

A final lesson from Rachel's well: Jacob cannot partake without rolling away the heavy stone so that all can drink. By slaking his thirst, he becomes a source of refreshment to all. He drinks, and rivers of living water flow from his inmost being on behalf of others. Like Jacob, I cannot get to the true water without making it available to those around me.

For the journey: Messiah promises not only to satisfy my spiritual thirst, but to make me a source of satisfaction to others. How do I roll away the stone at the mouth of the well, so that I can drink and supply water to others as well?

"TURNED INTO ANOTHER MAN"
Parashat Vayishlach, Genesis 32:4–36:43

A little old Jewish lady decides to make the long journey to speak with a guru in India. She flies into New Delhi and takes a train to a small town in the mountains, where she catches a rickety old bus for another leg of the journey. At the end of the bus line, she hires a porter to schlep her bags as she walks the last few miles. Finally, she arrives at the ashram and demands to speak with the guru right away. His attendants refuse her request at first, but she is so insistent that they let her in on the condition that she agrees to speak only three words. "Fine," says the old lady. When she comes into the guru, she looks up at him and says, "Sheldon, come home!"

People of all sorts long to escape the commonplace and be transformed into someone more holy. What they often discover, however, is that such a change can only come from an encounter with the God of Israel. Along with the covenants and ordinances so often emphasized in Jewish tradition, the Torah speaks of such encounters. Indeed, we might say that without the transformation that Torah describes, we cannot fulfill the precepts that Torah teaches us.

Thus, our last parashah opened with Jacob departing from the land of promise. As night falls, the text says literally, "he encountered the place" (*vayifga bamakom*; Gen. 28:11). Jacob spends the night in that place and has a vision of a ladder joining heaven and earth. He recognizes that in reality he has encountered God, who sometimes appears in rabbinic literature as ouenv, *HaMakom*, or the Place. This encounter with HaMakom prepares Jacob for the journey that lies ahead of him.

At the end of the parashah, as Jacob is about to return to the land, we see the same verb: "And angels of God encountered him" (Gen. 32:2). Now he will be prepared to return to the land from which he departed decades before. "Encounter" in these contexts implies something out of the ordinary, the heavenly realm breaking into the earthly. Jacob is not equipped for his departure or his return without this heavenly breakthrough.

We see the same verb in the story of King Saul. Samuel anoints him as king and sends him back to his father's house to await the time of his public revelation. Samuel tells Saul that he will "encounter a band of prophets . . . Then the Spirit of the LORD will come upon you, and you will prophesy with them and be turned into another man" (1 Sam. 10:5–6).

"Turned into another man . . .": this is the appeal of Jacob's story. We believe there is a transformed world waiting, the restored Creation of which Torah speaks. But like Jacob—and Sheldon—we desire transformation ourselves. In the end, we learn that only a divine encounter will make us different people.

More than the other patriarchs, Abraham and Isaac, Jacob is like us. Abraham, despite the flaws that Genesis honestly reports, appears on the scene as a visionary from the very first, a pioneer of faith in the one true God. Isaac is more passive, but he never veers from the faith of his father Abraham. Jacob, in contrast, is the patriarch with whom we can most identify, the Everyman of Genesis. Like us, he is a person in process, whose potential for greatness is evident, but nearly always mixed with qualities that are more ordinary.

Thus, for example, Jacob has the greatness to recognize and desire the spiritual legacy of his father Isaac, unlike his brother Esau who despises his birthright (Gen. 25:34). But he gains the birthright ignobly, taking advantage of Esau's shortsightedness to buy it for a bowl of lentil stew. It will take twenty-two years serving the wily Laban to transform Jacob into the man who can return to the Promised Land and take up the legacy of his forefathers. We may sympathize with his trials at the hand of Laban, but we realize that they are necessary—just like the trials that mold us.

In *Parashat Vayishlach*, however, we learn that such trials do not give the final shape to Jacob, but the divine encounters do. This parashah is a tale of homecoming. Jacob discovers that you *can* come home again, but you cannot come home unchanged. The Jacob who returns is different from the Jacob who departed:

> Then Jacob was left alone; and a Man wrestled with him until the breaking of day. Now when He saw that He did not prevail

against him, He touched the socket of his hip; and the socket of Jacob's hip was out of joint as He wrestled with him. And He said, "Let Me go, for the day breaks." But he said, "I will not let You go unless You bless me!" So He said to him, "What is your name?" He said, "Jacob." And He said, "Your name shall no longer be called Jacob, but Israel; for you have struggled with God and with men, and have prevailed." (Gen. 32:24–28)

Jacob undergoes two changes on his way home. His hip joint is dislocated, and his name is changed.

Concerning Jacob's injury, we read, "The sun rose upon him as he passed Penuel, limping because of his hip" (32:31). Literally, the Hebrew can read, "the sun rose *for* him," as Sforno interprets:

> After he passed Penuel limping, the sun rose and its rays healed him, as it will come to pass in the future, as it says, *But to you who fear my name, the sun of righteousness will rise with healing in its wings.* (Mal. 3:20)

Sforno sees Jacob's wound as temporary, but others see Jacob as permanently impaired. He bears in his flesh the reminder of the divine encounter for the rest of his life. How long Jacob's wound lasts, however, is not nearly as important as the simple fact that God touched him and left a mark on Jacob's soul that he would never forget.

Likewise, Jacob's renaming evokes a variety of translations and interpretations, such as that of Everett Fox:

> Then he said:
> Not as Yaakov/Heel-Sneak shall your name be henceforth uttered,
> but rather as Yisrael/God-Fighter,
> for you have fought with God and men
> and have prevailed. (Gen. 32:29)

Ramban sees Jacob's new name as the opposite of his old one:

> Thus the name *Ya'akov,* an expression of guile or of deviousness, was changed to Israel [from the word *sar* (prince)] and they called him *Yeshurun* from the expression *wholehearted 'v'yashar' (and upright).*[25]

Jacob's new name, like his injury, proclaims the transforming encounter with the divine. Jacob experiences two encounters—one as a young man setting out on his journey with nothing, and one as a mature man surrounded by possessions and cares, dependents and responsibilities. Apparently, the transforming encounter is not only for the young and adventurous, but also for the middle-aged (or beyond) and established. Whether we are caught up in youthful self-absorption or in the complacency of mature age, only a touch from God will really change us.

The earliest stories of Genesis hint at the hope of new birth that is central to the work of Messiah and the writings of the New Covenant millennia later.

Through his encounter with God, Jacob *becomes* Israel, representing us all. The Everyman of Genesis becomes the one-man embodiment of the chosen people of God. His story reminds us that we all must be changed by a divine encounter to find our place in the fulfilled Creation, as Messiah taught, "Most assuredly, I say to you, unless one is born again, he cannot see the kingdom of God" (John 3:3).

For the journey: Only an encounter with God can bring the transformation that prepares me for a life of faithful obedience. I will remain alert to the divine encounters that await me, and embrace them as essential stages in the journey.

CONTEST FOR CONTINUITY
Parashat Vayeshev, Genesis 37:1–40:23

> These are the generations of the heavens and of the earth when they were created, in the day that the Lord God made the earth and the heavens . . . (Gen. 2:4, KJV)

> From generation to generation, we shall tell of your greatness; forever and ever, we shall declare your holiness. (Conclusion of the *Kedushah* prayer of the *Siddur*)

Generations—*tol'dot* in Hebrew—appears as a key word throughout the book of Genesis. In the second chapter (v. 4), the word summarizes the entire creative process that which is pictured in Genesis 1, and introduces the more concrete and earthy portrayal of Genesis 2. In the following chapters, the formula "these are the generations"—*eleh tol'dot*—will appear ten more times to introduce the nations of humankind, and especially the descendants of Abraham.

The term tol'dot frames the whole drama of Genesis. The Lord seeks to establish a godly line of humankind that will follow in his ways and preserve the knowledge of him from generation to generation. But this desire encounters repeated opposition as humans rebel against, or simply ignore, the divine will. Genesis portrays a contest for generational continuity, and nowhere is this contest more evident than in the story of Joseph, which begins with the final occurrence of the phrase, eleh tol'dot:

> These are the generations of Jacob. Joseph, being seventeen years old, was feeding the flock with his brethren; and the lad was with the sons of Bilhah, and with the sons of Zilpah, his father's wives: and Joseph brought unto his father their evil report. (Gen. 37:2)

The text says, "These are the generations of Jacob," and immediately moves on to focus on Joseph, designated by Jacob as the heir apparent. Reuben, who had the right of inheritance as the firstborn, had already disqualified himself when he "went and lay with Bilhah his father's concubine" (Gen. 35:22). Simeon and Levi, next in line, proved their unworthiness by their violent and treacherous behavior toward Shechem (Gen. 34; 49:5). Later in this parashah, the action will shift to Judah, who follows Simeon and Levi in birth order. Will he prove himself worthy to be Jacob's heir? The choice between Joseph and Judah will not be resolved until the end of Genesis, and will indeed play out in biblical history far beyond that point. But for now, the focus is on Joseph.

Throughout Genesis, God is calling forth a human line that will truly represent him and be his partner on the way from Creation to completion. In his infinite wisdom, God decides that the roadmap for this journey must pass from generation to generation in one extended family. He favors Abraham because he has proven faithful in this task of generational transmission:

> Shall I hide from Abraham what I am doing, since Abraham shall surely become a great and mighty nation, and all the nations of the earth shall be blessed in him? For I have known him, in order that he may command his children and his household after him, that they keep the way of the LORD, to do righteousness and justice, that the LORD may bring to Abraham what He has spoken to him. (Gen. 18:17–19)

Likewise, in Exodus, the Lord says to Moses, "Go in to Pharaoh; for I have hardened his heart and the hearts of his servants, that I may show these signs of Mine before him, and that you may tell in the hearing of your son and your son's son the mighty things I have done in Egypt . . . that you may know that I am the LORD" (Exod. 10:1–2).

God's strategy of self-revelation, which is central to the whole biblical narrative, moves forward on one-by-one telling—"that you may tell your son and your son's son." When we tell our children, or any younger generation, about what God has done, we too have a share in declaring his name, that is, his reputation and glory, to those around us.

Because this generation-to-generation transmission is essential to God's plan, it entails a battle, the contest for continuity. At the beginning of Joseph's story, his brothers threaten his life. They spare him, but then the life of his whole generation is threatened by famine. Joseph must pass through many trials—rejection, slavery, imprisonment—as well as unparalleled success, before he establishes a new generation of his own. He endures all to ensure the survival of the next generation. In his own estimation, this is a battle well worth fighting, as he will tell his brothers at the end of the story. "You meant evil against me; but God meant it for good, in order to bring it about as it is this day, to save many people alive. Now therefore, do not be afraid; I will provide for you and your little ones" (Gen. 50:20–21).

It is a contest for the Lord, through Joseph, "to save many people alive." In the same way, there is a contest today to preserve the next generation. It is bad enough (from the standpoint of those who oppose God) for a few individuals to have an encounter with God, but a multi-generation movement for Yeshua—never! Anyone seeking to raise a family in the 21st century knows this contest for continuity firsthand.

In this struggle, we pass on not only the remembrance of events, but an immediate and intimate knowledge of the Lord, as Moses said, "What he did for me." God desires that through our story, a new generation "may *know* that I am the Lord" (Exod. 10:2b).

The God revealed in Torah, who moves and acts redemptively on the stage of history, has most fully revealed himself in Yeshua the Messiah. He now moves and acts redemptively in our lives. We pass his legacy on by displaying "what the Lord did for me . . ." concretely in the way we behave, the way we speak, and the way we treat each other.

For the journey: How can I display "what the Lord did for me" through Messiah Yeshua in my life? What am I doing to pass that story on to the next generation?

ELECTION AND ENVY
Parashat Mikketz, Genesis 41:1–44:17

In *The Hiding Place*, set in World War II Holland, Corrie Ten Boom asks a visiting pastor to hide a Jewish mother and newborn infant. He replies, "No, definitely not. We could lose our lives for that Jewish child." Corrie writes, "Unseen by either of us, Father had appeared in the doorway. 'Give the child to me, Corrie,' he said. Father held the baby close, his white beard brushing its cheek, looking into the little face with eyes as blue and innocent as the baby's. 'You say we could lose our lives for this child. I would consider that the greatest honor that could come to my family.'"[26]

When Father Ten Boom taught his daughters to love the Jewish people in the years before World War II, he spoke as a prophet. He was countering a centuries-old European legacy of anti-Semitism that would soon reach its horrible climax in the Nazi Holocaust. Today, in an unparalleled reversal, countless Christians have become lovers of Israel and the Jewish people. We live in a day of reconciliation between Jews and Christians, between Church and Synagogue.

The story of Joseph and his brothers, which continues through *Parashat Mikketz*, provides startling insights into this reconciliation. A key issue in the story, as in the Jewish-Christian story over the centuries, is election, the father's choice of one son above all others. Orthodox Jewish scholar Michael Wyschogrod sees Joseph and his brothers as a sign of God's choice of the Jewish people.

> Because [God] said, "I will bless those who bless you, and curse him that curses you; in you shall all the families of the earth be blessed" (Gen. 12:3), he has tied his saving and redemptive concern for the welfare of all humankind to his love for the people of Israel. Only those who love the people of Israel can

36

love the God of Israel. Israel is thus God's first-born, most precious in his eyes.

From this, two great dangers follow, both of which have come to pass. The first is Israel's vain pride in its own election and the second is the nations' jealousy at that same election. This twofold drama is prefigured in the tale of Joseph and his brothers, *but so is the reconciliation that awaits us in the end of time.*[27]

Joseph is the favorite of his father, Jacob, and he seems to flaunt that privilege in his brothers' faces. He reports their bad behavior to Jacob. He gloats over his dreams of dominating his brothers (and his parents as well). He sports the special garment, an ornamented tunic that Jacob gives him, even when he goes out to the fields of Dothan to check up on his brothers.

Joseph is indeed chosen, but as yet has no idea of what he is chosen for. His brothers can only see Joseph's self-absorption and react with envy. Wyschogrod—a loyal Jew—sees a parallel to Joseph in the Jewish people, who are equally chosen. He also sees the Gentile nations reenacting the envy of Joseph's brothers:

Just as Joseph's brothers rebelled against the favor shown by their father toward this one child of his, so the nations refuse to accept the election of Israel. And just as Joseph was not guiltless in the matter in that he did not accept his election as he should have, in humility, in fear and trembling, so Israel has not often made it easy for the nations to accept its election. Just as Joseph suffered for his deeds, so has Israel; just as Joseph retained the election, proving worthy of it, so has Israel.[28]

If this comparison is apt, the ending of the story is especially encouraging. Wyschogrod writes that this ending prefigures "the reconciliation [between Israel and the nations] that awaits us in the end of time." As followers of Yeshua, we believe this reconciliation will be accomplished only in him. Here we must depart from Wyschogrod's reading, for he sees reconciliation coming as the nations learn to accept "the mystery of their non-election."[29] But in Messiah, a remnant from the nations *is* elect. The mystery is that this election in no way diminishes Israel's election. Indeed, the election of Gentiles in Messiah depends upon Israel's election, as God said to Abraham, "In your seed all the nations of the earth shall be blessed" (Gen. 22:18).

Likewise, in Joseph's story, once the brothers accept his uniquely favored position, they are able to benefit from it. They never replace Joseph as the chosen son. Even as Jacob approaches death, he bestows a double portion upon Joseph, the traditional right of the first-born, by adopting both of his sons and including them in the number of the tribes of Israel (Gen. 48:15–16, 22). Nevertheless, he goes on to bless each of his other sons, and to articulate each one's destiny as part of the people of God. We might say that all twelve tribes are chosen, yet Joseph remains uniquely chosen, and the source of blessing to the rest.

The story of election and envy reveals the need for Jewish-Christian reconciliation. For centuries, the Church has taught that it replaces Israel as the chosen people of God, and that the covenants and promises first spoken to Israel now apply only to it. In this mistaken view, since the Church represents a new elect, Israel can no longer be elect, and Jews who accept Yeshua are no longer to live as Jews.

At the same time, Jews have often had difficulty acknowledging God's election of a remnant from among the nations through the Messiah Yeshua. Instead, both Jews and Christians have imagined themselves in a zero-sum game in which favor upon one group meant the rejection of the other. But these are the rules of man, not God. Reconciliation will mean affirming the election, both of Israel and of the faithful of all nations in Messiah Yeshua. The affirmation of Israel's election does not diminish the election of a remnant from the nations.

Those who see a need for reconciliation in their own lives will find a lesson here. Reconciliation means overcoming envy, and a zero-sum mentality that fears that the other's blessing will diminish our own. Instead, we must embrace the vastness of God's blessing for ourselves, and others as well.

When Messianic Jews and Christians read the Joseph story, they often see the rejected and suffering Joseph as prefiguring Yeshua. He too is rejected by his own brothers, and he too becomes the agent of salvation for the sons of Jacob and for the surrounding nations as well. If the story prefigures "the reconciliation that awaits us in the end of time," as Wyschogrod writes, it is foremost a reconciliation between Yeshua and his brothers, the Jewish people. Both readings stand, however. Joseph prefigures Israel the chosen people, *and* the chosen one among the chosen people, Yeshua the Messiah. Reconciliation between Israel and the nations is inextricably tied to reconciliation between Yeshua and the Jewish people.

The Son of God has come among us as the Jew Yeshua. He embodies God's irrevocable gifts and calling upon Israel, and he will never abandon his people. The consummation of Creation must involve the restoration of Israel and its reconciliation with the Gentile church.

Israel continues to be the elect of God, despite our wanderings and unbelief. An assembly from the nations is also the elect of God, despite its wanderings and unbelief. The mystery is that God is at work in both elect groups, despite the failings of each. As Joseph— the chosen one rejected by his brothers—declares at the end of his story: "But as for you, you meant evil against me; but God meant it for good, in order to bring it about as it is this day, to save many people alive" (Gen. 50:20).

For the journey: If I am part of God's chosen people, whether Jewish or Gentile, I must ask myself what I am chosen *for*. I can express my thanks to God for choosing me by seeking to be a source of blessing to others. What special assignment can I fulfill today as one chosen by God?

"AND HE DREW NEAR..."
Parashat Vayigash, Genesis 44:18–47:27

The gates of prayer are never closed.[30]

As the story of Joseph and his brothers reaches its climax, Judah draws near to Joseph to make an unusual request:

> Rabbi Judah said: He came near for battle, as in the verse, *So Joab and the people that were with him drew nigh unto battle* (2 Sam. 10:13). Rabbi Nehemiah said: He came near for conciliation, as in the verse, *Then the children of Judah drew near unto Joshua* (Josh. 14:6)—to conciliate him. The Rabbis said: Coming near applies to prayer, as in the verse, *And it came to pass at the time of the evening offering, that Elijah the prophet came near* . . . (1 Kings 18:36). Rabbi Leazar combined all these views: I come whether it be for battle, for conciliation, or for prayer.[31]

The phrase, "draw near," has different implications in different passages, and Rabbi Leazar combines three meanings: Judah draws near to *battle* against a terrible fate that has befallen one of the brothers; he draws near to bring *conciliation* to the whole family; and he draws near to *pray* for mercy from Joseph.

To understand Judah's action fully, we remember that the deeds of the fathers are a sign for the sons. Joseph is a sign to Israel that one whom they reject and cast out will become their deliverer. Joseph is destined to rule over the tribes of Israel, but first, like the deliverer to come, he must suffer rejection by his brothers because of this very destiny.

> Now when they saw him afar off, even before he came near them, they conspired against him to kill him. Then they said to one another, "Look, this dreamer is coming! Come now then, let us kill him, and cast him into one of these pits and say,

'Some wild beast has devoured him!' Then we will see what becomes of his dreams!" (Gen. 37:18–20)

The Messiah tells the story of another son, rejected like Joseph. A father owns a vineyard that he rents out to vinedressers. When he sends messengers to collect his share of the fruit, the vinedressers beat and kill them one by one. Finally, the father sends his son, saying, "They will respect my son." But when the vinedressers see the son, they conspire against him to kill him, saying to one another, "This is the heir. Come now then, let us now kill him, and seize his inheritance." So they take him and cast him out of the vineyard and kill him (Matt. 21:37–39).

Yeshua, of course, tells this story about himself. Like Joseph, he is rejected and cast out to die, and, like Joseph, he will be raised up from death to be exalted as ruler. Joseph emerges from the dungeon to become second only to Pharaoh in all of Egypt. He becomes the source of salvation to all nations, honored among them, but still a stranger to his own brothers. Indeed, as the famine spreads and all nations go down to Egypt for food, only the sons of Israel do not know where to obtain bread. "When Jacob saw that there was grain in Egypt, Jacob said to his sons, 'Why do you keep looking at one another?' And he said, 'Here, I have heard that there is grain in Egypt; go down to that place and buy for us there, that we may live and not die'" (Gen. 42:1–2).

Finally, the sons of Israel come to Egypt to appear before Joseph, whom they do not yet recognize. The story ends as God intended, when Joseph reveals himself to his brothers and saves them from famine. Now we understand that God sent Joseph to save the nations, so that he might in the end save Israel. Likewise, the other rejected son, unrecognized by his own brothers, brings salvation to the nations, so that in the end "all Israel will be saved" (Rom. 11:26).

At the climactic scene, however, the focus shifts from Joseph, who is a sign of Messiah to come, to Judah, who is also a sign for us.

Before Joseph reveals himself to his brothers, he tests them. They had rejected Joseph years before, wounding not only him, but also their father, Jacob, who spent the next twenty years mourning for Joseph. Have the brothers realized their sins against both their brother and their father? To test them, Joseph arrests the youngest brother, Benjamin, telling the rest, "Benjamin shall be my slave. And as for you, go up in peace to your father" (Gen. 44:17).

At this, Judah steps out from among his brothers, for he has promised his father that he will bring Benjamin home safely, and offer himself in place of Benjamin. Thereby, without knowing it, he passes the test:

> Then Judah drew near to him and said: "Please my lord, pray let your servant speak a word in my lord's hearing, and do not let your anger burn against your servant, for you are like Pharaoh! . . . So now, pray let your servant remain instead of the lad as slave to my lord, and let the lad go up with his brothers. For how can I go up to my father if the lad is not with me, lest I see the evil that would come upon my father?" Then Joseph could restrain himself no longer. (Gen. 44:18, 33–34; 45:1)

If Joseph is a sign of Messiah and the brothers are a sign of Israel, who is Judah? He is a sign of a believing remnant within Israel, interceding for the whole. Indeed, he is a sign of all—Gentiles, as well as Jews—who are willing to make real sacrifices for the restoration of Israel. Therefore, he becomes a sign for each of us.

We can imagine Judah as father and husband, a man with attachments and duties, whose only desire is to get food for his household and return home. Now he faces a terrible choice. He remembers his word to his father and knows he cannot return home without his younger brother. So he turns his back on his own desires and puts himself into Joseph's hands as a slave for life, for the sake of his brother. Because Judah draws near in this way, Joseph will call his brothers, all Israel, to draw near as well. "And Joseph said to his brothers, 'Please draw near to me.' So they drew near. Then he said: 'I am Joseph your brother, whom you sold into Egypt'" (Gen. 45:3–4).

The gates of prayer are never closed. Judah is a sign of the one who goes through those gates not for his own purposes, but on behalf of his brothers. The journey toward Creation's consummation cannot go forward without such prayers. Just as God raises up Joseph as the savior of Egypt and the surrounding nations, so that he might save Israel, so is the salvation of Israel central to his purposes for the whole human race in our day and into the future.

Judah is a sign of our calling as followers of Messiah to remain in solidarity with all Israel as we draw near to him, anticipating the day when the rest of the sons of Jacob will draw near to Messiah as well.

For the journey: The gates of prayer are never closed, but what will I do when I enter those gates? Will I go beyond concern for my own needs to practice unselfish concern for others? Specifically, like Judah, will I intercede for the whole family of Israel?

A COFFIN IN EGPYT
Parashat Vayechi, Genesis 47:28–50:26

In the next to last scene of the old Star Wars movie, *The Empire Strikes Back,* the hero Han Solo is frozen solid in carbonite by his imperial captors. As they lower the inert Solo into a vault, a frosty mist swirls about him and the music fades away. All you can think is, "sequel coming." It seems like a moment of defeat, but it signals the victory that is sure to come.

Like *The Empire Strikes Back,* Genesis concludes with an image of seeming defeat—a coffin in Egypt—that conveys the promise of victory to come:

> Then Joseph took an oath from the children of Israel, saying, "God will surely visit you, and you shall carry up my bones from here." So Joseph died, being one hundred and ten years old; and they embalmed him, and he was put in a coffin in Egypt. (Gen. 50:25–26)

At first reading, this seems like a disappointing ending for the magnificent first book of the Torah. The rabbinic commentators do not say a great deal about it, perhaps reflecting some embarrassment over Joseph's embalming, since later Jewish law forbids it. Likewise, Christian commentators often see the conclusion of Genesis as negative, suggesting the hopelessness of the human condition apart from divine redemption.

The book of Hebrews however, provides the key to understanding this conclusion: "By faith Joseph, when he died, made mention of the departing of the children of Israel; and gave commandment concerning his bones" (Heb. 11:22).

The coffin in Egypt becomes an emblem of hope, a sure sign that this story is not over yet. Joseph "made mention of the departing of the children of Israel," telling them twice that God would "surely visit" them and bring them up out of Egypt (Gen. 50:24–25). God promises redemption, and Joseph believes that promise.

As Genesis concludes, then, we may believe that we have only to wait for the sequel, when the promise will surely be fulfilled. We might think that the route from the coffin in Egypt to redemption is all in God's hand, but actually, the actors in this drama must provide a crucial element themselves. The sequel will be another step on the way from Creation to completion, the overarching theme of all the Torah, and therefore it will require human participation.

The Book of Exodus reveals the human element in the transition from the coffin in Egypt to the deliverance to come:

> It was, many years later,
> the king of Egypt died.
> The children of Israel groaned from the servitude,
> and they cried out;
> and their plea-for-help went up to God from the servitude.
> God hearkened to their moaning,
> God called-to-mind his covenant with Avraham, with Yitzchak, and with Yaakov,
> God saw the Children of Israel,
> God knew. (Exodus 2:23–25, Fox)

The simple language of Torah describes four divine actions. When the children of Israel groan, the Lord hears, remembers, looks, and knows. Of course, God knows everything all the time. Hence, numerous translations supplement this final phrase with words like, "God took notice of them" (NJPS), or "God acknowledged them" (NKJV). But the Hebrew is clear enough: "God knew," period.

God knows all things, but he has assigned to human beings the responsibility of reminding him. Our ancestors were groaning under their bondage, but they still bore the image of God and represented him. They had the authority to call upon him to intervene in human affairs, as they "cried out" with a "plea-for-help." In response to this cry, God hears, remembers, looks, and knows, thereby reminding us of both the power and simplicity of prayer.

Beyond this simple cry for help, we can see a second level of prayer, which is reflected in the traditional service of the synagogue, to this day. Even after the redemption from Egypt, the Jewish people remain in exile, but we possess the promise of redemption.

Our ancestors in Egypt may not have remembered God's promise to redeem them until Moses came to fulfill it, but God heard their anguished groaning anyway. Now we have the assurance of redemption revealed in Scripture, and call upon God on that basis.

Jewish liturgy abounds with examples of such a call. The final line of the *Kaddish* prayer says, "He who makes peace in his high places, may he make peace upon us and upon all Israel" (from the *Siddur*). Peace, *shalom*, is central to the prophetic vision of Creation consummated, revealed throughout the Book of Genesis. In the *Kaddish*, repeated daily in the synagogue, we call on the Lord to establish that shalom in our midst even now. When we sing this prayer, we repeat the refrain, *ya'aseh shalom alenu v'al kol Yisrael*, literally, "He *will* make peace upon us and upon all Israel." This is a prophetic and intercessory cry for the Lord to do as he has promised.

Likewise, preparing to take the Torah out of the ark in the synagogue service, we recite the words, "When the ark went forth, Moses would say, 'Arise, O Lord, and let your enemies be scattered, and let those who hate you flee from before you.'" (from the *Siddur*). As the Word of God goes forth in our service, we pray that the spiritual forces that oppose God and Israel will be defeated and driven back. In this weekly enactment, we pray for all Israel, and ultimately for the whole human race, looking forward to the day when "The Torah will go forth from Zion, and the word of the Lord from Jerusalem" (Isa. 2:3).

With such prayers, Israel has taken on its priestly responsibility throughout the centuries, and these prayers remain precious in the sight of God. For believers in Yeshua, whether Jewish or Gentile, the redemption of which they speak is even more immediate. Messiah has already launched the restoration of all things through his death and resurrection. Through him, these prayers will be fulfilled in the end of days, and through him, we come to a third level of intercession.

The first level is the simple cry to God for relief. A second level comes in response to the promises revealed in Scripture. We call out in the language of divine revelation to remind God to act as he has said he would. The third level responds to the *fulfillment* of the promise in Messiah Yeshua. We still await the Age to Come, but in Messiah, the spirit of God is at work among us here and now. We participate in this third level as we pray in the name of Yeshua, proclaiming his victory and life. For us, Joseph's coffin in Egypt pictures not defeat but the promise of resurrection, a promise already realized in Messiah Yeshua, and guaranteed to his followers.

Genesis opened with the account of Creation, which included the plan for its completion. God created human beings in his image, to have dominion over the earth under his rule. Through disobedience to God, however, human beings obstructed the way for the plan to be fulfilled. But even in the midst of human failure, even in the presence of a coffin in Egypt, God's promise remains. And humankind, including you and me, are responsible for believing the promise and calling on God to bring it to pass.

For the journey: God knows all things, but he awaits our cry. It is our responsibility in prayer to remind him of his promise, and to proclaim the fulfillment of that promise in Messiah Yeshua. The journey toward restoration advances through divine-human cooperation. How fully am I cooperating with God's plan?

שמות

THE BOOK OF EXODUS

Exodus brings us back to the closing scene of Genesis—Egypt, where Joseph has led the tribes of Israel. Now God is going to act upon his promise to Abraham to bring Israel out of bondage in Egypt and back to the land of Canaan. The Hebrew title for Exodus is שמות (*Sh'mot*), or "Names," from its opening line, "Now these are the names of the children of Israel who came to Egypt." But Exodus is no mere census, nor just a record of ancient events in an alien land. Rather, it retells such events to advance the narrative of Creation-Revelation-Completion that began in the book of Genesis.

- *Creation*. This theme underlies the entire Bible, but Exodus especially revisits and develops it. As one modern translator says, "The book of Exodus is Israel's second book of origins."[1] Throughout Exodus, as in Genesis, God acts to restore and protect the original order and blessing of Creation, despite human resistance and failure.

- *Revelation*. The entire story of Israel's deliverance from Egypt centers on God making himself known, as in the recurring phrase, "that you [or they] may know that I am the LORD." When God sends the plagues upon Egypt and delivers the Israelites in a great display of power, it is to make himself known both to Israel and Egypt as the true and living God. Because Exodus reveals God so fully, it becomes the foundational story of the rest of the Hebrew Scriptures, as well as of the account of Yeshua's life recorded in the Gospels. And it remains the foundational story of the Jewish people to this day.

The theme of Revelation reaches a climax when Israel arrives at Mount Sinai in Exodus 19. Here, before the eyes of 2,000,000 men, women, and children, God reveals his presence upon the mountain in fire, in the midst of thunder, lightning, and a thick cloud. Far greater than this vision of God's presence, however, is the word of God revealed at Sinai. Exodus records the Ten Commandments written by the finger of God, the basis for the entire body of divine instruction, which continues through the rest of the Torah.

One specific instruction, or set of instructions, in Exodus is especially designed to reveal God. He charges the Israelites with building the tabernacle, which takes up the final sixteen chapters of the book. The tabernacle is a model of the restored Creation, in which God dwells in the midst of his people, and reveals himself from there to all humanity.

- *Completion.* The restoration of all things does not yet take place in Torah, of course, but Exodus points toward it continually. We will see how specifics of the Mosaic legislation point toward the fulfillment of the Age to Come. Through obedience to God's word, human beings take on their responsibility to represent God within his Creation. Every commandment is a preview in the present age of the restored order and peace of the Age to Come.

In addition to advancing the story of Creation to completion, Exodus develops the themes of Covenant and Redemption introduced in Genesis. A covenant is a solemn and binding agreement that defines the relationship between God as the sovereign ruler, and human beings, his grateful subjects. God makes such covenants, first with all humankind through Noah, and then with one specific human family through Abraham.

In Exodus, he will act upon the covenant he made with Abraham to deliver his descendants from slavery and bring them into a new and expanded covenant as his chosen people. This action invokes the theme of Redemption. Redemption rescues God's people from the forces that disrupt his purpose in Creation and block his self-revelation. It reopens the way toward the fulfillment of Creation. Thus, redemption becomes an essential element in the big story of Creation-Revelation-Completion.

The message of Exodus is clear. God, the creator of all things, is a God who makes covenant with the humans that he created in his image. There are spiritual forces that oppose God and his people, but God is faithful to act in human history and in the end to make himself known upon the earth.

GOD REDISCOVERED
Parashat Shemot, Exodus 1:1–6:1

> The knowledge that we acquire by being in the ten plagues school is primarily the knowledge of God and how he works in contrast to Pharaoh and how he works. Pharaoh employs size and force and prestige to control and oppress. God employs only an eighty-year-old desert shepherd and his brother, their only weapon a stick, and a ragtag company of despised slaves to bring about freedom and salvation for the whole world. [2]

Exodus is a book of renewal, in which all the themes sounded at the beginning of Genesis reach a new crescendo. In Egypt, Israel becomes a new humanity, fulfilling the original blessing of fruitfulness from Genesis 1. "But the children of Israel were fruitful and increased abundantly, multiplied and grew exceedingly mighty; and the land was filled with them" (Exod. 1:7). When Moses is born, his mother sees *ki tov*, that he is good, using the same phrase that appears seven times in Genesis 1. In Exodus, Israel, in the person of Moses, is saved from the waters by an ark and restored to an Eden-like land flowing with milk and honey.

The renewal of Exodus, like all spiritual renewals, entails a renewed understanding of God. Here we acquire anew "the knowledge of God and how he works."

Thus, Moses' renewal begins when he encounters God at the Burning Bush. Whether you're a dedicated student of Scripture or not, you probably remember this encounter, which is so dramatic, so unexpected, and so decisive in shaping the rest of Moses' life. At the Burning Bush, God calls Moses back to Egypt to stand before Pharaoh and deliver the children of Israel.

You may also remember that Moses resists this calling with some heat. When God sends him back to Egypt, Moses says, "Who am I, that I should go to Pharaoh and bring forth the children of Israel out of Egypt?" The Lord encourages Moses, "I will certainly be with you." (Exod. 3:11–12). The real issue, of course, is the ability of God, not of Moses. God, not Moses, will get the glory as he intervenes in a situation that seems utterly hopeless.

Exodus shows us that in the face of great challenge, we are not to look to who we are, but to the God who is with us. This story preaches so well, however, that we might forget that God's answer doesn't quite satisfy Moses. He had first asked, "Who am I?" Now in response to God's promise to be with him, he asks, "and who are you?"

> Then Moses said to God, "Indeed, when I come to the children of Israel and say to them, 'The God of your fathers has sent me to you,' and they say to me, 'What is His name?' what shall I say to them?" (3:13)

The children of Israel have probably spoken of the God of their forefathers, but they have seen little evidence of God. Now God is going to use this "eighty-year-old desert shepherd and his brother . . . and a ragtag company of despised slaves to bring about freedom and salvation for the whole world." Just who is this God who says he is going to do such amazing things?

> And God said to Moses, "I AM WHO I AM." And He said, "Thus you shall say to the children of Israel, 'I AM has sent me to you.'" Moreover God said to Moses, "Thus you shall say to the children of Israel: 'The LORD God of your fathers, the God of Abraham, the God of Isaac, and the God of Jacob, has sent me to you. This is My name forever, and this is My memorial to all generations.'" (3:14–15)

The Lord says at first that he cannot be named: I am who I am. Jewish tradition considers the personal name of God, spelled with the four Hebrew letters equivalent to Y-H-V-H, too holy to pronounce, so that it is read as Adonai, or LORD. Rambam notes that YHVH is derived from the root vhv *hyh*, meaning, "to be." This name, therefore, "is not indicative of an attribute, but of a simple root and nothing else. Now absolute existence implies that He shall always be, I mean He who is necessarily existent."[3] From the Burning Bush, this eternally existent and unnamable God identifies himself as God of the patriarchs. Thus, he ties himself to time and place, apparently contradicting his "absolute existence." Scripture speaks of God's transcendence and of his presence among humankind, developing a tension that is not fully resolved until the coming of Messiah, who is Immanuel, God with us (Isa. 7:14).

There is another tension in the story of Exodus: "And God spoke to Moses and said to him: 'I am the LORD. I appeared to Abraham, to Isaac, and to Jacob, as God Almighty [*El Shaddai*], but by My name LORD I was not known to them'" (Exod. 6:2). But the patriarchs *did* use the name YHVH. Indeed, at the Burning Bush, God speaks of himself as "Adonai, God of your fathers." In what sense then was the name Adonai not known to the patriarchs?

We find a clue to this question in the name by which the Lord appeared to the forefathers, El Shaddai. This name sounds like the Hebrew word *dai*—enough—signifying that he is the God who is always sufficient. Sforno comments that El Shaddai identifies God as the Creator of all existence. But YHVH identifies God as he intervenes within his Creation to bring redemption. "I, who grant existence to all that exists, shall with this power bring them out by partially modifying nature."[4]

Abraham, Isaac, and Jacob know God as El Shaddai, the God who calls them, leads them to the land of Canaan, and promises them a great inheritance there. Even though they sometimes use the name Adonai, they all die without seeing the character of Adonai revealed. When the time comes to fulfill the promise, however, God reveals himself as Adonai, the one who acts within human history for his redemptive purposes.

In the Torah, as in our lives, God seeks to make himself more fully known. We often try to understand our life struggles in terms of our own happiness or success, and thereby often fail to understand. But perhaps we need to see our struggles as God's way of revealing himself as the One who is with us through it all, and who works in ways that don't always make sense to us.

As the biblical story unfolds, God does not grow more distant, but he draws nearer. And he draws near to accomplish redemption, not only to help the oppressed, but to reveal his character. "Then you shall know that I am Adonai your God who brings you out from under the burden of the Egyptians" (Exod. 6:6–7).

In our journey through Torah, we will find God becoming not more abstract, as we might expect, but more embodied and engaged, more knowable. Here is a *remez*, a hint, of the coming of Immanuel, God with us, in the person of Messiah. In Messiah, God makes himself known upon the earth more and more fully until the day of restoration arrives.

For the journey: All renewal entails a renewed vision of God. God never changes, but we must continually change in our understanding of him, as he seeks to reveal himself more fully to us. Am I ready to learn more of who God is, so I can share in the renewal that God brings?

YOU GOTTA SERVE SOMEBODY
Parashat Va'era, Exodus 6:2–9:35

> Well, it may be the devil or it may be the Lord
> But you're gonna have to serve somebody.[5]

Exodus is the Torah's book of worship. It takes Israel from the scene of oppression in Egypt, to Mount Sinai where they become a kingdom of priests, to the building of the tabernacle in the wilderness, where they will worship the Lord in the midst of the camp. Thus, when the Lord first calls Moses from the Burning Bush and sends him to deliver his people, he says, "This shall be a sign to you that I have sent you: When you have brought the people out of Egypt, you shall *worship* God on this mountain" (Exod. 3:12, emphasis added.).

Worship in Hebrew is *avodah*, which is also the word for service or labor. Israel has served Pharaoh, and now they must serve God. We might even say that Israel has worshiped Pharaoh—the verb is the same—and now they must worship God. They have devoted their time, abilities, and energies to the glory of Pharaoh, and now they must devote their time, abilities, and energies to the glory of God. Pharaoh, however, believes the people must serve him, so the Lord instructs Moses to tell him, "Thus says the Lord: 'Let my people go, that they may serve me'" (8:20 [16]).

Here in three Hebrew words we have the theme of the entire book of Exodus: *Shalach 'ami v'ya'avduni* שלח עמי ויעבדני—"Let my people go, that they may serve [worship] me." The first half of this phrase, "let my people go," describes the first half of Exodus, in which the God of Israel forces Pharaoh to release his people "by trials, by signs, by wonders, by war, by a mighty hand and an outstretched arm, and by great terrors" (Deut. 4:34). This half concludes with the crossing of the Red Sea. The second half, "that they may worship me," includes the encounter at Sinai and the building of the tabernacle, where Israel worships the Lord who has delivered them.

56

This drama of worship in Exodus teaches us much about our worship today.

1) Man is a worshiping being, created for a relationship with God.

Adam walks with God in the garden, in an intimacy with God that is at the heart of all worship. After the expulsion from the garden, men build altars, present offerings, and call upon the Lord. Worship is at the center of who we are as human beings. Hence, we are to worship with our whole being, not as an isolated event, but through all of our activities. Worship in the synagogue or church should reflect our entire lives given to worship.

2) There is a cosmic struggle for our worship.

We would like to imagine ourselves as autonomous beings that can choose whom to worship or whether to worship at all. But Exodus reveals that, as Bob Dylan sang, "You're gonna have to serve somebody"—God or Pharaoh. So when Moses makes a modest demand of Pharaoh to release Israel for three days to worship the Lord in the wilderness (Exod. 3:18; 5:3), Pharaoh cannot compromise. If he acknowledges God's claim here, he loses his claim on the very souls of the Israelites.

The temptation of Messiah reveals this same tug-of-war over worship:

> Once more, the Adversary took him up to the summit of a very high mountain, showed him all the kingdoms of the world in all their glory, and said to him, "All this I will give you if you will bow down and worship me." "Away with you, Satan!" Yeshua told him, "For the Tanakh says, 'Worship ADONAI your God, and serve only him.' Then the Adversary let him alone, and angels came and took care of him." (Matt. 4:8–11, CJB)

Satan seeks to draw our worship away from the Lord, thus diminishing his glory and disrupting the divine order established at Creation. He entices us with worldly power and comfort. Scripture does not promote asceticism or a narrow religiosity, but it does alert us to the power of the materialistic culture that surrounds us. We need to resist the images of greed, lust, and vanity that bombard us in the name of entertainment or success. The adversary does not insist on being worshiped directly; he is satisfied to simply divert our worship away from God.

3) *This struggle for worship centers upon Israel.*

In Exodus, the Lord identifies Israel as his firstborn son, a representative humanity, the priestly nation. If their worship can remain diverted, then the worship of the rest of the nations will be as well. This contest over worship may help explain the intense struggle that has characterized Jewish history over the centuries, and continues today. It is a struggle not just over Israel's destiny, but over the fulfillment of God's plan for all humanity.

4) *Falsely directed worship results in bondage.*

So the Egyptians made the children of Israel *serve* with rigor. And they made their lives bitter with hard *bondage*—in mortar, in brick, and in all manner of *service* in the field. All their *service* in which they made them *serve* was with rigor. (Exod. 1:13–14, emphasis added)

The Hebrew root עָבַד *avad*—serve or worship—appears five times in these two verses, to highlight the bondage of misdirected service. In contrast, through the sacrifice of Messiah, we are delivered out of bondage and set free to serve God alone. This personal story of salvation is just a part of the big story of humankind restored to God. The message of Scripture proclaims deliverance to all who are serving false gods—whether the gods of paganism, or the gods of secular materialism.

5) We are set free from bondage so that we can worship the true God.

The goal of our deliverance is not autonomy, but worship. God leads Israel out of Egypt, not just to enjoy freedom and prosperity, but to establish the tabernacle and priesthood; Messiah comes not just to forgive us from sin, or to bring us into God's blessing, but to establish us as worshipers.

The biblical drama ends with worship. The book of Revelation is the New Covenant counterpart to Exodus as the book of worship. There we see,

[A] great multitude which no one could number, of all nations, tribes, peoples, and tongues, standing before the throne and before the Lamb, clothed with white robes, with palm branches in their hands, and crying out with a loud voice, saying, "Salvation belongs to our God who sits on the throne, and to the Lamb!" . . . [T]hey are before the throne of God, and serve Him day and night in His Temple. And He who sits on the throne will dwell among them. (Rev. 7: 9–10, 15)

We were created to worship in the beginning, and worship will be our destiny in the end. The first man and woman walked with the Lord in the Garden of Eden in the cool of the day. We will regain such intimacy in the Age to Come when the purpose of Creation is fulfilled. In Messiah, we have a foretaste of this worship even now.

For the journey: Am I a worshiper, or just someone who squeezes a few minutes of worship into my busy schedule? Does my worship on *Shabbat*, or Sunday, or other "religious" times, reflect a life of worship through the week? Do I spend my time, abilities, and energies to increase God's name and reputation or only my own?

THE HEART OF PHARAOH
Parashat Bo, Exodus 10:1–13:16

> Rabbi Akiva used to say . . . "All is foreseen, yet free choice is given."[6]

The Lord commands Pharaoh to let the children of Israel go, but he hardens Pharaoh's heart so that he refuses to let them go (Exod. 10:20). This paradox has puzzled readers of Exodus since the earliest times. God desires to deliver his people from Egypt, but he ensures that the king of Egypt will not release them. Furthermore, God judges Pharaoh and his whole nation for keeping the Israelites in bondage, yet God hardened Pharaoh to do the very thing for which he judges him! Pharaoh seems to have no free choice in the matter, so why is he condemned?

One clue to this paradox is the verb translated "hardened" in Exodus 10:20. It is from the root חזק *hazak*, most commonly meaning "to strengthen, to make firm." We repeat this word in the synagogue at the conclusion of our reading of each book of Torah: *hazak, hazak, v'nit'chazek!* "Be strong, be strong, and let us be strengthened," to fulfill the teachings of this book.

The Lord does not simply harden Pharaoh, but he strengthens him to do *what he really wants to do*. God does not override Pharaoh's freedom of will, but reinforces it. Pharaoh might waver under the mounting weight of the plagues, but the Lord helps him to persevere and do what he really desires to do.

Still, a paradox remains. Solomon says, "The king's heart is in the hand of the LORD, like the rivers of water; He turns it wherever He wishes" (Prov. 21:1). God strengthens Pharaoh to do what he wants to do, but at the same time God is carrying out his own purposes. And indeed, in a few references in Exodus we read, not that the Lord strengthens the heart of Pharaoh, but that he "hardens" it (Exod. 7:3) or makes it "stubborn" (Exod. 8:28).

Sforno, in his comment on Exodus 7:3, says that the Lord hardens Pharaoh's heart so that he does not buckle under the pressure and release Israel without truly repenting.

> Without a doubt, were it not for the hardening of Pharaoh's heart he would have sent forth Israel, not because of repentance or submission to God, the Blessed One, (nor because) he regretted his rebellion, recognizing God's greatness and goodness—but because he could no longer abide the anguish of the plagues. . . . Now this would not have been repentance.

God's goal in Exodus is not only to deliver Israel out of the bondage of Egypt, but also to bring the oppressor to genuine repentance. This goal in turn leads to a greater one: Revelation—to make himself known to the entire human race. Accordingly, the Lord says to Pharaoh, "But indeed for this purpose I have raised you up, so that I might show you My power, and that My name may be declared in all the earth" (Exod. 9:16). God "raised up" Pharaoh, not only by making him king, but by helping him to stand until he genuinely repents, and thereby becomes a model for the multitudes. Sforno comments on this verse:

> *So that I might show you My power* . . . that you might repent, for *I do not desire the death of him who dies* (Ezekiel 18:32). *And that My Name may be declared* . . . thereby turning many away from sin.

Exodus might seem like the account of an ancient struggle between two local nations, but in reality, it tells of the struggle to bring the Creation to its divine goal. God seeks to reveal his sovereignty to all human beings, so that they can truly know him and reflect his image. He enlists human participation in this divine self-revelation, even from those who oppose him. As Akiva said, "All is foreseen"—God will fulfill the blessing and promise of the original Creation; "yet free will is given"—human beings have a genuine part in bringing this fulfillment.

Pharaoh is a free moral agent, genuinely responsible for his own deeds, yet God is behind it all, orchestrating everything for his own redemptive purposes. In the end, of course, Pharaoh does not repent. Instead, he is finally crushed by the weight of the plagues, culminating in the death of his own firstborn, and releases the Israelites under duress. *Parashat Bo* describes the first Passover, commemorating this moment of deliverance. Jewish families, as far back as the days of Yeshua, reenact this Passover every year through sharing a ceremonial meal, called a *Seder*.

> On the first day for *matzah*, the talmidim [disciples] came to Yeshua and asked, "Where do you want us to prepare your Seder?" "Go into the city, to so-and-so," he replied, "and tell him that the Rabbi says, 'My time is near, my talmidim and I are celebrating Pesach at your house.'" The talmidim did as Yeshua directed and prepared the Seder.
>
> When evening came, Yeshua reclined with the twelve talmidim; and as they were eating, he said, "Yes, I tell you that one of you is going to betray me." They became terribly upset and began asking him, one after the other, "Lord, you don't mean me, do you?" He answered, "The one who dips his matzah in the dish with me is the one who will betray me. The Son of Man will die just as the Tanakh says he will; but woe to that man by whom the Son of Man is betrayed! It would have been better for him had he never been born!" Judas, the one who was betraying him, then asked, "Surely, Rabbi, you don't mean me?" He answered, "The words are yours." (Matt. 26:17–25, CJB)

All is foreseen, yet free choice is given. The Son of Man must "die just as the Tanakh says he will," but woe to the one who betrays him!

In this paradox, we glimpse our profound responsibility as followers of God. In modern terms we might say, God has everything under control . . . and what I do still matters. Now we can understand why our own spiritual journeys are filled with tough choices, ambiguities, and unanswered questions. If the pathway to redemption were paved entirely by God, it would be smooth all the way. But God has given us a share in its construction, so the pavement is rough and rocky.

Sometimes we spend more energy trying to discern what God is doing on the way to redemption than on contributing our share. We may end up unprepared, like Yeshua's disciples on that same

Passover night. When an armed band came to arrest him, he submitted, saying, "'But all this has happened so that what the prophets wrote may be fulfilled.' Then the talmidim all deserted him and ran away" (Matt. 26:56, CJB). The divine plan goes forward as it must, but the disciples have lost their way within it. The moment of crisis arrives and they are missing from the Master's side.

At the end of the story, Yeshua gathers his disciples, except for the betrayer. And at the end of Pharaoh's story, God's plan goes forward without him. Such endings are God's responsibility. For us, the challenge is to remain near to the Master, even at the darkest moments.

For the journey: God has a plan that will not fail, *and* my choices still matter. I need to remain alert so that I don't fail to play my part, or worse, like Pharaoh, resist it. Instead, I have real responsibility in making God known in the earth. How do I fulfill my share of this responsibility today?

SPLITTING THE SEA
Parashat B'shallach, Exodus 13:17–17:16

> Once, Rabbi Shmelke of Nikolsburg said the Song at the Sea [Exod. 15:1–19] as prayer leader with such holy power that when the congregation recited with him the verses about the crossing of the Red Sea they all lifted up the hems of their kaftans to keep them from getting wet, for it actually seemed to them that they had gone down into the Sea which had split before them.[7]

As Exodus nears its climax, Israel departs from Egypt, but Pharaoh—who refused to repent through nine plagues—repents now for letting them go. He gathers his chariots and army to pursue the Israelites, and overtakes them as they are encamped on the shore of the Red Sea. With Pharaoh's army behind them and the Sea before them, the Israelites are trapped and terrified. Moses tells them, "Do not be afraid. Stand still, and see the salvation of the Lord, which He will accomplish for you today" (Exod.14:13). Salvation is something to be *seen*, a mighty revelation of God's power and glory.

At the shore of the Red Sea, the drama of Exodus returns to the original drama of "In the beginning." There, in the story of Creation, the sea is the primordial chaos out of which God will bring the order and beauty of our world. On the second day of Creation, the Lord makes a "firmament" to divide the waters above from the waters below. On the third day he says, "Let the waters under the heavens be gathered together into one place, and let the dry land appear" (Gen. 1:9). The work of Creation goes forth in this newly divided land and sea.

Now, in Exodus, the Lord divides the sea again, this time to bring salvation to the Israelites. But here the Hebrew uses a different word for "dividing." The root word in Genesis is בדל *badal*, from which we derive the word *Havdalah*, the prayer service that concludes Shabbat, dividing it from the rest of the week.

> Blessed are you, O Lord our God, King of the universe, who distinguishes between holy and ordinary, between light and darkness, between Israel and the nations, between the seventh day and the six days of labor. Blessed are you, O Lord, who distinguishes between holy and ordinary. (From the *Siddur*)

Through this prayer, the individual becomes a participant in dividing the week between Shabbat and the ordinary days. Like the parting of the Sea, this is an event of cosmic proportions, yet each member of the community has a share in it by reciting the blessing.

The word for the parting of the Sea, *baka*, meaning to split or cleave, is a more dramatic term than *badal*, and signals the divine intervention into a scene of disorder. But the parallels to Genesis remain. The waters are divided by a *ruach*, a "strong east wind" (14:21), just as the ruach, or Spirit, of the Lord hovered over the waters in the beginning. As at the Creation, the waters are tamed to reveal dry land, but here the dry land emerges as the scene of divine rescue and judgment. The same waters that part and become a wall to the Israelites "on their right hand and on their left" (14:22) become the means of judgment upon the Egyptians. Thus, the story echoes not only the first days of Creation, but also the flood of Noah, generations later, when God brings judgment by means of water.

In another echo of the Creation account, the pillar of cloud moves between Egypt and the Israelites, dividing the chosen people from their oppressor. On the Egyptian side, it appears as cloud and darkness. To the Israelites, it brings light by night, just as the Lord spoke "Let there be light" into the primordial darkness of the first day. Chaos confronts Egypt; Creation confronts Israel, both carried by the same cloud of divine glory.

Salvation is a new Creation, a foretaste of the renewed Creation of the Age to Come. Humankind was not present in the original Creation until the final day, but human beings are present in the drama of salvation and must respond. Therefore, after the splitting of the Sea, Moses and the Israelites sing a song of praise to the Lord,

> I will sing to the LORD,
> For He has triumphed gloriously!
> The horse and its rider
> He has thrown into the sea! (Exod. 15:1)

The rabbis of the Talmud noted that, "Moses *and the children of Israel* sang this song to the Lord" (Exod. 15:1, emphasis added). They saw the song as a responsive reading, with Moses taking the lead and the children of Israel responding line by line.[8] Every individual participated. The salvation of all Israel included the salvation of each individual Israelite who walked across the Sea on dry ground. This responsive song of worship became part of the traditional Jewish prayers, as recited by Rabbi Shmelke and his congregation in Nikolsburg, an invitation to every Jew in every age to personally embrace this incomparable event.

Like the parting of the Sea, the resurrection of Messiah was an event of cosmic proportions that demands an individual response. Matthew notes that at the moment of Yeshua's death the earth quaked, rocks split apart, and graves opened up, as saints were raised up from the dead to appear to many in Jerusalem. Three days after Messiah was placed in a tomb, "there was a great earthquake; for an angel of the Lord descended from heaven, and came and rolled back the stone from the door and sat on it. His countenance was like lightning, and his clothing as white as snow. And the guards shook for fear of him, and became like dead men" (Matt. 28:2–5).

In the midst of these awesome displays, Yeshua reveals himself to one faithful, bewildered follower by simply speaking her name, "Miryam," or Mary (John 20:16). The scope of God's salvation is far greater than our individual lives. His acts of salvation are part of the divine self-disclosure initiated at Creation and revived throughout the ages. At the same time, he calls each one of us to enter into this salvation. Sometimes he calls, as Yeshua did to Miriam, by simply speaking our name.

For the journey: God beckons each of the Israelites and each of us, like the worshipers of Nikolsburg, to respond with lively faith to his deeds of salvation. Do I recognize every day God's mighty deeds, past and present, and respond accordingly?

HUPPAH OF GLORY
Parashat Yitro, Exodus 18:1–20:23

Why do we drink four cups of wine at the Passover Seder, the ceremonial meal that commemorates the Exodus from Egypt? One tradition says that the four cups are a reminder of the Lord's fourfold promise of redemption:[9]

> I am the LORD;
> I will bring you out from under the burdens of the Egyptians,
> I will rescue you from their bondage,
> and I will redeem you with an outstretched arm and with
> great judgments.
> I will take you as My people, and I will be your God.
> (Exod. 6:6–7a)

"I will take you as my people . . ." The Lord is speaking the language of courtship. The whole story of God's deliverance of Israel from Egypt is like a romance. God finds Israel captive in Egypt and battles with the oppressor to rescue her. He sweeps her away into the wilderness, where the two can be alone. Through the prophet Jeremiah, the LORD says to Israel: "I remember you, the kindness of your youth, the love of your betrothal, when you went after Me in the wilderness, in a land not sown" (Jer. 2:2).

The climax of this romance comes at Mount Sinai, where the Lord brings Israel into covenant with himself, under the canopy of smoke and glory-cloud.

> Owing to the brevity of the summer nights, and the pleasantness of the morning sleep in summer, the people were still asleep when God had descended upon Mount Sinai. Moses betook himself to the encampment and awakened them with these words: "Arise from your sleep, the bridegroom is at hand, and is waiting to lead his bride under the marriage-canopy."

Moses at the head of the procession hereupon brought the nation to its bridegroom, God, to Sinai, himself going up the mountain.[10]

In this version of the story, the tablets of the Ten Commandments are the *ketubah*. This essential part of the traditional Jewish wedding is a marriage contract signed by the bride and groom before the ceremony can begin. Likewise, the glory-cloud over Sinai is the *huppah*, the marriage canopy, under which the bride and groom stand as they are joined in matrimony. With these essentials in place, God seals his union with Israel: "I will take you as my people, and I will be your God."

In the beginning, God created marriage because he decreed, "it is not good that man should be alone" (Gen. 2:18). Woman completes man and is his true counterpart. "Therefore a man shall leave his father and mother and be joined to his wife, and they shall become one flesh" (Gen. 2:24). Marriage became a social institution and a means to various ends, but in the beginning, it was an end in itself. God's relationship with Israel reflects this primal reality. His betrothal to Israel is a marriage not of convenience, but of passion. God does not rescue Israel from Egypt to accomplish some task within the divine agenda, but, as he tells her, "to take you as my people."

Still, out of this relationship that is an end in itself comes much fruit. Most obviously, especially in the context of the Genesis story, marriage leads to bearing children. But even couples without children often have an impact and fruitfulness beyond the sum of the two parts. Thus, at Mount Sinai, the Lord anticipates great things from his marriage to Israel. Through Moses, he reminds his people (19:4–6):

> You have seen what I did to the Egyptians,
> and how I bore you on eagles' wings and brought you to Myself.
> Now therefore, if you will indeed obey My voice and keep
> My covenant,
> then you shall be a special treasure to Me above all people;
> for all the earth is Mine.
> And you shall be to Me a kingdom of priests and a holy nation.

We can derive three lessons from these words, not only for Israel gathered at Mount Sinai, but for ourselves today.

First, God's love and mercy are the framework of the entire story. He took the initiative to rescue Israel from Egypt, to split the waters of the Sea, to bring them out into the wilderness, and to reveal himself there in all his glory. The metaphor of eagles' wings captures the sense of God's transcendent power and mercy. The fantasy classic *The Return of the King*, by J.R.R. Tolkien, beautifully employs the same metaphor. The heroes Frodo and Sam have accomplished an impossible mission, casting the evil Ring of Power into the volcanic heart of Mount Doom to be destroyed. As the mount itself collapses, trapping Frodo and Sam, they too are rescued by eagles' wings.

> And so it was that Gwaihir [the Eagle] saw them with his keen far-seeing eyes, as down the wild wind he came . . . two small dark figures, forlorn, hand in hand upon a little hill, while the world shook under them, and gasped, and rivers of fire drew near. And even as he espied them and came swooping down, he saw them fall, worn out, or stricken down by despair at last, hiding their eyes from death.
>
> Side by side they lay; and down swept Gwaihir, and down came Landroval and Meneldor the swift; and in a dream, not knowing what fate had befallen them, the wanderers were lifted up and borne far away out of the darkness and the fire.[11]

When we were helpless and lost, God sent Messiah Yeshua to rescue us and bring us to himself. We may face difficulty and disillusionment in the years that follow this rescue, but God's love and mercy overshadow the entire journey.

Second, God requires that we take our place in this story through obedience. This may sound contradictory to the first point, but we must embrace both truths. The story depends entirely on God's initiative, yet we have a part in it only as we respond to him. The Lord says, "*If* you will indeed obey My voice and keep My covenant, *then* you shall be a special treasure to Me" (Exod. 19:5, emphasis added). We need to cultivate obedience if we are going to play out our part in the divine story.

And what is our part? This question leads to a final point.

God chose us for a purpose far beyond ourselves. Israel saw what God did to their oppressors (negatively) and to them (positively), but there was still more—they were to be a source of blessing to all the earth. The Lord says, "All the earth is Mine. And you shall be to Me a kingdom of priests and a holy nation." A priest is one who lives for the benefit of others. Israel's deliverance from Egypt was ultimately for the benefit of all the nations, that they might know that the God of Israel is the one true and living God.

Peter applies this calling to all who follow Yeshua. "But you are a chosen generation, a royal priesthood, a holy nation, His own special people, that you may proclaim the praises of Him who called you out of darkness into His marvelous light" (1 Pet. 2:9). As followers of Yeshua, we need to remember that our salvation in him isn't just about our salvation. It is part of a far grander, divine purpose of representing the goodness and mercy of our God to those around us. This is how we respond in gratitude to him who bore us on eagles' wings and brought us to himself.

For the journey: We cannot have a big vision of God and a narrow vision of our own lives. In Messiah Yeshua, God brought us to himself for a purpose far beyond ourselves—to represent him before our loved ones, neighbors, associates, and those far off as well. How does this purpose expand my vision for my own life?

YOUR ENEMY'S DONKEY
Parashat Mishpatim, Exodus 21:1–24:18

Rabbi Alexandri said: Two donkey drivers who hated each other were walking on a road when the donkey of one lay down under its burden. His companion saw it, and at first passed on. But then he reflected: Is it not written in the Torah, "If you see your enemy's donkey lying down under its burden . . ."? So he returned, lent a hand, and helped his enemy in loading and unloading. He began talking to his enemy: "Release a bit here, pull up over there, unload over here." Thus, peace came about between them, so that the driver of the overloaded said, "Did I suppose that he hated me? But now look how compassionate he has been." By and by, the two entered an inn, ate and drank together, and became fast friends. What caused them to make peace and become fast friends? Because one of them kept what was in Torah.[12]

The three synoptic Gospels—Matthew, Mark and Luke—all tell of Yeshua's temptation in the wilderness, but Mark's account is unique in at least two ways. He writes:

> Immediately the Spirit drove Him into the wilderness. And He was there in the wilderness forty days, tempted by Satan, and was with the wild beasts; and the angels ministered to Him. (Mark 1:12–13)

In Matthew and Luke, Yeshua is *led* by the Spirit into the wilderness. Only here is he *driven* by the Spirit. The verb in Greek is *ekballo* and its use here is a remez, or hint, of another layer of meaning in the story. This same Greek verb appears in the Septuagint, the ancient Greek translation of the Hebrew Scriptures, widely used during Yeshua's time. The Septuagint uses ekballo to tell of Adam and Eve being "driven out" of the Garden in Genesis 3:24.

Adam is tempted and then driven out. Yeshua is driven out and then tempted. This reverse order reminds us that Yeshua reversed Adam's failure and prevailed over temptation. In Adam's story, angels guard the way to the Tree of Life, to prevent Adam's return. In Yeshua's story, the angels minister to him. They receive him after his temptation, in contrast with the cherubim of Eden who close the way to Adam after his temptation.

The second unique feature of Mark's account supports this interpretation of the temptation as a reversal of Adam's fall. Before Adam's temptation, he names the animals (Gen. 2:19–20). After Yeshua's temptation, he is "with the wild beasts." Adam's naming is a sign of his mastery. As the divine image bearer, he has dominion over the beasts and over all Creation. Naming the beasts is an act of dominion. In contrast, when we read that Yeshua is with the wild beasts, we are reminded of Isaiah's vision of the Age to Come, when,

> The wolf also shall dwell with the lamb,
> The leopard shall lie down with the young goat,
> The calf and the young lion and the fatling together;
> And a little child shall lead them.
> The cow and the bear shall graze;
> Their young ones shall lie down together;
> And the lion shall eat straw like the ox. (Isa. 11:6–7)

Neither Isaiah nor Mark is advocating animal rights in the current political sense. But they are looking forward to the restoration of order and peace intended at Creation, in which there is harmony between humans and animals, and among the animals themselves.

This vision of restoration underlies the instruction that appears in Rabbi Alexandri's story, which deals with part of *Parashat Mishpatim*.

> If you meet your enemy's ox or his donkey going astray, you shall surely bring it back to him again. If you see the donkey of one who hates you lying under its burden, and you would refrain from helping it, you shall surely help him with it. (Exod. 23:4–5)

Through obedience to the mitzvah, one becomes an agent of restoration, not only on a human level, but also beyond. The animal that is lost or suffering is property, but it is also a creature of God, an aspect of his Creation that has succumbed to the disorder of the age we live in. The mitzvah of protecting the animal helps restore the goodness of Creation and move us toward completion.

As Rabbi Alexandri points out, obedience to the divine command brings peace—peace between God and man, peace between man and man, and even peace within the created order. God gives the command, the donkeys, even the ability to work, but we must supply the obedience. We needn't go to the extremes of the animal rights movement to show concern for animal life, both domesticated and wild. As we respond to the command with the required compassion toward animals, it transforms the way we look at humans as well.

Yeshua summarized this whole strain of teaching within Torah with his command to love our enemies (Matt. 5:44). The commandment in this parashah reminds us that this mandated love is no mere sentiment, but requires action. We may not like to admit that we have enemies, but we all do—perhaps not enemies bent on our destruction, but people who have wronged us, disappointed us, or failed us in some way or another. These are the people Messiah expects us to help.

A final contrast between Yeshua and Adam: Adam names the wild beasts in the Garden; Yeshua is "with the wild beasts" in the desert. If Yeshua's temptation provides a reversal of Adam's temptation and failure, why does it leave him in the desert? Should not Yeshua's victory over temptation immediately open the way for him to re-enter the Garden? But this is precisely the point—in this age, redemption advances not in some ideal and secluded garden, but in the desert, the world of disorder and challenge that we know so well. There we have enemies, there animals go astray or stumble under a heavy load. And there Messiah goes before us to set right what has been damaged.

For the journey: As followers of Yeshua, we must ask ourselves, "When was the last time I wandered from my own busy or pleasurable course to help someone else—especially someone whom I cannot count as a friend?"

I am indebted to Rabbi Paul Saal for the reference to the Rabbi Alexandri story, and some of the ideas in this commentary on Parashat Mishpatim.

CREATION AND REST
Parashat T'rumah, Exodus 25:1–27:19

> One Shabbat during that time, Yeshua was walking through some wheat fields. His talmidim were hungry, so they began picking heads of grain and eating them. On seeing this, the *P'rushim* said to him, "Look! Your talmidim are violating Shabbat!" (Matthew 12:1–2, CJB)

What is lawful and unlawful on Shabbat? Torah's instructions seem straightforward enough. Shabbat is to be a day of rest that is honored and kept separate from the ordinary days of the week. On Shabbat, we and all those with us are to rest and do no work. But the Torah does not define work, or prohibit specific acts, beyond the instruction, "You shall kindle no fire throughout your dwellings on the Sabbath day" (Exod. 35:3).

Traditional Jewish law, or halakhah, has developed detailed and rigorous Shabbat restrictions. Traditional Jews will not drive a car or flip a light switch on Shabbat, both to avoid anything like kindling a fire, and to keep the day as free as possible from ordinary activities. Some Christian groups apply similar rigor to Sunday. The movie *Chariots of Fire* (Warner Bros., 1981) tells the story of Eric Liddell, a British runner in the 1924 Paris Olympics, who refused to race on Sunday, even after the members of the Olympic Committee, including the Prince of Wales, urged him to do so.

Outsiders sometimes criticize such strictness, but anyone who seriously attempts to keep a day of rest will soon understand the need to define what is permitted and what is not. Just what constitutes work? The Talmud mentions thirty-nine categories of work "taught to Moses at Sinai" as forbidden on Shabbat.[13] These turn out to be the various categories of work that were required to build the tabernacle, or *mishkan*, the dwelling-place of God in the camp of Israel.

How did the ancient rabbis make this connection between Shabbat and mishkan? The connection is actually hidden in the narrative structure of the entire section of Exodus that begins with *Parashat T'rumah.* This structure is what scholars call a *chiasm,* from the Greek letter *chi,* or X. A narrative chiasm tells a story detail by detail, reaches a turning point, and then repeats the details in reverse order, to arrive at the end of the story. The chiastic structure often reveals a deeper level of meaning. On the following page is the chiasm of the final sixteen chapters of Exodus.

A   The glory of the Lord is revealed at the top of Mount Sinai. 24:15–18

>   B   Instructions for building the mishkan, chapters 25–30, opening with instructions for the offering and ending with the call of Bezalel, 31:1–11

>   >   C   Instructions to keep Shabbat, 31:12–17

>   >   >   D   The two tablets given: 31:18

Turning point: the two tablets broken in the golden calf incident, chapters 32–33

>   >   >   D-1   The two tablets restored, chapter 34

>   >   C-1   Instructions to keep Shabbat repeated, 35:1–3

>   B-1   Building the tabernacle 35:4–40:33, opening with the taking of the actual offering, and a renewal of the call of Bezalel

A-1   The glory of the Lord revealed in the mishkan within the camp, 40:34–38

Note the central place of Shabbat in this narrative structure. After the instructions for building the tabernacle in B come the instructions for keeping Shabbat in C. Before the building begins in B-1, the instructions for Shabbat are repeated in C-1. In addition, B is subdivided into six sections, each beginning with the words, "And the Lord spoke (or said) to Moses" (Exod. 25:1; 30:11, 17, 22, 34; 31:1). The seventh "And the Lord spoke . . ." (Exod. 31:12) introduces the discussion of Shabbat, the seventh day.[14]

A further connection between Shabbat and the mishkan is in the use of the word *m'lakhah*, or work. This word appears three times at the conclusion of the Creation account (Gen. 2:2–3):

> And on the seventh day God finished His work which He had done, and He rested on the seventh day from all His work which He had done. Then God blessed the seventh day and sanctified it, because in it He rested from all His work that God had created and made.

In the same way, m'lakhah appears three times in the instructions for Shabbat that come after the directions for building the holy place (Exod. 31:14–15):

> You shall keep the Sabbath, therefore, for it is holy to you. Everyone who profanes it shall surely be put to death; for whoever does any work on it, that person shall be cut off from among his people. Work shall be done for six days, but the seventh is the Sabbath of rest, holy to the LORD. Whoever does any work on the Sabbath day, he shall surely be put to death.

The word appears again in the instructions for Shabbat after the golden calf incident, and before the building of the mishkan. "Work shall be done for six days, but the seventh day shall be a holy day for you, a Shabbat of rest to the Lord. Whoever does any work on it shall be put to death" (Exod. 35:2).

M'lakhah appears an additional twenty-one times in the account of building, concluding with the completion of the undertaking (Exod. 40:33): "And Moses finished the work." These words reflect the conclusion of the Creation account: "On the seventh day God finished His work" (Gen. 2:2). M'lakhah is a dominant theme in both accounts, of Creation and tabernacle.

Since the tabernacle and Shabbat are so clearly linked, the halakhah derived that the thirty-nine categories of work involved in building the mishkan are the thirty-nine categories of work forbidden on Shabbat.

Thus, the Talmud seeks to answer the question of what is lawful and unlawful on Shabbat. It takes us far beyond that question, however, to reveal that the work of the tabernacle reflects the work of

Creation itself. "This explains why the Tabernacle was finally erected 'on the first day of the first month' [Exod. 40:2], which is New Year's Day, a powerful symbol of the beginning of the Creation of the world, the transformation of chaos into cosmos."[15]

This connection also explains the significance of our daily work. Shabbat, the day of rest, sanctifies all work because it defines it as sharing in the act of Creation. Work becomes not just a means of earning a living (although there is nothing wrong with that), but a participation in God's work. All of our labors have the potential of expressing the order and vitality with which God imbued his Creation. Therefore, all work is holy.

When Yeshua allowed his disciples to pluck and eat grain on Shabbat, he taught us an additional lesson. The Pharisees charged the disciples with violating Shabbat. Yeshua responded, "Have you not read in the Torah that on the Sabbath the priests in the Temple profane the Sabbath, and are blameless? Yet I say to you that in this place there is One greater than the Temple" (Matt. 12:5–6). Greater than the Temple? If the Temple, like the tabernacle before it, pictures the completed Creation, the one greater than the Temple must be great indeed! All work is holy, but work we pursue as we follow Messiah, whether as ministers or maintenance men, shares a unique holiness.

For the journey: Shabbat sanctifies all labor. Work is not just earning a living, or a means of personal fulfillment, but a share in God's creative process. Whether we are highly paid executives, or minimum wage earners, Shabbat defines our work as holy, an essential part of following Yeshua. How can I see my daily work as holy?

STONES OF REMEMBRANCE
Parashat Tetzaveh, Exodus 27:20–30:10

My wife and I occasionally visit an elderly Russian Jewish couple who came to America in the early 90s. They had served as doctors with the Red Army through World War II. The husband was a field surgeon who followed the troops from the Soviet heartland to the gates of Berlin, performing 14,000 surgeries on the way. Now they are well into their 80s, elderly, and in failing health. When the time comes to say good-bye, the wife always says, "Don't forget us."

"We won't forget you," we reply. "We'll never forget you."

True enough, but our friend is not merely asking that we keep them in mind. Rather, she is saying, "Give us a phone call. Come back and visit . . . and don't be so long next time!"

Our friend's remark may be in the long tradition of Jewish maternal guilt, but it also reflects the biblical concept of remembrance. Remembering is more than just storing something in our mental database. It is re-enactment, paying a visit to the things we might be tempted to neglect.

Even God, who never forgets, remembers in this way, as we see in *Parashat Tetzaveh*. Here, in the midst of his instructions for building the mishkan, the Lord prescribes the garments for the High Priest. Moses is to have two onyx stones engraved with the names of the sons of Israel and set in gold. And then, the Lord tells him,

> You are to place the two stones on the shoulder-pieces of the
> *efod*,
> as stones of remembrance for the Children of Israel.
> Aharon is to bear their names before the presence of *Hashem*
> on his two shoulders, for remembrance. (Exodus 28:12, Fox[16])

The stones that the High Priest bears on his shoulders ensure that the Lord will remember the children of Israel. But how could God ever forget his chosen people, or anyone else for that matter?

Why does the creator of all things require a reminder? Yet even though we ask these questions, we all have experienced times when it seems as though God has forgotten *us*; times when we'd be thankful if someone with connections in the heavenly court could mention our name in his presence.

This is exactly what God provided through the stones of remembrance that the High Priest wore. When we face deep disappointments—an illness that does not respond to treatment, children or loved ones who wander from God's ways, financial pressures that seem to only increase with time—what a comfort it would be to imagine a High Priest who comes into God's presence daily carrying our names upon his very clothing.

With this in mind, we can understand the anguish of the Jewish people over the loss of the Temple and priesthood at the hands of the Roman army in 70 C.E. After this disaster, the people might wonder who would bring their remembrance—both individually and as the whole house of Israel—before God. Hence, to this day, observant Jews pray continually for the restoration of the Temple and priesthood. For example, the Amidah, a major part of the daily prayer service, concludes, "May it be pleasing in your sight, O Lord our God and God of our fathers, that the holy Temple be rebuilt, swiftly, in our days" (from the *Siddur*).

But thanks be to God, we have a living High Priest, Yeshua the Messiah! He bears the stones of remembrance, engraved with our names, continually before God. "He, because He continues forever, has an unchangeable priesthood. Therefore He is also able to save to the uttermost those who come to God through Him, since He always lives to make intercession for them" (Heb. 7:24–25). Because Yeshua intercedes for us, God never forgets us. And God's remembrance does not mean that our names are stored somewhere in the vastness of his cosmic data base. It means that he comes to visit when we call upon him in prayer.

Remembrance has another, human side to it that also relates to prayer. We must remember in the same way God remembers, the way my old Russian friends desire—not just by storing data, but by visiting again and again. Prayer involves revisiting the goodness, power, and mercy of God continually. In prayer, we not only ask God to remember us and our needs, but we remember him with thanksgiving and a sense of awe.

The stones of remembrance teach another lesson that is perhaps the most striking. In the presence of God, the priest does not bear his own name, but the names of his fellow Israelites. Indeed, the names of the children of Israel are part of the clothing the priest *must* wear if he is to come into the Holy Place at all. Without them, he has no priesthood.

As we learn about prayer from Yeshua our High Priest, we will begin to bear the names of others, as he does, into the presence of God. Prayer is not just a satisfying spiritual activity; it is a discipline we practice on behalf of others. For Messianic Jews, and Gentiles who stand in solidarity with Israel, prayer will include reminding God of the names of the children of Israel.

In this way, we not only *benefit* from Messiah's priesthood, but we *participate* in it as well. As Samuel said to the children of Israel, "Moreover as for me, God forbid that I should sin against the LORD in ceasing to pray for you" (1 Sam. 12:23).

Through Messiah, we have access into God's presence, but we do not use this access just for ourselves. Rather, we bear the stones of remembrance before God on behalf of others, and especially on behalf of Israel. And because Israel is the priestly nation among the nations, the redemption of Israel for which we pray is the key to Tikkun Olam, the repair of the world that includes the redemption of all humankind.

For the journey: Prayer involves remembrance: God remembers us, we remember God, and we remember others when we come into his presence. How can I grow in my practice of prayer so that it is not just a means of personal fulfillment, but a way of serving others as well?

THE TEST OF INTERCESSION
Parashat Ki Tissa, Exodus 30:11–34:35

Once Moses saw that Israel would not be able to withstand God's wrath at the Golden Calf, he bound his soul to them and smashed the tablets. Then he said to God, "They have sinned and I have sinned, for I smashed the tablets. If you forgive them, forgive me also," as Scripture tells us: "Now if you will forgive their sin . . . then forgive mine as well. But if you do not forgive them, do not forgive me either, but rather 'wipe me out of your book that you have written.'"[17]

Jewish tradition speaks of *Moshe rabbenu*—Moses our teacher. Like all true teachers, he teaches by example as well as precept. Nowhere is Moses' example more inspiring than in his response to the incident of the golden calf. Here he faces a spiritual test that we may someday face as well: Will we live for ourselves or others? Will we content ourselves with seeking a personal relationship with God, or will we look beyond this relationship, precious as it is, to serve those who may lack it?

Moses has just received detailed instructions for building the mishkan and equipping its priests. This instruction includes a reminder to keep Shabbat. Since the tabernacle is a model of Creation, the work of building it reenacts the work of the six days of Creation. Hence, the instruction to rest on Shabbat even from the work of the tabernacle, just as the Lord rested from his labors of creating. Building the mishkan is exalted work that foreshadows the restored Creation. It is most striking, then, that the Lord assigns this work to a band of escaped slaves.

Before Moses can return to give the people this glorious assignment, however, they make themselves a calf of gold to worship. They set aside the work of Creation completed to work on the statue of a cow!

This depraved project begins with a free-will offering. "And Aaron said to them, 'Break off the golden earrings which are in the ears of your wives, your sons, and your daughters, and bring them to me.' So all the people broke off the golden earrings which were in their ears, and brought them to Aaron" (Exod. 32:2–3). Later, when the people finally get back on track, the work of building the holy place will begin with a similar free-will offering. "They came, both men and women, as many as had a willing heart, and brought earrings and nose rings, rings and necklaces, all jewelry of gold, that is, every man who made an offering of gold to the LORD" (Exod. 35:22).

In this way, the Torah portrays the golden calf as a reversal of the tabernacle. Both projects are meant to provide a visible image of the Lord in the midst of his people, but of course, the calf is an image of the people's own making. Therefore, it allows for worship based on their human desires and inclinations, instead of the holy worship ordained by God. Thus, with one act, the children of Israel break the first two commandments that Moses brought down to them from Sinai, worshiping other gods and making a graven image (Exod. 20:3–4). They violate the very purpose for which God had delivered them from Egypt—"that they may serve Me."[18] A catastrophic failure, but not irreversible. God will punish the idolaters, but spare the people as a whole. In the end, the Lord promises to continue to accompany them in their journeys: "My Presence will go with you, and I will give you rest" (Exod. 33:14).

What turns this story around? How can the people be restored to God after the disaster of the golden calf? This is where Moses makes all the difference, and becomes an example to us.

When Moses was still on Mount Sinai, the Lord told him that the people had fallen into idolatry. Then he added, "I have seen this people, and indeed it is a stiff-necked people! Now therefore, let Me alone, that My wrath may burn hot against them and I may consume them. And I will make of you a great nation" (Exod. 32:9–10).

Here is the test: Will Moses distance himself from Israel because of their sin, or will he continue to identify with his people *despite* their sin? Leading this band of former slaves filled with contention, doubt, and rebellion has already proven to be a great burden. Now God seems to offer a far less troublesome way to accomplish his purposes. Let the people receive their well-deserved punishment for idolatry, and the Lord will make a new nation of Moses.

Moses refuses this offer, however, and remains with his people. The midrash even pictures him deciding to sin by breaking the tablets of the Ten Commandments, so that he can be in the same situation as the rest of Israel. Now, he who has communed with God face-to-face pleads for the people, as one of them.

When we read this story, we can hardly compare ourselves to Moses. We have certainly not attained his spiritual stature or endured his tests. But we can learn much about prayer from Moses. He went far beyond praying for his own needs to pray for the whole Jewish community of his day, and so can we. As Moses stood with his people in all their wanderings, so can we. As Moses would not allow his privilege with God to distance him from his people, but employed it to intercede for his people, so must we.

Identifying with imperfect people, while drawing near to a perfect God, is an essential part of prayer. We see those who take this position throughout Scripture, from Abraham pleading for Sodom, through Esther pleading for Israel in exile. Finally, we see Messiah himself, "who did not consider it robbery to be equal with God, but . . . humbled Himself and became obedient to the point of death, even the death of the cross" (Phil. 2:6–8).

Messianic Jews are in a similar position. Even though the great majority of the Jewish people do not recognize Yeshua as Messiah, we remain part of our people. There, like Moses, we can petition God on their behalf. A similar choice faces all followers of Yeshua. Do we maintain a position of intercession on behalf of others, or develop a religious movement designed for our own comfort and self-fulfillment?

When Moses persisted in asking God to restore his Presence, not just to himself, but to all Israel, God rewarded him. "I will also do this thing that you have spoken; for you have found grace in My sight, and I know you by name" (Exod. 33:17). As we focus not on ourselves, but on God and his people, we too will find grace in his sight.

For the journey: Spiritually oriented people often isolate themselves from those who most need their influence. How can I overcome isolation today and reconnect with my people, whoever they may be, as an influence and intercessor for God's purposes?

BEZALEL
Parashat VaYakhel, Exodus 35:1–38:20

In 1906, Boris Schatz, court sculptor to the king of Bulgaria, brought six of his students to the land of Israel to found a school of arts and crafts. Schatz sought to establish a center that would affect the cultural life of the whole Jewish settlement. Donors helped to find a market for the weaving, needlework, metalwork, and carvings the students would produce. Within five short years, 460 students and craftsmen labored in the school and its workshops. What is the name of this school, which continues to thrive in Israel today? It is named after the greatest craftsman of the Torah, the one in charge of building the tabernacle and its furnishings—Bezalel.[19]

Schatz and his colleagues were undoubtedly thinking of Bezalel's artistry when they named their school after him. But equally prominent in the biblical account is Bezalel's spiritual empowerment. To equip him for his great task of artistry, God fills Bezalel with the Spirit more abundantly than any other person mentioned in Torah. Exodus describes this infilling twice, both before and after the crisis of the golden calf:

> See, I have called by name Bezalel the son of Uri, the son of Hur, of the tribe of Judah. And I have filled him with the Spirit of God, in wisdom, in understanding, in knowledge, and in all manner of workmanship. (Exod. 31:2–3)

> See, the LORD has called by name Bezalel the son of Uri, the son of Hur, of the tribe of Judah; and He has filled him with the Spirit of God, in wisdom and understanding, in knowledge and all manner of workmanship. (Exod. 35:30–31)

When we compare the language here with that describing other Spirit-empowered leaders, such as Joshua, Bezalel seems to be uniquely endowed:

> And the LORD said to Moses: "Take Joshua the son of Nun with you, a man in whom is the Spirit, and lay your hand on him." (Num. 27:18)

> Now Joshua the son of Nun was full of the spirit of wisdom, for Moses had laid his hands on him; so the children of Israel heeded him, and did as the LORD had commanded Moses. (Deut. 34:9)

The Spirit fills Joshua, but upon Bezalel it abounds "in wisdom, in understanding, in knowledge, and in all manner of workmanship." This ancient Israelite receives an abundant spiritual endowment, which hints at a similar endowment God is still ready to give today.

When Moses ascended Mount Sinai, says the Midrash, he not only reached the top of the mountain, but he ascended into heaven. There he saw the heavenly court, the model for the earthly tabernacle (Exod. 25:40; Heb. 8:5). Moses imagined that he would be the one to build this structure for God. The Lord told him, however, that he was like a king, and a king does not make anything himself. Rather, he issues orders and others do the work. Moses wondered who would be able to carry out such a project, so the Lord "brought him the book of Adam and showed him all the generations that would arise from Creation to Resurrection, each generation and its kings, its leaders, and its prophets, saying unto him: 'I have appointed all these for their destinies from Creation, and Bezalel too I have appointed from that time.' This is why it says, *See, I have called by name Bezalel.*" [20]

Why does the Torah describe the calling of Bezalel, who is after all only a craftsman, in such rich terminology? Why does God so abundantly fill him with the Spirit, beyond the measure he gives to Joshua, the successor of Moses himself? Because building the tabernacle reenacts the work of Creation, and Bezalel has been chosen from Creation to oversee this work. When the Lord announces his appointment, he does not use the usual formula, "See I call by name Bezalel," but "See, I *have called* by name Bezalel." The past tense here is the remez, or hint, that Bezalel's calling originated long before, as it says: "I have appointed all these for their destinies from Creation, and Bezalel too I have appointed from that time."

Just as the Spirit is essential to the whole process of Creation, so it is essential to the journey from Creation to completion. Before the work of Creation begins, "the Spirit of God was hovering over the face of the waters" (Gen. 1:2). Before the work of the tabernacle begins, the Spirit of God fills Bezalel, empowering him to carry out the work.

Remarkably, the Midrash links the creative Spirit to the coming Messiah, commenting on the phrase, "the Spirit of God was hovering. . ." "This alludes to the spirit of Messiah, as you read, *And the spirit of the Lord shall rest upon him* (Isa. 11:2)."[21] When the Messiah appears, his Spirit, the same Spirit that hovered over the primeval waters, comes upon all who follow him.

> And it shall come to pass afterward
> That I will pour out My Spirit on all flesh;
> Your sons and your daughters shall prophesy,
> Your old men shall dream dreams,
> Your young men shall see visions.
> And also on My menservants and on My maidservants
> I will pour out My Spirit in those days. (Joel 2:28–29 [3:1–2])

Despite Bezalel's spiritual greatness, however, God does not call him alone, but raises up Aholiab at the same time. Aholiab is from the least of the tribes, Dan, while Bezalel is from the greatest, Judah.

> God said: 'Let him [Dan] come and be associated with him [Judah], so that no man may despise him or become arrogant, for both great and small are equal in God's sight; Bezalel comes of the tribe of Judah and Ahaliab from Dan, yet [the latter] is associated with him.' Rabbi Hanina said: The great and the small are equal, and one should never ignore his help.[22]

Here is another hint of the great outpouring to come, for just as Bezalel is an agent of re-Creation, so are those who live in union with Messiah. In Messiah's spiritual outpouring, there is no longer great or small, but all are gifted and all need each other, as it is written, "But the manifestation of the Spirit is given to each one for the profit of all . . ." (1 Cor. 12:7)

For the journey: Like Bezalel, we have an assignment in the work of re-creation, and like him we have partners who might appear less gifted than we are. How well do we recognize our need for just such partners? How well do we work with them to accomplish the divine task?

THE CLOUD FILLS THE TABERNACLE
Parashat P'kudei, Exodus 38:21–40:38

A recent book on Jewish pastoral care introduces a Hebrew phrase, *hitlavut ruchanit,* or spiritual accompanying:

> The root of this term, *lvh,* is used in biblical and rabbinic texts to refer to one who "walks with" another. Ministering angels, God's presence, friends, priests, peers all are described as *lvh,* accompanying people as they go on their path. The reflexive form of the verb [*hitlavut*] connotes a person involving himself or herself in the journey with the other.[23]

The book goes on to outline the power of hitlavut ruchanit, simply being there for others as they go through life's challenges and transitions. A rabbi or pastor may have much to give to those he serves, but the essential thing is often simply walking with them through the key moments of life.

Indeed, accompanying others in this way is so vital that one of the greatest obstacles to serving others effectively is the urge to "*do* something." When someone has lost a loved one, we rush to say, "I understand," when we really cannot understand. We respond to distress or despair by dispensing advice like a talk show host, instead of just listening deeply, which is often what the suffering person needs most. Suffering makes us insecure, and we respond by trying to alleviate it in some way, but what our friends need most is for us to just be with them. Often, it is through our simple presence in the midst of suffering that the Lord himself is present.

The final chapters of Exodus apply this idea of spiritual accompanying to God himself. After the incident of the golden calf, the Lord tells Moses,

> Depart and go up from here, you and the people whom you have brought out of the land of Egypt, to the land of which I

swore to Abraham, Isaac, and Jacob, saying, 'To your descendants I will give it.' And I will send My Angel before you . . . for I will not go up in your midst, lest I consume you on the way, for you are a stiff-necked people. (Exod. 33:1–3)

Moses pleads with the Lord, "If Your Presence does not go with us, do not bring us up from here" (Exod. 33:15). Moses cannot envision Israel apart from the presence of God in their midst. It is more important to him than the Promised Land and deliverance itself. Moses' plea for divine accompaniment reminds us that the presence of the Spirit is essential to us as well. Beyond all that God tells us, vital as it is, we long for him simply to be with us.

Even as Moses is presenting his case, however, the Lord has already relented. He promises Moses, "My Presence will go with you, and I will give you rest" (Exod. 33:14). The Lord had threatened to send "My Angel before you." Now he promises "My Presence will go with you." He will indeed practice hitlavut ruchanit, spiritually accompanying his people Israel.

Accordingly, the Lord tells the people to begin building the tabernacle. He had given the instructions before the incident of the golden calf, and now, after the people are punished and restored, the tabernacle can be built. The glory cloud, the Presence of the Lord, that was within the tent of meeting outside the camp (Exod. 33:7ff.) will now be present in the holy place in the heart of the camp. Hence, it is called "the tabernacle of witness" (Exod. 38:21), because "it witnessed to Israel that God had truly forgiven them for making the Golden Calf, for now He was causing His presence to dwell among them."[24]

All this prepares us for the glorious conclusion of Exodus:

> Then the cloud covered the tabernacle of meeting, and the glory of the LORD filled the tabernacle. And Moses was not able to enter the tabernacle of meeting, because the cloud rested above it, and the glory of the LORD filled the tabernacle. Whenever the cloud was taken up from above the tabernacle, the children of Israel would go onward in all their journeys. But if the cloud was not taken up, then they did not journey till the day that it was taken up. For the cloud of the LORD was above the tabernacle by day, and fire was over it by night, in the sight of all the house of Israel, throughout all their journeys. (Exod. 40:34–38)

Note the poetic cadence of these final verses. In each one, the word "cloud" appears. In addition, the phrase, nearly synonymous in this context, "glory of the Lord" appears twice, for a total of seven mentions of the divine presence. Seven, of course, is the number of Creation completed. The tabernacle as a model of Creation is complete only now as the glory-cloud fills it. To underline this truth the identical phrase, "and the glory of the Lord filled the tabernacle," is stated twice. The tabernacle fulfills God's purposes in bringing Israel forth from Egypt, and the Israelites will journey continually with a sense of this fulfillment.

This noble conclusion is echoed in the conclusion of another book of Scripture, where Messiah says, "Lo, I am with you always, even to the end of the age" (Matt. 28:20). This conclusion provides lessons for all who seek to walk in God's ways.

First, if he whose glory is unapproachable was willing to accompany Israel in its desert wanderings, how much more should we accompany those who are passing through one of life's deserts. We live in community, which means that we break out of isolation and make ourselves available to those around us.

Second, it is the greatest of gifts that God chose us and called us to be near to him. For us to be who we are meant to be, to reach our true destination, God must accompany us. Or rather, we must not depart from his Presence. All of us need to seek the Lord, to discern and detect the moving of the cloud, before we set out on our way.

Finally, in a narcissistic age, it is good to remember that the big story is not about us, but about God. He delivers Israel, not simply to free us from bondage, or to give us his good instructions in the Torah, but ultimately to reveal himself. The narrative concludes as the glory-cloud of God fills the tabernacle and no man can enter in. His glory, not our deliverance, is the point of the story.

For the journey: The story is not about me, but about God and his glory. Therefore, I am here to accompany others, to simply be with them as they pass through life's difficulties and challenges. Who is the one who needs my spiritual accompaniment even today?

THE BOOK OF LEVITICUS

אָרְקְרָא

Leviticus is the heart of Torah. Named for its opening word, וַיִּקְרָא (*Vayikra*), meaning "And he called," it is the third book, the mid-point of the Five Books of Moses. Leviticus is the only one of the Five Books that takes place entirely at the foot of Mount Sinai. It records no journeys and very little narrative. In Leviticus, Israel has arrived at the destination established at the beginning of Exodus, the mountain of revelation, to receive the Torah. Throughout the book, Israel does not move from that exalted point.

The instructions of Leviticus are at the heart of Torah as well. In Exodus, the tabernacle is constructed and the priesthood is or-dained, but in Leviticus the priesthood begins their actual ministry. After it gives guidance to the priests, the book provides a law of ho-liness that shapes the identity of Israel. In Leviticus 19, this law of holiness restates the ten words given at Sinai, known as the Ten Commandments. In this aspect, too, Leviticus is at the heart of To-rah, since the ten words are given first in Exodus 20, and then re-counted in Deuteronomy 5. But halfway between the two, here in Leviticus, we have another version.

Despite this centrality, Leviticus is an inaccessible book to many readers. It details rituals of priesthood and sacrifice that have not been carried out for nearly 2000 years, rituals that hardly seem rel-evant to life in the 21st century. Even its ethical instructions deal with matters that have largely passed from the scene of contempo-rary life. We learn about dietary laws and agricultural practices that seem remote from our demanding lives. Chapters are taken up in discussing a category of diseases and symptoms that most of us have never seen.

But this summary ignores a central theme of Leviticus that ties it into the meta-narrative of Torah—the theme of Creation to completion. The tabernacle that takes up so many of its pages is a model of Creation, the Creation that was "very good," which is yet to be brought to its fulfillment. The commandments of Leviticus are acts of restoration, each one anticipating this fulfillment. Even the arcane practices of purity and separation reenact the creative act of havdalah, of separating darkness and light, dry land and sea, which characterized God's work in the beginning.

Translator Robert Alter comments:

> There is a single verb that focuses the major themes of Leviticus—"divide" (Hebrew, *hivdil*). That verb, of course, stands at the beginning of the . . . story of creation: "And God saw the light, that it was good, and God divided the light from the darkness. . . . And God made the vault and it divided the water beneath the vault from the water above the vault, and so it was." . . . What enables existence and provides a framework for the development of human nature, conceived in God's image, and of human civilization is a process of division and insulation—light from darkness, day from night, the upper waters from the lower waters, and dry land from the latter. That same process is repeatedly manifested in the ritual, sexual, and dietary laws of Leviticus.[1]

This process of setting apart and creating order is captured in the theme of holiness, a theme that has been present in the earlier books, but comes to the fore in Leviticus. Holiness is the point of all the myriad details of instruction throughout the book. As we go through these instructions we will see that the holiness that God intends is not fussy and prudish, but a reflection of his own glory. The refrain of Leviticus is, "You shall be holy, for I the Lord your God, am holy" (Lev. 11:44–45, 19:2, 20:26).

If we can see it, Leviticus describes a way of life for God's chosen people that reveals his own character in the midst of a world that is distant and estranged from him.

FEARSOME NEARNESS
Parashat Vayikra, Leviticus 1:1–5:26

The Israeli postal service, which sorts more than 2 million pieces of mail a day, comes across several addressed to God, the Holy Land or Jesus. Rather than relegate the letters to bins of undeliverable mail, they are brought to the Western Wall, Judaism's holiest site, a few times a year. Postal authorities consider the letters private conversations with God and do not open them. Letters come from all corners of the globe, including a few from predominantly Muslim nations like Indonesia. "This place is the holiest place for the Jews, and it is the first gate for prayers. That's why a prayer in this place is important and these notes are important," said Shmuel Rabinovitch, chief rabbi at the site. The Western Wall is considered a remnant of the second Temple, and many people come to the wall to pray and slip notes with requests between the ancient stones.[2]

Where can we draw near to God? This story makes us wonder if there is a physical location that is somehow closer to the divine than any other.

Exodus closes with a description of such a location, the tabernacle or Tent of Meeting, which is a model of the restored Creation of which the entire Torah speaks. Here the visible glory of God, or *Shechinah*, dwells so that no one can approach. Leviticus opens with a word of invitation from within that very tent. Indeed, Leviticus seems to open in mid-sentence, connecting to Exodus with its first word: "*And* He called to Moses, and the Lord spoke to him from the Tent of Meeting . . ." The Lord does not want to leave us with the awe-inspiring distance of the end of Exodus, but is eager to call us close to himself, to approach the place that is closer to the divine than any other.

Rashi notes that this invitation in Leviticus is not just, "And he called," but "And he called *to Moses*," a phrase that is far more personal.

"Calling" . . . is the language of affection, language that the ministering angels use, as it says, "One called to the other and said, 'Holy . . .'" The voice of God would go, and reach Moses' ears, and all of Israel would not hear it.[3]

"And he called" is one word in Hebrew, *vayikra*. Its use here reveals a unique characteristic of the God of Israel. He is ultimately unknowable, unapproachable, other, but he is also the One who calls us close to himself, out of his own mercy and kindness. He is the transcendent God who issues eternal instructions to Moses, but he does so in words of intimacy and affection. He is the omnipresent God who fills the universe, but he provides a location where we can draw near to him. Thus, when the Israeli postal service treats letters addressed to God as private and confidential conversations, it reflects a biblical perspective.

A tiny detail in the handwritten Torah scroll used in every synagogue around the world sheds additional light on God's desire for nearness with us. The final letter of the opening word of Leviticus, vayikra, is alef—t. According to tradition, this letter is written in a smaller font than the rest of the letters, almost as if it doesn't belong there. Without this alef, the word would be *vayikar*, "and he met" or "and he encountered," a word that appears in the story of Balaam the false prophet: "Then the LORD *met* Balaam, and put a word in his mouth . . ." (Num. 23:16).

The similarity between these two words helps explain the small alef in vayikra.

In his monumental humility, Moses wished to describe God's revelation to him with the same uncomplimentary word used for Balaam—without an א—but God instructed him to include the א *as an expression of affection*. Too humble to do so wholeheartedly, Moses wrote a small t.[4]

Vayikra, the word spelled with the small alef, brings us back to Genesis, the account of beginnings. There we encountered the word in the story of the Garden of Eden: "*Vayikra Adonai Elohim el ha-adam*—And the LORD God *called* to the man. . . ." But when Adam and Eve hear this call, they hide because to them God is fearsome and best kept at a distance. Yet, this same God is seeking them, calling out to them to return to him. And calling, as Rashi notes, "is the language of affection."

The God of Israel is both fearsome and near. He continues reaching out to Adam as he asks him, "Where are you?" God invites Adam to come clean and come near. Adam, however, responds only to God's fearsomeness: "I was afraid because I was naked; and I hid myself" (Gen. 3:10). God desires restored intimacy with Adam and Eve, but in the end, he must expel them from the Garden because of their sin. Nevertheless, he covers their nakedness, clothing them in the skins of animals. They are sent into exile, but not abandoned. The skins serve as a reminder that they need not (and of course cannot) hide from God.

Likewise, in Leviticus, the God who is holy and unapproachable seeks to bridge the distance between himself and his people. He calls out to Moses and instructs him how to draw near. He provides the way of access through a detailed system of sacrifices—first hinted at in the skins of animals he gave as a covering to Adam and Eve.

Throughout Leviticus, as in all its texts, Scripture portrays God's fearsome nearness, a unique combination of unapproachable holiness and an extended hand of welcome. This combination reaches its fullest expression in the person of Messiah, in whom the transcendent God comes near to humankind. "God in the Messiah was reconciling mankind to himself . . ." (2 Cor. 5:19, CJB).

The Western Wall in Jerusalem is the holiest site in Judaism today, a place where many believe they are closer to God than anywhere else. But the real question is not *where* we can draw near to God, but *how*. God in his holiness and power is unapproachable, but through the sacrifice that he provides we can draw near. In Messiah, as in the tabernacle long ago, we find a place of meeting.

When it comes time for this Messiah to choose those who will represent him before others, he first calls them near to himself. "And He went up on the mountain and called to Him those He Himself wanted. And they came to Him. Then He appointed twelve, that they might be with Him and that He might send them out to preach, and to have power to heal sicknesses and to cast out demons . . ." (Mark 3:13–15).

God calls us to his fearsome nearness. Only as we respond and come near are we able to bear his image before a world that needs a glimpse of the divine.

For the journey: Those who follow Messiah must live a hidden life near to God if they are to live a public life representing God. Am I responding fully to God's invitation to draw near to him?

CONTINUAL WORSHIP
Parashat Tsav, Leviticus 6:1–8:36

> Concerning the words in the Scriptures: "When any man of you bringeth an offering to the Lord . . ." [Lev. 1:2] the rabbi of Rizhyn said: "Only he who brings himself to the Lord as an offering may be called a man."[5]

The first altar builder in the Bible was Noah, as we read, "Then Noah built an altar to the LORD, and took of every clean animal and of every clean bird, and offered burnt offerings on the altar. And the Lord smelled a soothing aroma" (Gen. 8:20–21a).

We might imagine that Noah built this altar to make a sin offering before the Flood came, so that he and his family could enter the ark confident in their right relationship with the Lord. Or we might imagine that he made an offering even earlier, to call on God to have mercy and hold back the waters of the Flood. But, no, Noah became the first altar builder *after* the great crisis of the Flood had passed, to express his gratitude and reverence for God. From this, we learn that the altar is not only a place for seeking mercy and forgiveness, but above all a place for worship. There will indeed be sacrifices upon the altar to provide forgiveness of sin, but first we see an offering of worship, presented to the Lord as "a soothing aroma."

Likewise, in all of the details about offerings and priesthood in the early chapters of Leviticus, it is possible to lose the larger picture. The sacrificial system is about worship, and all worship, all coming-near-to-God, involves an offering. The sacrifices do not all deal with sin and forgiveness. Indeed, the instructions for the first type of sacrifice, the *olah* or elevation offering, do not mention sin at all. But all the sacrifices do express worship of God.

The lesson for us: worship always involves an offering, something we present to the Lord that ultimately represents us. As the Rabbi of Rizhyn taught, a person must bring himself or herself to the Lord as an offering.

Since worship requires an offering, it requires fire as well, for it is by fire that the offering actually ascends to the Lord. Thus, this week's parashah opens with this instruction:

> This is the law of the burnt offering: The burnt offering shall be on the hearth upon the altar all night until morning . . . And the fire on the altar shall be kept burning on it; it shall not be put out. And the priest shall burn wood on it every morning, and lay the burnt offering in order on it; and he shall burn on it the fat of the peace offerings. A fire shall always be burning on the altar; it shall never go out. (Lev. 6:9–13 [6:2–6])

The name of the daily elevation offering, olah, derives from a verb meaning "to go up." Since it is by means of fire that the offering "goes up" to the Lord, olah is frequently translated as "burnt offering." Translator Robert Alter notes the central role of fire in the sacrifices of Leviticus:

> Fire and blood are the two substances that are the key to the sacrificial rites, but the present passage gives preeminence to . . . fire—the element associated with God's fiery epiphany at Sinai and with his first appearance to Moses in the Burning Bush. Hence an altar with a fire that "shall not go out."[6]

The fire "shall not go out" because it represents Adonai, the ever-present and unchangeable God. The instructions about sacrifice are not an esoteric list of rules and regulations, but a way of revisiting the grand narrative of God's self-revelation to Israel. The fire, as Alter says, reminds Israel of their encounter with God at Mount Sinai—"The sight of the glory of the LORD was like a consuming fire on the top of the mountain in the eyes of the children of Israel" (Exod. 24:17). As the fire burns continually, it reminds Israel that God abides in the camp throughout all their journeys.

Here is an additional lesson for us as worshipers of the God of Israel. It is the priests, the representative humans, who must keep the fire burning continually. We are to worship steadily and continually. Surely there will be high moments of worship, when we gather as the holy community on special days to offer praise before the Lord. But, like the priests, we are to keep the fire of worship burning in our lives at all times, and not let it go out.

Traditional Judaism promotes this sense of continual worship in numerous ways, such as by providing blessings for a great number of daily actions and events. It considers it a great mitzvah to recite one hundred blessings each day, and every blessing is itself an act of worship, beginning with the words: "Blessed are you, O Lord our God, king of the universe. . . ." Thus, the flame of worship is kept burning continually.

Likewise, in the B'rit Hadashah, Paul instructs us, "Always be joyful. Pray regularly. In everything give thanks, for this is what God wants from you who are united with the Messiah Yeshua" (1 Thess. 5:16–18, CJB).

True worship requires an offering, and a true offering represents the offer of oneself to God. Such worship is continual, a fire that is not quenched. Such worship defines the holiness to which Leviticus calls us in every chapter. It requires us to make worship the central focus of our lives and to resist the self-centered, consumerist values of our day that would treat worship as one commodity among many. As the Lord brought us out of the bondage of Egypt, so Messiah brought us out of the bondage of sin, not just to improve our circumstances, but that we might worship him.

For the journey: Real worship means that I offer myself to God, not just on special occasions, but continually. What can I offer to God today that will genuinely represent an offering of my whole self?

MISREPRESENTING GOD
Parashat Sh'mini: Leviticus 9:1–11:47

> Now Aaron's sons Nadab and Abihu each took his fire pan, put fire in it, and laid incense on it; and they offered before the Lord alien fire, which He had not enjoined upon them. And fire came forth from the Lord and consumed them; thus they died at the instance of the Lord. Then Moses said to Aaron, "This is what the Lord meant when He said:
>
>> Through those near to Me I show Myself holy,
>> And gain glory before all the people."
>
> And Aaron was silent. (Lev. 10:1–3, NJPS)

Nadab and Abihu must have sinned greatly to deserve such swift and decisive punishment. Yet, Scripture says only that they offered "alien fire," which God had not commanded them. Nadab and Abihu are priests, mediators between God and his people. Whatever the exact nature of their sin, it is clear that they somehow misrepresented God, because the Lord responds to their sin by saying, "Through those near to Me I show myself holy." Such misrepresentation is a grave offense indeed.

Moses learns the same lesson at the waters of Meribah. There, the Israelites complain because there is no water. The Lord tells Moses to speak to the rock, and it will bring forth water. Instead, Moses castigates the people for their complaining, and strikes the rock. Water comes forth, but the Lord tells Moses,

> Because you did not have-trust in me,
> to treat-me-as-holy before the eyes of the Children of Israel, therefore:
> you shall not bring this assembly into the land that I am giving them! (Num. 20:12, Fox)

As Moses tells Aaron after the death of his sons, the Lord will show himself holy through those near to him and will be glorified

99

before all the people. At Meribah, however, Moses, like his nephews earlier, misrepresents God before the people—and receives harsh judgment himself.

During most years, the reading of the story of Nadab and Abihu in the synagogue comes not long before *Yom HaShoah*, Holocaust Remembrance Day. One of the essential books for understanding the Holocaust and its horrific impact upon the Jewish people is *Night* by Elie Wiesel. In his foreword to the book, the venerable French author François Mauriac writes of his first meeting with the young Wiesel. Wiesel tells Mauriac how his childhood faith perished in the living hell of Auschwitz, and Mauriac writes,

> What did I say to him? Did I speak of that other Israeli, his brother, who may have resembled him—the Crucified, whose Cross has conquered the world? Did I affirm that the stumbling block to his faith was the cornerstone of mine, and that the conformity between the Cross and the suffering of men was in my eyes the key to that impenetrable mystery whereon the faith of his childhood had perished? Zion, however, has risen up again from the crematories and charnel houses. The Jewish nation has been resurrected from among its thousands of dead. It is through them that it lives again. We do not know the worth of one single drop of blood, one single tear. All is grace. If the Eternal is the Eternal, the last word for each one of us belongs to Him. This is what I should have told this Jewish child. But I could only embrace him, weeping.[7]

Mauriac is right not to speak. Those who represented the Messiah whom Mauriac wanted to share with Wiesel had so *misrepresented* him that there was nothing left to say." Hitler, of course, was no Christian. But the seedbed for the Holocaust had been prepared by centuries of Christian anti-Semitism throughout Europe, and the Church had done little to protest the destruction of the Jews. We must remember the ten Booms and many other Christians who helped. We must give thanks for Christians since the Holocaust who have worked to overcome anti-Semitism and seek true reconciliation with the Jewish community. But we must also remember that during the Holocaust the vast majority of Christians, and especially the visible institutions, did not help.

In the Protestant Netherlands, the Nazis offered a deal to the churches that were opposing the deportation of the Jews. If they would stop their protest, the Nazis would refrain from deporting those Jews who had become Christians. The Dutch Reformed Church accepted the deal and went silent concerning the fate of the majority of the Jewish community. On the other side of the European continent, a Lithuanian Catholic bishop met occasionally with the chief rabbi in his area. As the Nazi vice was tightening, the rabbi asked if the bishop could arrange for Jewish children to be hidden in monasteries. The bishop refused to intervene, saying that the monasteries were autonomous and, besides, "their abbots and priors did not excel in mercy and love." Later that same year, 1943, the Nazis occupied Rome and rounded up its Jews under the windows of the Vatican, which made no public statement of concern or protest.[8] Hitler and the Nazis were the great culprits of the Holocaust, but the Church was guilty of its own sin—misrepresenting God by refusing to help the Jews. Those with a claim to be near to God failed to display his holiness in this tragic time.

Nearly sixty years after the deportation of the Roman Jews, John Paul II became the first Pope to visit Israel—in itself an act of apology. He visited Yad VaShem, the Holocaust Memorial in Jerusalem, and prayed at the Western Wall, where he placed a prayer for forgiveness between its stones:

> God of our fathers, you chose Abraham and his descendants to bring your name to the nations. We are deeply saddened by the behavior of those who in the course of history have caused these children of yours to suffer. And asking your forgiveness, we wish to commit ourselves to genuine brotherhood with the people of the covenant. Jerusalem, 26 March 2000. Signed: John Paul II.[9]

Today, Messianic Jews often meet with resistance or even rejection as we seek to follow Messiah in the midst of the larger Jewish community. Some resistance to the word of Messiah seems inherent to human nature, but *Parashat Sh'mini* reminds us of the reason for a particularly Jewish resistance—the misrepresentation of God in the name of Yeshua. Many Jews resist the message of Yeshua because he has been so tragically misrepresented among the Jewish people for so long.

If we respond to this resistance by distancing ourselves from the Jewish community, we risk misrepresenting God ourselves. Instead, we have an opportunity to emulate Yeshua, who above all others is near to God . . . and who resolutely remains near to Israel, despite rejection. "For I say that the Messiah became a servant of the Jewish people in order to show God's truthfulness by making good his promises to the Patriarchs" (Rom. 15:8, CJB).

Nadab and Abihu were priests, mediators between God and Israel, who somehow went astray and misrepresented God. Their story teaches us how disastrous such misrepresentation can be. The Holocaust teaches us a further lesson. We can misrepresent God not only by doing the wrong thing, but simply by failing to do anything.

Messiah represents God by offering God's mercy, healing, and restoration, especially to the whole house of Israel, to "confirm the promises given to the patriarchs." Those who claim to follow Messiah are to do the same. Our hope is that among us, God might in some way "show himself as holy and be glorified before all the people" (Lev. 10:3).

For the journey: We can misrepresent God by doing nothing in the face of evil or need. What opportunities to represent God's love and mercy have I been overlooking—opportunities that might be right in front of me today?

EIGHTH DAY, FIRST DAY
Parashat Tazria, Leviticus 12:1–13:59

All of Creation is in need of redemption, as Scripture says: ". . . which God created to do." (The *Sefat Emet*[10])

Creation and redemption: we have been tracing these two great themes throughout the Torah from the beginning. The nineteenth century commentary called the *Sefat Emet*, or "language of truth," claims that one verse, Genesis 2:3, summarizes both of these themes: "Then God blessed the seventh day and sanctified it, because in it he rested from all his work which God created to do" (literal translation). The phrase "which God created to do," according to this view, means that after God *created* all things, he began to *do* the work of redemption.

The *Sefat Emet* goes on to note that human beings, created on the sixth and final day of Creation, have a share in this work of redemption. "The human was created last in deed, but first in the order of redemption. It is through humanity that Creation and redemption are joined together."[11]

On the sixth day, just before God entered the rest of the seventh day, he gave instructions to the newly formed human couple: "Be fruitful and multiply; fill the earth and subdue it" (Gen. 1:28). After six days of Creation, the work was not entirely finished. Humankind still had the task of filling and subduing the earth. This process is part of the redemption to which the *Sefat Emet* refers, not just redemption from sin (which hasn't even happened yet), but fulfillment of all that God intends for his Creation.

In a similar vein, over three hundred years earlier, Sforno comments on Genesis 2:1. "'Thus the heaven and the earth were finished' . . . having reached the end purpose of existence in general." That is, heaven and earth are not *finished* in the sense that there is nothing left to be done, but in that they express the purpose of Creation "in general." And what is that purpose? Redemption, or *Tikkun* in Hebrew, "the restoration of all things, which God has spoken by the mouth of all His holy prophets since the world began" (Acts 3:21).

In a conversation spanning centuries, Sforno and the *Sefat Emet* agree on a point that has tremendous implications for us today. Creation holds within itself the seed of a new Creation. We have noted this theme throughout our study of Torah and it comes to the fore again, as we reach the midway point through Torah here in *Parashat Tazria*. The completion of God's original plan of Creation requires a new Creation, a spiritual rebirth for every human being. Thus, in *Parashat Tazria*, we read,

> Then the LORD spoke to Moses, saying, "Speak to the children of Israel, saying: 'If a woman has conceived, and borne a male child, then she shall be unclean seven days; as in the days of her customary impurity she shall be unclean. And on the eighth day the flesh of his foreskin shall be circumcised.'" (Lev. 12:1–3)

The eighth day is the first day of new Creation. In Genesis, the seven days are the week of Creation, but here they are seven days of impurity, followed by an eighth day that designates a new beginning. This is not to indicate that the "old Creation" is somehow corrupt and must be replaced by the new. Rather, the creation of the male child, which is in itself holy, does not reach its fulfillment, or redemption, until the eighth day, through circumcision. The holiness of Creation is elevated to a new level.

God gives the original instruction concerning circumcision, of course, to Abraham:

> God further said to Abraham, "As for you, you and your offspring to come throughout the ages shall keep My covenant. Such shall be the covenant between Me and you and your offspring to follow which you shall keep: every male among you shall be circumcised. You shall circumcise the flesh of your foreskin, and that shall be the sign of the covenant between Me and you. And throughout the generations, every male among you shall be circumcised at the age of eight days." (Gen. 17:9–12, NJPS)

Circumcision on the eighth day becomes *havdalah*, the boundary that distinguishes the household of Abraham, which is joined to the Lord through covenant, from the rest of humankind. We might say that God creates humanity on the sixth day, as the culmination of his work of Creation, and then creates a new humanity on the eighth day through circumcision.

> The eighth day is particularly significant because the newborn has completed a seven-day unit of time corresponding to the process of Creation. In like manner, Exodus 22:29 stipulates that the first-born of an animal is dedicated only on the eighth day after birth, and Leviticus 22:27 lays down that an animal is not fit for sacrifice before that day.[12]

The eighth day, then, is a day of new Creation that carries forward the purpose of the original Creation. Now we understand why the gospels emphasize the first day of the week in recounting the resurrection of Messiah. "After Shabbat, as the next day was dawning, Miryam of Magdala and the other Miryam went to see the grave" (Matt. 28:1, CJB). "In the evening that same day, the first day of the week, when the talmidim were gathered together behind locked doors out of fear of the Judeans, Yeshua came, stood in the middle and said, 'Shalom aleikhem [Peace to you]!'" (Yochanan [John] 20:19, CJB). The first day is the eighth day, the first day of redemption.

God himself accomplishes and guarantees this work of redemption, but he does so in partnership with humankind, ultimately embodied in Messiah himself. The eighth day reminds us that God created us not just to await redemption and certainly not just to await our "heavenly reward" in some other realm. Rather, we are to be active participants in the cosmic drama planned from Creation, a drama that reaches its turning point in the resurrection of Messiah.

The *Sefat Emet* says, "It is through humanity that Creation and redemption are joined together." Messiah, the Son of God, becomes Son of Man to accomplish redemption, above all through his resurrection on the eighth day. As we respond, we join a new, reborn humanity that shares in the work of redemption until all comes to completion.

For the journey: In humanity, Creation and redemption join together. We see this reality in Yeshua the Messiah, the Son of Man who brings redemption, but do we see it in ourselves? How do I participate in Tikkun, restoration of Creation, even today?

THE LEPER PRIEST
Parashat M'tzora, Leviticus 14:1–15:33

> What is the Messiah's name? . . . The Rabbis said: His name is
> "the leper scholar," as it is written, Surely he hath borne our
> griefs, and carried our sorrows: yet we did esteem him a leper,
> smitten of God, and afflicted.[13]

Leviticus speaks of a mysterious disease, or group of diseases, called
tzara'at, which we often translate as "leprosy." A passage in the Talmud speaks of the Messiah as bearing this disease, a tremendous insight into our spiritual condition as human beings.

Tzara'at as described in the Torah differs from the leprosy that we
know today in its symptoms and progression. Furthermore, tzara'at
afflicts garments and even the walls of houses as well as the skin of
humans. Accordingly, tzara'at must be a term for either a wide variety
of diseases, or else a specific disease that existed only in the days when
Israel lived under the priestly system in the Land of Israel.

The person who suffers from this condition is a *m'tzora*, which is
the name of this week's parashah. The m'tzora's diagnosis is mysterious, but clearly he embodies the opposite of the holiness that should
characterize the people of Israel. For holiness to be preserved, the
m'tzora must be separated to live outside the camp, identifying himself as unclean so that no one will inadvertently touch him.

> Now the leper on whom the sore is, his clothes shall be torn
> and his head bare; and he shall cover his mustache, and cry,
> "Unclean! Unclean!" He shall be unclean. All the days he has
> the sore he shall be unclean. He is unclean, and he shall dwell
> alone; his dwelling shall be outside the camp. (Lev. 13:45–46)

Even if a leper recovers from his disease, as in this week's reading, he is still not allowed within the camp. First, the priest must go
to him outside the camp, and examine him for signs of the disease.

If he passes this exam, the leper returns to the camp, but then undergoes a long and demanding process before he can be reintegrated into the community of Israel (Lev. 14:1–32).

When he suffers from the disease, his separation from Israel must be complete; when he is restored to Israel, his separation from the disease must be complete. The disease and the camp of God's people are utterly incompatible. Yet, though the leper is separated, he does not depart altogether; he remains "outside the camp," apart yet waiting for the day of restoration.

The text speaks of tzara'at as a "plague" or *nega*, which provides the connection between Messiah and leprosy made by the sages of the Talmud. Isaiah writes of the one he calls the Servant, "Yet we esteemed him stricken [*nagua*], smitten by God, and afflicted" (Isa. 53:4), or as the Talmud translates, "Yet we did esteem him a leper, smitten of God, and afflicted." And again, "For he was cut off from the land of the living; for the transgressions of my people he was stricken [nega]" (Isa. 53:8). Since the Talmud recognizes that Isaiah's Servant in this passage is the Messiah, it portrays Messiah as a leper.

Another Talmudic passage carries this connection even further.

> Rabbi Joshua bar Levi met Elijah standing by the entrance of Rabbi Simeon bar Yohai's tomb. He asked him: 'When will the Messiah come?'—'Go and ask him himself,' was his reply. 'Where is he sitting?'—'At the entrance.' 'And by what sign may I recognize him?'—'He is sitting among the poor lepers: all of them untie their sores all at once, and rebandage them together, whereas he unties and rebandages each separately, thinking, should I be wanted, it being time for my appearance as the Messiah, I must not be delayed through having to bandage a number of sores.'[14]

This remarkable midrash catches a great irony of the Jewish story. The messianic hope underlies the scriptures and prayers of the Jewish people. The messianic ideal is at the heart of Jewish thought. And yet, the one who fulfills this ideal, the Messiah himself, now dwells outside the camp of Israel, estranged from the Jewish people as a whole. He sits as a leper among the lepers "at the entrance," that is, at the entrance of Rome, according to the rabbis. With uncanny insight, they imagined the Messiah in exile at the gates of Rome, the center of the Gentile—and especially Christian—world. There the Messiah waits for the call back to Jerusalem, back to his own people Israel, to whom he will reveal himself at the proper time.

This great irony in the Jewish story leads to the great challenge for the Messianic Jewish community—can we maintain our identification with this Messiah and with our Jewish people at the same time? We claim to be a bridge between the Jewish world and the Messiah whose name is a scandal in the Jewish world. Like the Messiah we follow, we often find ourselves outside the camp of Israel. Can we, like him, remain loyal to our own people within the camp?

The same issue confronts all who would follow Yeshua. Nearness to Messiah often creates distance from friends and loved ones. In the 21st century, as in the first, Yeshua is often found outside the established religious world, and even beyond the bounds of social acceptability. Are we willing to follow him there?

The instructions for restoring a leper will help us answer this question. A cleansed leper must go through a ritual of restoration that resembles the ritual of consecration for the priests. Like the new priest, the leper brings an elaborate offering and undergoes a seven-day period of consecration (Lev. 14:1–32; cf. 8:1–9:1). On the eighth day of the priest, he begins his ministry in the tabernacle; on the eighth day of the leper, he appears before the Lord at the door of the tabernacle. There the leper brings a trespass offering, and then, "The priest shall take some of the blood of the trespass offering, and the priest shall put it on the tip of the right ear of him who is to be cleansed, on the thumb of his right hand, and on the big toe of his right foot" (Lev. 14:14)—the same ritual that Moses performs to consecrate the sons of Aaron (Lev. 8:24).

The leper is like a priest because he preserves holiness in the camp of Israel by bearing impurity out from the camp in his own body. His solitary affliction is for the benefit of the whole community. Surely, this is true of the afflictions of Messiah, the leper scholar. Furthermore, the leper was "like one dead" (Num. 12:12), and now that he is cleansed he is alive, cast out and now restored. He is like a priest in this way as well, because he dwells among his people as a sign of God's restorative power. Likewise, our life in Messiah is incomplete unless it is a sign of Messiah's restoration to those estranged from him.

For the journey: The restoration of the leper reminds us of our restoration in Messiah. We have been restored to the camp to be a sign of restoration to others. Messiah cannot imagine the day of redemption apart from his return to his people. How can we imagine our redemption to be complete apart from the redemption of all Israel, which is a key to the redemption of all peoples?

TO AZAZEL . . . AND BACK
Parashat Acharei Mot, Leviticus 16:1–18:30

If God lived on earth, people would break his windows.
(Yiddish proverb)

This proverb, like the Torah itself, recognizes a certain perverseness in human nature. When God "lived on earth" within the cloud of glory that rested upon the tabernacle, his people did "break his windows" through sin and unbelief. But God in his mercy provided a Day of Atonement, or Yom Kippur, a day of cleansing and restoration from sin, which allowed him to remain in the midst of Israel.

The central figure in the Yom Kippur ritual of old is sometimes called the "scapegoat." We use this term in ordinary speech to refer to someone who bears the blame for the misdeeds of others, but it may actually represent a misunderstanding of the biblical ordinance of Yom Kippur.

There, the Lord instructs Aaron to bring two goats on the Day of Atonement: "[A]nd he shall place lots upon the two goats, one marked for the LORD, and the other marked for Azazel." Aaron sacrifices the goat marked for the Lord, and takes the other goat, marked for Azazel, lays both his hands on its head "and confess[es] over it all the iniquities and transgressions of the Israelites, whatever their sins, putting them on the head of the goat; and it shall be sent off to the wilderness through a designated man" (Lev. 16:8, 21, NJPS).

Azazel in this passage is often translated as "scapegoat", but commentators have struggled over its meaning for centuries and have developed three possible interpretations, only one of them yielding this translation:

1. Azazel can designate the *place*, the "inaccessible region" to which the goat is sent (Lev. 16:22, NJPS). Thus the Talmud interprets the first syllable of Azazel as *'az*, meaning "strong" or "fierce," so that the word means "a fierce land."[15]

2. Azazel may name the *goat* itself, as a contraction of *'ez* (goat) and *'azal* (to go away). This is the source of the English "scapegoat," a contraction of "escape-goat."
3. Azazel may be the name of a *demonic power* ruling over the wilderness to which the goat is sent. Ibn Ezra refers to this interpretation in his commentary on 16:8.

> If you would understand the hidden meaning behind the word *Azazel*, you would also understand the hidden meaning behind its concept, for it has its associations in the Torah. I will give you a hint: when you reach thirty-three you will know.[16]

This third possibility is the most puzzling to our modern ears, and worth some exploration. If we take Ibn Ezra's hint and count thirty-three verses past the introduction of Azazel in Leviticus 16:8, we come to Leviticus 17:7: "[T]hat they may offer their sacrifices no more to the goat-demons after whom they stray" (NJPS). Now we're even more puzzled. If Azazel is a demonic power, offering the goat to it appears to be just the sort of offering to "the goat-demons" that the Torah prohibits here. Certainly, God is not telling us that on Yom Kippur we must purchase our holiness by appeasing the demons!

Ramban seeks to resolve this difficulty.

> Now the Torah has absolutely forbidden to accept other gods as deities, or to worship them in any manner. However, the Holy One, blessed be He, commanded us that on the Day of Atonement we should let loose a goat in the wilderness, to that "prince" which rules over wastelands, and this goat is fitting for it because he is its master, and destruction and waste emanate from that power, which in turn is the cause of . . . the sword, wars, quarrels, wounds, plagues, division and destruction.[17]

Ramban goes on to explain that the goat is not *sacrificed* to Azazel; indeed, there is no sacrifice involved at all, for its blood is not shed. Instead, this goat "shall be left standing alive before the LORD, to make expiation with it, and to send it off to the wilderness for Azazel" (Lev. 16:10, NJPS). The goat does not involve worship of Azazel the "prince" of the wastelands, God forbid. Rather, the goat belongs to the Lord who uses it as a means of separating between the holy and the unholy. He commands Israel to send it away to this other power, along with all their sins and impurities, so the camp of Israel may remain holy.

In his interpretation, Ramban brings together the three alternatives listed above. He sees "Azazel" as a compound of two words, *ez* (goat) and *azal* (going). Thus, it can refer to the "going-goat" itself, to the place where the goat goes, and to the power resident in that place. Such a place is utterly apart from Israel in its holiness; by casting out the goat bearing all unholiness into another place , Israel remains holy.

Hundreds of years after this ordinance was given, the prophet Isaiah used similar terms to speak of a mysterious figure he called the Servant, who is "despised" and "rejected" and "cut off out of the land of the living" (Isa. 53:3, 8). The prophet reveals that the cast out Servant is bearing the sins of Israel, just as the goat bore the sins of Israel. Indeed the same three categories—sin, iniquity, and transgression—that appear in Leviticus 16:21 reappear throughout Isaiah 53. The rabbinic literature centuries later understood these three terms to describe the full range of sin, all that would require atonement on Yom Kippur (for example *Soncino Talmud*, Yoma 36b).

Messianic Jews and Christians, of course, see the sin bearer of Isaiah 53 as Yeshua the Messiah. When his time comes to offer himself up, he does not do so within the holy city as a Temple sacrifice. Instead he is cast out of the city, and finally outside the boundaries of Jewish life and identity, out to Azazel—the wilderness of estrangement from God.

Remarkably, Ramban identifies this wilderness, the land of Azazel, with Rome: "In short, it is the spirit of the sphere of Mars, and its portion among the nations is Esau [a code word throughout rabbinic literature for Rome], the people that inherited the sword and the wars . . ."[18]

Yeshua is handed over to Esau-Rome and crucified. Then, through his resurrection he returns from this exile, no longer bearing our sins but bearing forgiveness and new life.

> Therefore I will divide Him a portion with the great,
> And He shall divide the spoil with the strong,
> Because He poured out His soul unto death,
> And He was numbered with the transgressors,

And He bore the sin of many,
And made intercession for the transgressors. (Isa. 53:11–12)

If God lived on earth, we would break his windows. In Yeshua, God has borne such rejection, removed it from us, and brought forgiveness in its stead. "For on that day he shall make atonement for you, to cleanse you, that you may be clean from all your sins before the LORD" (Lev. 16:30, literal translation). The p'shat, or plain sense, of this verse is that "he" who makes atonement is the High Priest, but another interpretation says that "he" is the Lord himself.[19] The one most offended by sin is the one who ultimately bears away our sins, that we might be restored to him.

For the journey: On Yom Kippur, the one who has been offended, the only one innocent of sin, is the one who brings forgiveness and restoration. In those relationships in which I have been offended and wronged, is there a way that I can take the initiative in bringing restoration?

JUSTICE AND BEYOND
Parashat K'doshim, Leviticus 19:1–20:27

"These people who can see right through you never quite do you justice . . . ." [20]

Justice is a dominant theme throughout Leviticus, an aspect of the holiness that must characterize God's people. Hence, when Leviticus introduces a code of holiness in *Parashat K'doshim* it details the justice required of Israel.

The code's most famous line, however, envisions a limit to justice, or perhaps a more profound justice than can be captured by any code: "You shall not avenge, nor bear any grudge against the children of your people, but you shall love your neighbor as yourself; I am the LORD" (Lev. 19:18). Here in a word, Torah's vision of holiness and justice is fulfilled.

The Torah does not imply that all our grudges are misdirected, or that there is never anything to avenge. We will indeed encounter injustice in the course of our lives, and we are normally to join with the Lord in the pursuit of justice. But here at its heart, the code of holiness focuses not on strict justice, but on love of neighbor. And the Lord reminds us who is ultimately responsible for justice by concluding this instruction with the words, "I am the LORD." He is the one who will pursue justice in any given situation, but here he assigns us other responsibilities.

In the Pulitzer Prize-winning novel *Gilead*, the narrator, an elderly Iowa pastor, tells the story of his grandfather. As a boy, in the early 1800's, the grandfather had seen a vision of Jesus as a slave—"the Lord, holding out his arms to him, which were bound in chains. My grandfather said, 'Those irons had rankled right down to His bones.'" [21] Unable to forget this dream, the grandfather moved to Kansas, where he preached against slavery, sometimes with a loaded pistol in his belt, ready to do justice on behalf of the oppressed. When the Civil War broke out, he welcomed it as divine cleansing upon the sinful nation, and lost an eye in service as a chaplain with the Union Army.

The grandfather was zealous for the justice of God, but sometimes all too human in seeking it. He once caught his grandson, the narrator, in some misbehavior, and glared at him with his lone eye. The grandson remembered:

> But I was a child at the time, and it seems to me he might have made some allowance. These people who can see right through you never quite do you justice, because they never give you credit for the effort you're making to be better than you actually are, which is difficult and well meant and deserving of some notice.[22]

The Torah's code of holiness, like *Gilead*, reminds us that there is a human justice that serves no justice at all. The grandson turns tables on the grandfather by showing how the grandfather misses justice. Likewise, the code of holiness turns tables on us, lest we become too intent on justice and thereby unjust, too intent on pursuing purity and thereby become impure.

In the midst of its detailed rulings about holiness and purity, Leviticus assigns us the task of grace. Yeshua was once teaching about this commandment to love your neighbor when a lawyer asked him a reasonable enough question, "And who is my 'neighbor'?" (Luke 10:29, CJB) In other words, "Just how much is this commandment going to demand of me?" "How much justice must I pursue?" Leviticus reminds us that strict justice sometimes fails, and when it does, we must relinquish the desire for revenge. Indeed, we cannot even hold a grudge. In response to the lawyer's question, however, Yeshua goes even further. It is no longer enough to refrain from holding a grudge; now you must positively seek the good of the other.

> Taking up the question, Yeshua said: "A man was going down from Jerusalem to Jericho when he was attacked by robbers. They stripped him naked and beat him up, then went off, leaving him half dead. By coincidence, a priest was going down on that road; but when he saw him, he passed by on the other side. Likewise a Levite who reached the place and saw him also

passed by on the other side. "But a man from Shomron who was traveling came upon him; and when he saw him, he was moved with compassion. So he went up to him, put oil and wine on his wounds and bandaged them. Then he set him on his own donkey, brought him to an inn and took care of him. The next day, he took out two days' wages, gave them to the innkeeper and said, 'Look after him; and if you spend more than this, I'll pay you back when I return.' Of these three, which one seems to you to have become the 'neighbor' of the man who fell among robbers?" He answered, "The one who showed mercy toward him." Yeshua said to him, "You go and do as he did." (Luke 10:30–37, CJB)

The priest and the Levite may have good reasons to cross over to the other side. Perhaps they have found exemptions from the command to love your neighbor, some reason why it does not apply in their case, or under these circumstances. But *you,* Messiah says, are obligated nonetheless. Your neighbor is the one you encounter in need, the one you are able to love not in theory, but through practical and sacrificial action.

The lawyer who asked for a limit to the commandment wanted to justify himself. The commandment, however, ends with the words, "I am the LORD," reminding us that its focus is divine justice, not self-justification. The entire code of holiness is framed in the same terms. It opens with the Lord's words to Moses, "Speak to all the congregation of the children of Israel, and say to them: 'You shall be holy, for I the LORD your God am holy' (Lev. 19:1–2), and closes with the instruction, "And you shall be holy to Me, for I the LORD am holy . . ." (Lev. 20:26).

In Leviticus, justice and holiness are closely related. Both are found only in the emulation of God, who alone is holy and just. Forgetting this, we become self-righteous and holier-than-thou. We become like those "people who can see right through you," but "never quite do you justice." The justice and holiness of God do not gaze from a distance at the messy realities of life, but actively engage them. The Samaritan is a despised outsider, who might well have held a grudge against his Jewish neighbors. Instead, he fulfills the Torah far better than their experts do. The Samaritan who washed the wounded man, hoisted his body onto his donkey, and dug into his purse for extra coins to cover his expenses, is holy. The priest and Levite—who have kept their hands clean—are not.

The lawyer asks his question because he wants to justify himself. In response, Yeshua tells about an outsider who goes beyond self-justification to fulfill Torah. The moral for the lawyer and for us as well: "Go and do likewise."

For the journey: My neighbor is the one who needs a neighbor. Holiness requires that I find such neighbors and provide the help they need. When I ask "Who is my neighbor?" am I hoping to narrow my neighborhood or expand it? Am I ready to show mercy to a stranger?

TIMES OF ENCOUNTER
Parashat Emor, Leviticus 21:1–24:23

At a book tour event in 2000, author Tim LaHaye told the audience about the conception of the *Left Behind* series.

> In about 1985, one of my dearest friends, Shirley Peters . . . mentioned the idea of the rapture taking place on an airplane. Then a few days later, while I was flying in a 747 jet across the country to a prophecy conference . . . I got to thinking about the idea Shirley had mentioned: "What if the rapture took place?" According to a Gallup poll, about one-third of the population claim to be born-again; so about one-third of the people on the 747 would be gone. And the stewardess would discover their clothes and pound on the door and shout, "Captain, a hundred people are missing from our aircraft." And the rest is history.[23]

The *Left Behind* book series, by Tim LaHaye and Jerry Jenkins, has enjoyed vast popularity with its portrayal of the rapture (in which believers in Yeshua are removed from the earth to meet him in the air [1 Thess. 4:16–17]) and the Great Tribulation that follows. The series draws heavily on the book of Revelation to develop its particular midrash on the end of the age. Bible readers who are fascinated with this subject rarely turn to the book of Leviticus to gain insight into biblical prophecy. The Levitical festivals, however, provide a perspective on the Age to Come far different from *Left Behind*.

We saw that Leviticus opened with the Lord's call to Moses out of אֹהֶל מוֹעֵד *ohel mo'ed*, the tent of meeting, or the tabernacle, which had been the focal point of the final chapters of Exodus, and remained the focal point in Leviticus. In Leviticus 23, however, the focus shifts to מוֹעֲדִים *mo'adim*, the plural form of *mo'ed*, which refers to the appointed festivals of the Lord. The story turns from the *tent* of meeting, to the *times* of meeting. Israel encounters the divine not only in the tent of meeting, but also in the seasons of the year.

The tabernacle, as we have seen, is a model of the restored, ideal Creation. As the tabernacle—ohel mo'ed —is a symbol of restoration in the midst of the camp, so the festivals—the mo'adim—are moments of restoration in the midst of the ordinary days of the year.

The word mo'adim first appears in Genesis 1:14. "Then God said, 'Let there be lights in the firmament of the heavens to divide the day from the night; and let them be for signs and seasons [mo'adim].'" From the beginning of Creation, the Lord ordains the holy times to remind us for all generations of the original integrity of the Creation and of God's purpose of renewing all things.

Thus, Shabbat opens the list of festivals, because it is a memorial of Creation (Exod. 31:17). It also anticipates "the day that will be all Shabbat,"[24] when the goodness of Creation will be restored, and humankind will at last be at rest within it.

Every festival partakes of this prophetic quality of Shabbat. So, we are told on Shavuot, the Festival of Weeks: "When you reap the harvest of your land, you shall not wholly reap the corners of your field when you reap, nor shall you gather any gleaning from your harvest. You shall leave them for the poor and for the stranger: I am the LORD your God" (Leviticus 23:21–22).

Moses had already instructed the Israelites to leave the gleanings for the poor a few chapters earlier, in Leviticus 19:9–10. Why does he repeat it here? Because Shavuot is the festival of the grain harvest, and a holy harvest requires the Israelites to conduct it with respect for the poor and the stranger in their midst. The poor have a rightful share in the harvest, even though they have no land of their own, because they too are created in the image of God and have dominion over all the earth. In the Age to Come the divine image will be restored in every human being. Shavuot anticipates the conditions of that age, when there will be no more hunger and poverty, and no one will be a stranger, but all will have a share in the abundance of the Lord.

In addition, Shavuot is the anniversary of the giving of Torah on Mount Sinai, which was also a restoration of divine order. On the Shavuot following Yeshua's resurrection, he poured out the Spirit upon all of his followers gathered in Jerusalem (Acts 2:33). This outpouring anticipated the Age to Come, when the Spirit of God will be abundantly available to all, young and old, male and female, Jew and Gentile, and "the earth will be filled with the knowledge of the LORD as the waters cover the sea" (Isa. 11:9).

When the Spirit was poured out on Shavuot, Jews were present, "devout men, from every nation under heaven" (Acts 2:5). As members of the priestly nation of Israel, constituted at the first Shavuot at Mount Sinai, these men were the representatives of all the nations, which will partake of the Spirit in the Age to Come. The infilling of the Spirit is not primarily an individual experience of divine power, but a share in the powers of the Age to Come, already present through Messiah Yeshua.

The preview of the Age to Come that we see in Shavuot is evident in all the biblical festivals. Thus, for example, the instructions for Sukkot (the Feast of Tabernacles) include this: "And you shall rejoice in your festival, you and your son and your daughter, your male servant and your female servant and the Levite, the stranger and the fatherless and the widow, who are within your gates" (Deut. 16:14). On this day of joy, all are to be included in rejoicing. The conditions of this age—bondage, poverty, bereavement, and alienation—are overcome by the abundant joy of the Age to Come.

When the Torah anticipates the Age to Come, its focus is not so much on who is taken up and who is left behind, but on a restoration of divine order that includes the dignity and well-being of all humanity. In the appointed festivals, God commanded Israel to enact this restoration each year by ensuring that the poor were fed, the lonely were enabled to rejoice, and the outsiders were brought near. In those high points of the year, at least, in God's design, no one was left behind.

For the journey: The biblical festivals reveal that when we practice ethical behavior or show compassion for the disadvantaged, we are doing a dress rehearsal for the kingdom of God. Who are the gleaners—the strangers, fatherless, and widows—who need to be included in my harvest?

JUBILEE IS COMING
Parashat B'har, Leviticus 25:1–26:2

> Forever young, forever young,
> May you stay forever young.[25]

Have you ever wished that you could start over? That you could be "forever young," as in the Bob Dylan song—going back to your earliest years of life to erase all your mistakes, cancel all your debts, undo all your sins?

This may sound like wishful thinking, but it was a reality in the Torah legislation of the Jubilee. From one Jubilee to the next, the Israelites counted forty-nine years—seven sevens of years. Seven, the number of perfection, was itself perfected. Then came the fiftieth year, in which Moses instructed the people to "proclaim liberty throughout all the land," so that "you shall return, each man to his holding and you shall return each man to his family" (Lev. 25:10). The liberty of Jubilee restores to its original owners any land holding that had been sold, and to his family any Israelite who had fallen into slavery. Jubilee returns Israel to the original order that the Lord intended for it, the order that he will restore forever in the Age to Come.

The count of forty-nine years between one Jubilee and the next reminds us of the count of forty-nine days leading up to Shavuot outlined in the previous parashah. There we saw that Shavuot, like all of the festivals, anticipates the conditions of the Age to Come. The laws of Shavuot provide a share of the harvest to all who live in Israel, anticipating the restored justice of the kingdom of God. Even more than Shavuot and the rest of the festivals of Leviticus 23, however, Jubilee provides a foretaste of "the day that will be all Shabbat, and rest for everlasting life."[26]

Jubilee expresses the themes of holiness and havdalah, which sound throughout Leviticus. It distinguishes one year as separate from and uncorrupted by ordinary pursuits, thereby making holy the passage of all the years.

As the year of restoration in Israel, Jubilee shapes the messianic hope of restoration described in the Scriptures and beyond. Thus, Ezekiel employs Jubilee language to rebuke the false shepherds of Israel. They have not done for Israel what the Jubilee is designed to do: "The weak you have not strengthened, nor have you healed those who were sick, nor bound up the broken, nor brought back what was driven away, nor sought what was lost; but with force and cruelty you have ruled them" (Ezek. 34:4).

Ezekiel proclaims that the Lord intends the liberty of the year of Jubilee for all who are broken and estranged. God promises that the day will come when he himself will accomplish what the shepherds of Israel have failed to do. "I will feed my flock, and I will make them lie down. I will seek what was lost and bring back what was driven away, bind up the broken and strengthen what was sick; but I will destroy the fat and the strong, and feed them in judgment" (Ezek. 34:15–16).

The hope of Jubilee restoration echoes through the prophets and into the prayers of Israel. In the second blessing of the *Amidah*, the traditional series of blessings recited every day, we address the Lord as the One who "upholds the living in lovingkindness, raises the dead in great mercy, supports the fallen, heals the sick, releases the bound, and keeps his faith to those asleep in the dust" (from the *Siddur*).

The accounts of the life of Messiah also echo this hope. When Yochanan, or John the Baptist, was bound in prison, he sent two of his disciples to ask Yeshua, "Are you the one who is to come, or should we look for someone else?" Yeshua answered, "Go and tell Yochanan what you are hearing and seeing—the blind are seeing again, the lame are walking, people with *tzara'at* [a skin disease resulting from God's judgment upon sin] are being cleansed, the deaf are hearing, the dead are being raised, the Good News is being told to the poor—and how blessed is anyone not offended by me!" (Matt. 11:3–6, CJB).

Why would one be offended by Yeshua? Because he claims to be Messiah at a time when the Jubilee is not fully established. Yochanan remains imprisoned. Roman armies occupy the land of Israel. But Yeshua shows that the Jubilee has indeed begun with his arrival in Israel, and so will inevitably be fulfilled. In the meantime, do not be offended, but maintain hope.

Once during a discussion with a group of intermarried Jewish-Christian couples, one of the Jewish men said, "OK, Yeshua is a great guy. I'll even accept that he is the greatest guy, but Messiah—who knows? Besides, who needs a Messiah?"

I could have told my friend that *I* needed a Messiah and Yeshua proved himself as Messiah to me . . . and that if you ever figure out that you need a Messiah, Yeshua will be there for you too. Instead, I focused on the corporate aspect. You may not realize that you need a Messiah, but you cannot deny that this world does. Just look at the suffering, injustice, and oppression all around us. Yeshua embodies the hope of liberty, of a return to God's order and justice that is rooted in the Torah and reflected throughout our Scriptures and prayers. Yeshua has already launched a restoration that has had immeasurable impact on the world we live in, and is evidence of redemption to come. My personal story of salvation is a foretaste of the worldwide Jubilee that Messiah will bring in the end.

Jubilee decrees that each one is to return to his family and to his holding. In our day of isolation and estrangement, this promise is especially significant. In the final chapters of Leviticus, God provides a way of return to himself which anticipates the great restoration that is the underlying theme of all the books of Torah. This return restores us to families and friendships that have been damaged, and to our share in Scripture and the tradition that flows from it.

Those who follow Messiah Yeshua believe that he is the one who brings about this return. Therefore, we refuse to account our personal Jubilee complete apart from the Jubilee for all Israel, which ultimately is the Jubilee that restores all humanity.

For the journey: Jubilee must be proclaimed. Moses says, "You shall sound the *shofar*, and you shall proclaim liberty" (Lev. 25:9–10, paraphrased). As we await the Jubilee to come, may we proclaim the Jubilee that is already here in Messiah Yeshua, so that many in Israel and beyond may return to their families and their holdings.

POSSESSION AND DISPOSSESSION
Parashat B'chukkotai, Leviticus 26:3–27:34

Beruriah, the wife of the great Rabbi Meir, was a woman of godly wisdom and character. One Shabbat, when Meir is at prayer, she discovers that their two sons have died. Meir returns from prayer and asks after the two boys, but Beruriah puts him off until the close of Shabbat. Then she poses a question: "Some time ago, I was given a treasure to guard, and now the owner wants it back. Must I return it?" "Of course," replies Meir, probably wondering what his wife is thinking. Then she leads him into the bedroom and shows him the bodies of their two sons. "These are the treasures, and God has taken them back."[27]

Chief among the lessons of this story is this: the things that we hold most precious in life really do not belong to us, but to God. And if we cannot possess even these most precious things, we ultimately possess nothing at all. This dispossession, however, does not leave us impoverished. Dispossession implies loss, or even violation, but in God's design, it may draw us into boundless riches, as we may hope that Beruriah and Meir discovered.

The final chapters of Leviticus speak of possession and dispossession to reflect the big story of the Torah, that we are on our way from Creation to completion. As Leviticus concludes, it reminds us that all the narratives and instructions of Torah guide us on this journey.

In most years, we read the final parashiyot of Leviticus, *B'har* and *B'chukkotai*, together as one week's portion, and both take place in the same setting at the foot of Sinai. B'har opens, "And the LORD spoke to Moses on Mount Sinai . . ." (Lev. 25:1) B'chukkotai (and the entire book of Leviticus) concludes, "These are the commandments which the LORD commanded Moses for the children of Israel on Mount Sinai" (Lev. 27:34). Gathered at Mount Sinai, the Israelites receive a final set of instructions before they depart for the land of promise. No one imagined at this time that thirty-eight more years of wandering lay ahead. Instead, these instructions were to be the final orders before Israel entered its inheritance. Accordingly, Sforno notes: "Now, Moses our Teacher mentions this chapter here [Lev. 25:1] because he thought that they would immediately enter the Land, as he testified, saying, *We are journeying to the place* (Numbers 10:29)."[28]

Thus, at this crucial moment, as Israel thinks about taking possession of the Promised Land, it is even more striking to realize that this inheritance will not really belong to Israel at all. The land remains the LORD's property, and will revert every fifty years to the original division decreed by Moses to the first generation to enter the land. Thus, each share in the land of Israel is a *holding*, or *achuzah* in the Hebrew, not a *possession*. Every fiftieth year, the Israelites shall "proclaim freedom throughout the land for all its inhabitants. . . . Each of you shall return to his *holding* and each of you shall return to his family" (25:10).

In its final parashiyot, then, Leviticus introduces the principle of dispossession, a key to life in the Age to Come. Ownership implies the right to use one's property however one desires, including the right to sell it. But the Israelites cannot sell any holding within their inheritance.

> In buying from your neighbor, you shall deduct only for the number of years since the jubilee; and in selling to you, he shall charge you only for the remaining crop years: the more such years, the higher the price you pay; the fewer such years, the lower the price; for what he is selling you is a number of harvests. (Lev. 25:15–16, NJPS)

The same principle of dispossession concludes the instructions here at the end of Leviticus. "All tithes from the land, whether the seed from the ground or the fruit from the tree, are the LORD's; they are holy to the LORD. . . . All tithes of herd and flock, every tenth one that passes under the shepherd's staff, shall be holy to the LORD" (Lev. 27:30, 32). The tithe indicates that the produce of the land and of the flock does not ultimately belong to Israel, but to God.

As Rabbi Hillel noted long ago, "the more possessions, the more worry."[29] In our age of consumerism, an age that elevates greed into a virtue, we need to revisit this law of dispossession. It is meant to permeate all of life. We spend our energies worrying about what we have acquired or not acquired, but in the end, we acquire nothing. The law of dispossession relieves us of such worries, and does far more. It provides a way of nearness to God.

Possessions may sometimes be a gift from God, but they can stand between us and God. Thus, Messiah's invitation to follow him involves dispossession: "Whoever of you does not forsake all that he has cannot be my disciple" (Luke 14:33). Moreover, he enacts the story of dispossession to the fullest:

> Let your attitude toward one another be governed by your be-
> ing in union with the Messiah Yeshua:
>> Though he was in the form of God,
>> he did not regard equality with God
>> something to be possessed by force.
>> On the contrary, he emptied himself,
>> in that he took the form of a slave
>> by becoming like human beings are.
>> And when he appeared as a human being,
>> he humbled himself still more
>> by becoming obedient even to death—
>> death on a stake as a criminal! (Phil. 2:5–8, CJB)

Yeshua's act of dispossession is on our behalf. He endured death as the obedient son of Adam so that all the disobedient children of Adam may endure life instead of death. His act, however, is also an example for us, as Rav Shaul notes, "Let the same mind be in you that was in Messiah Yeshua." This mind places obedience to God ahead of the inheritance from God. It recognizes that even the true blessings from God—such as the Israelites' inheritance of the Land—can keep us from the simple obedience that God requires. To accomplish this purpose requires dispossession more often than possession.

We might paraphrase Hillel: "The more stuff we possess, the more stuff possesses us." Liberation comes as we realize that life in this age is a holding and not a possession. As we possess nothing in this world, the Lord takes possession of us for the world to come.

For the journey: All that I have is on loan from God, the one who owns it all. When I forget this, it brings anxiety, greed, and distraction from what matters most. Have I allowed my possessions to take possession of me?

במדבר

THE BOOK OF NUMBERS

The Hebrew title of Numbers—במדבר (*B'midbar*) or "in the wilderness"—says it all. The book opens in the wilderness of Sinai "on the first day of the second month, in the second year after they had come out of the land of Egypt . . ." (Num. 1:1), or less than a year after the Israelites arrived at Sinai (Exod. 19:1). It concludes in the wilderness, not at the foot of Mount Sinai, but "in the plains of Moab by the Jordan, across from Jericho" (Num. 36:13). Most of the forty-year period of desert wanderings, plus the reasons for it, are comprised within the book of Numbers.

Wilderness is not just the setting of Numbers, but one of its dominant themes. The wilderness and its challenges shape Israel into the holy nation God has called it to be. The forty years of wandering seem to be a tragic delay, the result of distrust in God's promise to give Israel the land of Canaan. But the same forty years prepare Israel to take the land. The desert, which seems to be a place of exile and fruitlessness, is also a place of encounter with God.

The Hebrew text provides a remez, or hint, of this remarkable quality. Wilderness is *midbar*, or מדבר in Hebrew. We can detect within this word another Hebrew word, *davar*, or דבר, which means "word." In many Hebrew words, the prefix mem, or מ, signifies location. For example, the root for "dwell" is *shachan* or שכן. The word for place of dwelling is *mishkan*, משכן, the term used for the tabernacle in the wilderness. Lamp is *ner*, נר; the place of lamps is *menorah*, מנורה, the lampstand within the tabernacle.

This pattern in the Hebrew language allows us to make an imaginative word study. Desert, midbar, is the place of the word, davar—the place of revelation. Accordingly, B'midbar, "in the wilderness," continues the story of God's self-revelation that began in Genesis. It also records, with realism and honesty, Israel's repeated failure to respond to that self-revelation, a failure that seems to threaten the heart of the divine plan. In the end, however, the plan goes forward and a new generation prepares to enter the Promised Land.

This story unfolds in Numbers in three major sections.

- 1:1–10:10. Here we read of the great census that gives the book its name in English, which also makes it seem rather unapproachable to many readers. The census takes up the first four chapters, and then is followed after a break by a repetitious list of the offerings of the tribes that have been counted. This seems tedious to a modern reader, but it conveys a sense of pageantry and splendor as Israel is about to begin its journey from Sinai to the Promised Land.

- 10:11–19:22. This section picks up the itinerary suspended after Exodus 19, when Israel arrived at Sinai. Wilderness is the place of testing and of revelation because it is also the terrain of journeying. The journey in the wilderness provides a metaphor that prepares us for the warnings of Exile that become dominant in the next book of the Torah, Deuteronomy, and the writings of the Prophets that follow.

- 20:1–36:13. In chapter 20, Miriam and Aaron die, signifying that a new generation has arisen, the generation that will finally enter the Promised Land. In this section, the Israelites engage in their first battles, defeating the kings Og and Sihon, who become symbols of the conquest to come. These accounts are followed by the story of Balaam, sent to curse Israel, who instead provides a blessing. After he and his Midianite handlers are defeated, Israel prepares to cross the Jordan.

This narrative is interspersed with sections of commandments and judgments that will guide Israel's future in the Promised Land. "These are the commandments and the judgments which the LORD commanded the children of Israel by the hand of Moses in the plains of Moab by the Jordan, across from Jericho" (Num. 36:13). Here, at the eastern bank of the Jordan, Israel is poised to fulfill the plan God set in motion when he called to Moses from the Burning Bush to deliver his people from Egypt. Numbers reminds us that at the heart of this plan is davar, the word, God revealing himself to his people Israel and, through them, to the world.

WILDERNESS OF REVELATION
Parashat B'midbar, Numbers 1:1–4:20

> All those who freely devote themselves to His truth shall bring all their knowledge, powers, and possessions into the Community of God, that they may purify their knowledge in the truth of God's precepts and order their powers according to His ways of perfection and all their possessions according to His righteous counsel. (From the Dead Sea Scrolls[1])

When I am in Israel, I love to visit the Dead Sea and surrounding area. It is desolate but beautiful at the same time—a refuge from the hectic and crowded streets of Jerusalem.

One of the sites by the Dead Sea is Qumran, the ruins of a large communal center connected with the Dead Sea Scrolls, which were found in a number of nearby caves. These scrolls are one of the greatest archaeological finds of the twentieth century, containing the earliest manuscripts that we possess of most of the Hebrew Scriptures, plus numerous other writings from the centuries just before the coming of Messiah. From scrolls like "The Community Rule" quoted above, we also learn about the communal life of Qumran, where pious Jews fled from the growing corruption of Jerusalem to seek God in the desert beginning in the second century BCE.

Yeshua began his ministry in this same region, where Yochanan (John) appeared as "a voice crying in the wilderness" (Isa. 40:3), a favorite phrase of the Qumran sect. He called Israel to turn away from sin, turn back to God, and be immersed in the waters of the Jordan. All the people of Judah and Jerusalem went out to the wilderness in response to Yochanan's preaching, and there Yeshua appeared to receive immersion and initiate his ministry.

The area around Qumran reminds us of "the great and awesome desert, in which were fiery serpents and scorpions and thirsty land where there was no water" (Deut. 8:15). Wilderness holds a special place in the continuing story of Creation and renewal that began in the book of Genesis. Indeed, Mark's account of the life of Messiah links the wilderness, which seems so uninhabitable, with the Garden of Eden, the site of humankind's first habitation. After Yeshua's immersion at the hand of Yochanan, we read:

> Immediately the Spirit drove Him into the wilderness. And He was there in the wilderness forty days, tempted by Satan, and was with the wild beasts; and the angels ministered to Him. (Mark 1:12–13)

As we noted in *Parashat Mishpatim*, the wording here is significant. In the other gospels, Yeshua is "led" by the Spirit into the wilderness; only in Mark is he "driven out." This phrase echoes the language of Genesis 3, in which Adam and Eve are "driven out" of the Garden after their great transgression. Another element unique to Mark is his mention of the "wild beasts." Perhaps this is a reminder of Adam's naming of the beasts in Genesis 2, his first activity within the Garden of Eden. And both accounts, of course, center on temptation, the temptation that defeats Adam and Eve, but which Messiah overcomes.

So, we can read the temptation of Messiah in Mark as a reversal of the sin of Adam and Eve. Adam is in the Garden, he names the beasts, he is tempted and defeated, and then he is driven out. In reverse order, Yeshua is driven out into the wilderness, then he is tempted and victorious, then he is with the beasts, and the angels minister to him, in contrast with the angelic cherubim that guard the way back into the Garden from Adam and Eve.

The wilderness in Mark is the place of restoration. It seems to be the opposite of Eden, but paradoxically becomes Eden-like as the place of restored fellowship with God. This vision of the wilderness led some Jews of the second Temple period out to the desert to find God's "ways of perfection and . . . righteous counsel," as the Dead Sea Scrolls stated.

The wilderness is barren and remote, but there—because of these very qualities—we can hear God's word. Thus, we come to the opening words of Numbers or *B'midbar*: "And the Lord *spoke* to Moses in the *wilderness* of Sinai" (Num. 1:1, emphasis added).

In the wilderness God speaks. Torah is teaching us that it is in the places of difficulty, challenge, and temptation that we find God. Adam and Eve lost God in a garden, but Yeshua regained God in the wilderness. Likewise, in our own lives, the difficulties that we face can become the source of new understanding and communion with God.

But the book of *B'midbar* reveals that the wilderness is also a place of complaining, rebellion, and failure. Life's difficulties can bring us into an encounter with God, but they can also embitter and destroy us.

B'midbar reveals some of Israel's greatest failures. The opening chapters describe the census that Moses takes at God's command as part of the military preparation to take the Promised Land. Not long after the census, Moses' brother and sister, Aaron and Miriam, rebel against him. Then, scouts sent out to assess the Land come back with an evil report, leading the people to rebel against God's plan of conquest. Shortly after the rebellion the scouts set in motion, a Levite named Korach leads another, massive rebellion that brings great destruction upon the tribes of Israel. Finally, before the book closes, Moses himself will rebel and lose his right to enter the Promised Land. Interspersed among these low points of disobedience are numerous complaints and murmurings among the children of Israel.

The same geography can be the place of revelation or rebellion. What makes the difference? Our response. The drama of Numbers turns on whether the Israelites in their desert wanderings will trust the Lord who has revealed himself to be so trustworthy, or will let the desert wanderings push them into complaining and disobedience.

Our greatest challenges in life can lead us into either revelation or rebellion. We can emerge from the wilderness experience as better and stronger people, or embittered and defeated. What makes the difference? Our response. As we trust in the God who reveals himself as trustworthy throughout the Torah, our wilderness becomes a place of encounter with him.

For the journey: Difficulties and disappointments in life can draw us into greater understanding of God and his ways—or they can drive us away from God altogether. It all depends on our response. How am I responding to the tough, frustrating situations that are in my life right now, and how will I respond to difficulties in the next few days or months?

A MERCIFUL CURSE
Parashat Naso, Numbers 4:21–7:89

A king had some empty goblets. He said: "If I put hot water in them, they will burst. If I put cold water in, they will crack." So the king mixed cold and hot water together and poured it in, and the goblets were uninjured.

Even so, God said, "If I create the world with the attribute of mercy alone, sin will multiply; if I create it with the attribute of justice alone, how can it endure? So I will create it with both, and thus it will endure."[2]

The longing for justice seems to be part of our human nature. We yearn to see the standards of right and wrong enforced in the world around us, and yet are disappointed more often than not. When the wicked escape punishment, it troubles us almost as much as when the innocent suffer.

This longing for justice lies at the root of the ordinance of the unfaithful wife in *Parashat Naso*. It not only answers the suspicions of a jealous husband, but it also restores justice to the community.

> If any man's wife goes astray and behaves unfaithfully toward him and a man lies with her carnally, and it is hidden from the eyes of her husband, and it is concealed that she has defiled herself, and there was no witness against her, nor was she caught—if the spirit of jealousy comes upon him and he becomes jealous of his wife, who has defiled herself; or if the spirit of jealousy comes upon him and he becomes jealous of his wife, although she has not defiled herself—then the man shall bring his wife to the priest. (Num. 5:12–15a)

The priest takes some of the dust from the floor of the tabernacle, mixes it with holy water in an earthen vessel to make "bitter water" (Num. 5:18). He gives it to the alleged adulteress declaring,

"'May this water that causes the curse go into your stomach, and make your belly swell and your thigh rot.' Then the woman shall say, 'Amen, so be it.' Then the priest shall write these curses in a book, and he shall scrape them off into the bitter water" (Num. 5:22–23). If the woman is guilty, the curse will enter her with the water, but if she is innocent, she will remain unharmed.

Ramban notes the miraculous element in this ordinance:

> Now there is nothing amongst all the ordinances of the Torah which depends upon a miracle, except for this matter, which is a permanent wonder and miracle that will happen in Israel, when the majority of the people live in accordance with the Will of G-d . . . so that they are worthy that the Divine Presence dwell among them.[3]

Normally justice depends on the wisdom of human judges. But no one can know whether the accused woman is guilty or innocent. Her husband has become infected by "the spirit of jealousy." Something must be done to restore justice, and God makes a special provision. Ramban notes that the miraculous nature of this ordinance reflects the unique condition of Israel at the time, newly delivered from bondage and living in the presence of the *Shechinah*, the glory-cloud of God. Later, as the spiritual condition of Israel declined and adultery became more widespread, the Talmud says, the bitter water ceased to be effective (Sotah 47b). But in better days, God intervenes to restore justice.

We saw a similar intervention in the case of Nadab and Abihu, who were struck down by a fire from the Lord's presence because they offered "strange fire" (Lev. 10), and we will see it again shortly in the rebellion of Korach (Num. 16). Centuries later, the early Messianic community experiences divine intervention in the judgment of Ananias and Sapphira (Acts 5). In each of these cases, God acts supernaturally to restore justice because he is so present within the community that he cannot allow disorder to remain. Later, as sin increases, God ceases to intervene so directly.

God's miraculous intervention in the ordinance of the accused woman does not come directly, however, but at the hands of the priest, who is empowered to call down a curse upon the guilty. In contrast, in the next chapter, God appoints this same priest as the agent of blessing.

> Speak to Aaron and his sons, saying, "This is the way you shall
> bless the children of Israel. Say to them:
> 'The LORD bless you and keep you;
> The LORD make His face shine upon you,
> And be gracious to you;
> The LORD lift up His countenance upon you,
> And give you peace.'" (Num. 6:24–26)

The same priests who are the instruments of cursing pronounce the blessing. Both judgment and blessing can be signs of
God's presence among his people.

Once some scribes and Pharisees brought a woman caught in
adultery, "in the very act," to Yeshua, saying: "Now Moses, in the law,
commanded us that such should be stoned. But what do You say?"
(John 8:5). Instead of answering, Yeshua wrote in the dirt, perhaps
as a reminder of the dust stirred into the bitter water of Numbers 5.
Then he said, "He who is without sin among you, let him throw a
stone at her first" (John 8:7). At this word, the woman's accusers
slipped off one by one, and the woman was not condemned. Where
sin is abundant, God may delay his judgment. Instead, he provides a
time of forgiveness so that the holiness of the community can be re-
established.

Complete justice awaits the Age to Come when the purity and
holiness of Creation are fulfilled. In the meantime, the ordinance of
bitter water reminds us of the pervasiveness of sin, which requires
that justice be tempered with mercy. God mixes mercy with judgment so the world may endure. No priest in Israel has employed the
bitter water for nearly two thousand years, but the descendants of
Aaron continue to pronounce the blessing of Numbers 6:24–26 to
this day. We may wonder why the wicked go unpunished, but we
must thank God that his mercy prevails over judgment.

For the journey: Yeshua said, "Blessed are the merciful for they shall
see God." Am I merciful? How often have I longed for God's justice
without realizing that I myself was in need of mercy?

GUIDE AND GLORY-CLOUD
Parashat B'ha'alotkha, Numbers 8:1–12:16

In the traditional morning service, before the Torah scroll is removed from the ark and carried out among the congregation, the worship leader calls out, "*Vay'hi binsoa ha'aron, vayomer Moshe*—And it came to pass, whenever the ark went forward, that Moses would say: 'Arise, O LORD! Let Your enemies be scattered, and let those who hate You flee before You'" (Num. 10:35).

The traditional Torah service reenacts the scene at Mount Sinai, when all Israel stood before the mountain to receive the word of the Lord from the hand of Moses. As the Torah scroll is carried through the congregation, we touch it with a prayer book, or the fringe of the prayer shawl, and then touch that object to our lips. Through this ancient custom, we repeat the words that our ancestors spoke when the Torah was first brought down from the mountain and offered to them: "All that the Lord has said, we will do" (Exod. 24:17).

The words from Numbers 10 that introduce the Torah service were first spoken as the Israelites prepared to depart from Mount Sinai and begin the final stages of the journey to the Promised Land. Since the middle of the book of Exodus, they have been encamped at the foot of Mount Sinai, receiving the instructions of Torah, especially those for building the tabernacle and establishing the priesthood and sacrifices. There, the Israelites build the tabernacle, inaugurate the sacrifices, and receive further instructions in the life of the holy community. All of this takes us through the rest of Exodus, all of Leviticus, and well into the book of Numbers.

Finally, in Numbers 10, Israel prepares to move on. The book opened with the census of Israel's fighting men because Israel is about to come into contact with its enemies, as Moses says, "Rise up, O LORD! Let your enemies be scattered." Hence, just as the Torah service reenacts the divine encounter at Mount Sinai, so it anticipates the day when the Torah will go forth throughout the world. Indeed, after we chant the line from Numbers beginning, "Arise, O LORD . . ."

139

we recite Isaiah 2:3, "For from Mount Zion will go forth the Torah, and the word of the LORD from Jerusalem." The ark of God goes before Israel, not just to push back the enemy tribes in the desert, but also to further the process of world redemption, which reaches fulfillment in the return of Messiah Yeshua to rule over all nations.

Numbers 10:35–36 captures a prophetic moment. This may explain why an inverted form of the Hebrew letter *nun* brackets these verses in the Torah scroll (as reproduced in *JPS Hebrew-English Tanakh*[4]).

הַמַּחֲנֶה: ז* ס

35 וַיְהִי בִּנְסֹעַ הָאָרֹן וַיֹּאמֶר מֹשֶׁה

קוּמָה | יְהוָה

וְיָפֻצוּ אֹיְבֶיךָ

וְיָנֻסוּ מְשַׂנְאֶיךָ מִפָּנֶיךָ:

36 וּבְנֻחֹה וּבְנֻחֹו יֹאמַר

שׁוּבָה יְהוָה

רִבְבוֹת אַלְפֵי יִשְׂרָאֵל: ז* פ

The commentators provide various explanations for this ancient, but unusual, feature of the Torah scroll. It is clear, however, that these verses mark a major turning point in the narrative flow. Moses pronounces these words as the ark goes forth to launch a completely new phase in Israel's journey, which will end only with the fulfillment of God's purposes for all humankind.

It seems strange, then, to remember that just a few verses earlier Moses had asked his father-in-law, Hobab (appearing in earlier passages as Jethro), to continue to guide the Israelites: "So Moses said, 'Please do not leave, inasmuch as you know how we are to camp in the wilderness, and you can be our eyes'" (Num. 10:31).

Why does Moses ask Hobab to guide them, when the LORD himself is about to go before them as guide? "The ark of the covenant of the LORD went before them for the three days' journey, to search out a resting place for them. And the cloud of the LORD was above them by day when they went out from the camp" (Num. 10:33–34). It is this very reality that Moses invokes when he says, "Arise, O LORD, and let your enemies be scattered."

Some interpreters suggest that Moses' words to his father-in-law should be translated in the past tense: "So Moses said, 'Please do not leave, inasmuch as you have known how we are to camp in the wilderness, and you have been our eyes'" (Num. 10:31). Perhaps he is not saying that the Israelites still need him as a guide, now that the ark goes before them, but simply that they want him to travel with them in honor of his past contributions.

The text, however, is more straightforward. The Israelites will follow the glory-cloud of God, and they will also follow Hobab, who has already proven himself a reliable guide. The Israelites do not choose between the guidance of God's cloud and the guidance of Moses' father-in-law. Rather, God guides his people through both means, acting together.

We see something similar in the Book of Ruth, read during Shavuot, not long before we read this parashah in the synagogue. Boaz employs a striking metaphor in his words to Ruth, "The LORD repay your work, and a full reward be given you by the LORD God of Israel, under whose wings you have come for refuge" (Ruth 2:12). The LORD is like a protecting eagle, sheltering its offspring under mighty, outstretched wings. Later, when Ruth approaches Boaz for help, she uses the same metaphor: "I am Ruth, your maidservant. Take your maidservant *under your wing*, for you are a close relative"(Ruth 3:9, emphasis added). Does Ruth come under the wing of the LORD, or under the wing of Boaz? But, of course, it is not an either/or situation. Ruth seeks refuge in the Lord, and the Lord brings her to Boaz, who will provide refuge. In a similar way, the Lord guides the Israelites and brings Hobab into the camp of Israel to be their eyes.

In the divine program of world redemption, everything depends on God's mercy and grace, but human beings have a genuine part to play. As Paul writes, "For we are of God's making, created in union with the Messiah Yeshua for a life of good actions already prepared by God for us to do" (Eph. 2:10, CJB). We are not passive observers, simply waiting for God to act, but are "created for good works." We even have a share in the plan of world redemption, the Word of God going out to all the world as pictured in the Torah service. Yet we cannot perform these works apart from him. Indeed, the Lord gives us genuine responsibility in his plan, so that we discover that we cannot fulfill this responsibility without his help. In the divine-human partnership of world redemption, we discover how dependent we are upon God.

For the journey: If I take someone under my wing, who knows whether he or she has really come under the wings of the Lord God of Israel? I will be on the watch for real-life opportunities to cooperate with God's redemptive purposes.

CLOTHES MAKE THE MAN
Parashat Shlach L'kha, Numbers 13:1–15:41

Years ago, when I worked as a salesman, our manager gave everyone a copy of the book *Dress for Success*.[5] This was more than a fashion book. Rather, it was a study of how different styles and colors influenced one's effectiveness. In one test, a man wearing a beige raincoat asked people passing by for handouts and collected a tidy sum. Later he did the same in a gray raincoat and came up empty-handed. The book abounds with examples like this. Apparently, at least on a human level, clothes do make the man.

The Torah turns this principle around—clothing cannot make us something we are not, but it can remind us what we are supposed to be. Moses instructs the Israelites "to make tassels on the corners of their garments throughout their generations, and to put a blue thread in the tassels of the corners. And you shall have the tassel, that you may look upon it and remember all the commandments of the LORD and do them" (Num. 15:38–39).

"Tassel" is *tzitzit* in Hebrew, and such tassels are worn by Jewish men to this day. Traditional Jews wear a four-cornered undergarment with tassels that either appear on the outside of their pants, hanging down from the waist, or remain under the outer clothing, out of sight. The traditional prayer shawl, or *tallit*, has a tzitzit at each corner, thus providing another way to fulfill the commandment.

In the ancient world, nobles wore garments with ornate hems as a sign of their status. "The more important the individual, the more elaborate the embroidery of his hem. Its significance lies not in its artistry but in its symbolism as an extension of its owner's person and authority."[6] Thus, a husband would divorce his wife by cutting off the hem of her garment. A seer in ancient Mari would send his report to the king and include a lock of his hair and a portion of his hem to attest its authenticity. From this we understand the significance of David's cutting a piece of the hem off the robe of Saul, why David's heart troubled him after he did so, and why Saul took it as a sign that David would succeed him as king (1 Sam. 24:6, 20).[7] Likewise, we see more clearly why a woman in need of healing grabbed the hem of Yeshua's garment (Matt. 9:20).

"Thus the significance of the *tzitzit* lies in this: It was worn by those who counted; it was the identification tag of nobility."[8] In Israel, the Torah decrees, it is not only the nobles, but every Israelite who is to wear such fringes on their garments.

The requirement to wear a thread of blue among the other threads of the tzitzit heightens its noble quality. Blue is the color of nobility, largely because of the cost of the dye in the ancient world. Indeed, the dye was so costly that the rabbis of the Talmudic era decreed that the blue thread was no longer to be worn, and the fringe should be white, so that all Jewish men would enjoy equal dignity.[9] Nevertheless, the original significance remains. Blue is the color of royalty, and therefore the color of the priestly garments and the tabernacle itself. The single blue thread of the tzitzit reflects the single blue thread that held the golden head plate of the High Priest, on which were inscribed the words *kodesh l'Adonai*, "Holy to the Lord" (Exod. 28:36). Just as the priestly garment was made of both linen and woolen strands—a combination forbidden to the ordinary Israelites—so the early rabbis ordained that the tzitzit contain both white linen and blue woolen strands. "Thus the *tzitzit*, according to the rabbis, are modeled after a priestly garment that is taboo for the rest of Israel!"[10]

It is clear, then, that the tzitzit not only reminds the Israelites to obey the commandments, but it also reveals that they receive these commandments as a holy priesthood. Obedience is not just a way to keep the Israelites in line. Rather, it expresses the holiness of their calling and the purpose of their redemption from Egypt. Hence, the Lord concludes the instruction of the tzitzit with the words, "I am the Lord your God, who brought you out of the land of Egypt, to be your God: I am the Lord your God" (Num. 15:41).

This is indeed a lofty calling. Yet, even more striking is its position in the text of Numbers. We are in *Parashat Shlach L'kha*, which opens with Moses sending twelve men, one from each tribe, to scout out the Land of Israel in preparation for its conquest. The story ends, of course, in disaster. Ten of the twelve scouts bring back an evil report. Only Joshua and Caleb encourage the people to take the Land. The people believe the majority, refuse to take the Land as God has commanded, and end up being condemned to perish in the wilderness. This incident is not the first trial Moses faces in the book of Numbers. In the chapter before we learned of the complaints of his own siblings, Aaron and Miriam, and the Lord's chastisement upon Miriam. Finally, just before the ordinance of the tzitzit, we hear of a man who breaks the Shabbat and is condemned to be stoned to death.

After the ordinance is given, things do not improve at all. The following chapter tells of the rebellion of Korach, who joins with Dathan, Abiram, and others to challenge the authority of Moses and Aaron. The Lord puts down this rebellion in the most drastic way, with the earth swallowing up Korach and his family, and fire from heaven striking down 250 other rebels.

The way Numbers tells the story makes it clear that when the Lord clothes the Israelites as priests, he does so fully knowing their tendency to rebel. The holy garment is not a reward for faithfulness because they have hardly been faithful. Instead, the tzitzit expresses the faithfulness of God. By it, he calls into being a holy priesthood out of the unqualified and unworthy.

Is it possible that God still views Israel as a holy priesthood, despite its corporate failure to acknowledge Yeshua as Lord and Messiah, and still has a holy destination in mind for the whole people? As Paul reminded the Gentiles who believed in Yeshua, "Concerning the gospel they are enemies for your sake, but concerning the election they are beloved for the sake of the fathers. For the gifts and the calling of God are irrevocable" (Rom. 11:28–29).

Clothes make the man. The tzitzit not only reminds Israel of the irrevocable commandments of the Lord, but of their irrevocable calling as a royal priesthood and a holy nation.

In our day, we are seeing a great move of reconciliation between Christians and Jews. Despite the Jewish "no" to Yeshua, God still has a glorious plan for them, a plan that will ultimately be fulfilled in this same Yeshua. As the tzitzit is a reminder to Israel of their holy calling, so may it be a reminder to Christians, after centuries of anti-Jewish attitudes and actions, to love and honor the Jewish people.

For the journey: God has an unchangeable purpose that brings together Jews and Christians. There are visible reminders of this purpose in the world around me. How might I display such a reminder, like the tzitzit, in my own life?

LAND OF MILK AND HONEY
Parashat Korach, Numbers 16:1–18:32

> "I don't think we want any more Kings . . . no more than we
> want any Aslans. We're going to look after ourselves from now
> on and touch our caps to nobody. See?"
>
> "That's right," said the other Dwarfs. "We're on our own
> now. No more Aslan, no more Kings, no more silly stories
> about other worlds. The Dwarfs are for the Dwarfs." And they
> began to fall into their places and to get ready for marching
> back to wherever they had come from.[11]

In the C.S. Lewis classic *The Last Battle*, Aslan the lion is the Messiah figure. A false messiah disguised as Aslan appears and misleads the people, including a band of Dwarfs whom he has taken captive. The followers of the true Aslan, led by King Tirian, arise, overturn the false messiah, and liberate the Dwarfs. They expect the Dwarfs to rejoice and welcome Aslan's imminent return, but the Dwarfs reject both the King and Aslan. From now on, "the Dwarfs are for the Dwarfs."

Parashat Korach records a similar disillusionment among the Israelites. They grow weary of wandering in the wilderness, living off manna and miraculous supplies of water, and begin to long for the well-watered bounty of Egypt. "We remember the fish which we ate freely in Egypt, the cucumbers, the melons, the leeks, the onions, and the garlic; but now our whole being is dried up; there is nothing at all except this manna before our eyes!" (Num. 11:5–6).

One of the Levites, Korach, leads a rebellion that takes this complaining even further, even calling Egypt, instead of Canaan, the "land of milk and honey" (Num. 16:13). With this phrase, they reveal the wicked heart of their rebellion and call down the unprecedented divine judgment that will end it.

We live in an era that exhorts us—in the words of a popular bumper sticker—to "Question Authority." The American Revolution gave birth to a great nation through resistance to authority, which seems in retrospect to have been principled and noble. Yet such resistance is risky. It can easily lead to anarchy and the reaction that inevitably follows, as evidenced by the French Revolution, which came just a few years after the American, and gave birth to the Reign of Terror and the career of Napoleon.

Question authority, perhaps, but beware of the rebellion of Korach, which would overturn all authority. Korach's followers equate Egypt with the Promised Land and accuse Moses, God's appointed leader, of mocking them when he speaks of another Promised Land.

> Not only have you perpetrated evil against us by taking us out of a land flowing with milk and honey and bringing us into the wilderness, but you also jest with us—for you have not brought us to the Land into which you said you would bring us and still you speak to us as though you have given us "an inheritance of fields and vineyards," by commanding us those commandments which are connected only to the Land . . . as though it was already ours and we have fields and vineyards in it![12]

Korach's followers not only question the authority of Moses, but they turn all authority on its head. They see Moses, the self-sacrificing leader, as Moses the self-serving leader, who even mocks those who follow him. The real Promised Land is no longer the place to which Moses is leading them, but Egypt, the place of servitude from which they had fled. It was all a big mistake, and the best course is to go back.

The Last Battle pictures the ultimate rebellion led by the false messiah at the end of the age (Rev. 13), which leads to the rejection of all authority. Likewise, Korach's rebellion does not simply propose to replace one authority structure with another, which at times may be a legitimate course of action. Instead, it questions authority altogether, even God's authority, and refuses to live under any of it. As a result, it undermines the divine project launched in Genesis of establishing the order and blessing of Creation over all the earth. In the end, the Dwarfs are for the Dwarfs and no one else.

When Moses speaks of the Promised Land in the book of Deuteronomy, he uses language that evokes the abundance of Creation and Eden before the exile of Adam and Eve:

> For the LORD your God is bringing you into a good land, a land
> of brooks of water, of fountains and springs, that flow out of
> valleys and hills; a land of wheat and barley, of vines and fig
> trees and pomegranates, a land of olive oil and honey; a land in
> which you will eat bread without scarcity, in which you will
> lack nothing. (Deut. 8:7–9)

By delivering Israel from Egypt and giving them the Torah, the Lord
is raising up Israel as a restored humanity, to dwell in the Eden of
the Promised Land and bear the divine image on behalf of the rest
of humankind. Korach sees all this as a fairy tale and yearns instead
for the security and control of life in Egypt.

Now we can understand why God's judgment upon Korach is
so harsh.

> Now it came to pass . . . that the ground split apart under them,
> and the earth opened its mouth and swallowed them up, with
> their households and all the men with Korah, with all their
> goods. So they and all those with them went down alive into
> the pit; the earth closed over them, and they perished from
> among the assembly. (Num. 16:31–33)

The very earth must swallow up Korach because his rebellion is
infectious. It would undermine the entire purpose of the Exodus
from Egypt.

In the end, however, God desires to remind the Israelites that
his purpose is one of blessing and life, even though his judgment
against the rebels has been so severe. He directs the Israelites to
gather twelve rods, one representing each tribe, and place them
within the tabernacle. In the morning, they discover that Aaron's
rod has come to life and produced blossoms and buds and ripe al-
monds (Num. 17:23), thus vindicating the leadership of Moses and
Aaron. God's final answer to rebellion is not suppression, but abundant life that only he can bring forth, life which only the obedient
can experience.

For the journey: Authority needs to be exercised with humility and
the fear of God. But rejection of authority can lead to mistaking
Egypt for the Promised Land. Have I in any way embraced the anti-
authority attitude that is so prevalent in our day?

WATER FROM THE ROCK
Parashat Hukkat, Numbers 19:1–22:1

> Surely it was taught: Ten things were created on the eve of the [first] Sabbath at twilight. These are they: the well, the manna, the rainbow, the writing and the writing instruments, the Tables, the sepulcher of Moses, the cave in which Moses and Elijah stood, the opening of the ass's mouth, and the opening of the earth's mouth to swallow up the wicked.[13]

On a recent trip to Israel, our tour group was driving north along the western shore of the Dead Sea. Our guide pointed to the mountains of Moab across the sea in present-day Jordan. Through the haze, we could see Pisgah, the high point to which the Lord directed Moses in Deuteronomy 3:27: "Go up to the top of Pisgah, and lift your eyes toward the west, the north, the south, and the east; behold it with your eyes, for you shall not cross over this Jordan." There, Moses begged the Lord for the chance to set foot in the land that had been the focus of his hopes and yearnings for the past forty years, but it was not to be. In an unknown and unmarked spot on that mountain, Moses lies buried to this day. Here is "the sepulcher of Moses . . . created on the eve of the first Sabbath."

This scene is sadly ironic. The great deliverer of his people has no share in the final stage of their deliverance. After bearing with the people for so long in their trials, he cannot partake of their joy with them. Ironic though it is, the scene is most fitting. Moses has been the mediator for Israel, representing the people before God in all their sins and shortcomings. It is fitting that he remain with his own generation, even in exile. Perhaps the Torah is anticipating here that much of Israel's history will be experienced outside the Promised Land. Moses our teacher dies in exile to identify not only with the generation that he led out of Egypt, but also with countless generations of Jews who have died in exile. His teachings guide us, whether in the Land or in dispersion.

Nevertheless, the question remains, why does God treat Moses so harshly? The answer lies in a familiar story in this week's parashah.

The people have arrived at Kadesh in the wilderness of Zin only to discover that there is no water. They raise their voices in complaint against Moses, and the Lord instructs him: "Take the rod; you and your brother Aaron gather the congregation together. Speak to the rock before their eyes, and it will yield its water; thus you shall bring water for them out of the rock, and give drink to the congregation and their animals" (Num. 20:8).

Moses and Aaron, however, deviate from this instruction, with terrible consequences:

> And Moses and Aaron gathered the assembly together before the rock; and he said to them, "Hear now, you rebels! Must we bring water for you out of this rock?" Then Moses lifted his hand and struck the rock twice with his rod; and water came out abundantly, and the congregation and their animals drank. Then the LORD spoke to Moses and Aaron, "Because you did not believe me, to hallow me in the eyes of the children of Israel, therefore you shall not bring this assembly into the land which I have given them." (Num. 20:10–12)

Now we know why Moses must die on the far side of the Jordan, in the land of Moab.

The passage from the Talmud cited above provides further insight. The "well . . . created on the eve of the first Sabbath" is the rock that Moses struck. We first read of it in Exodus 17, when the previous generation of Israelites arrived at a waterless place—perhaps the very same place as in Numbers 20—and the Lord supplied them with water from the rock. From that time on, despite all their wanderings and difficulties, the Israelites always had a supply of water . . . until now.

A midrash portrays this rock following the children of Israel in all their wanderings, a miraculous well created from the very beginning to supply them with water. One variation of the story links this miraculous supply to Miriam. In Exodus 15, she is the prophetess who leads the daughters of Israel in dance and exalted praise before the Lord. In her honor, the Lord supplies water to Israel in Exodus 17. But when the Israelites arrive at Kadesh in Numbers 20, Miriam dies and the water ceases.

Apparently, a form of this midrash was current when Paul wrote his letter to the Corinthians:

> For, brothers, I don't want you to miss the significance of what happened to our fathers. All of them were guided by the pillar of cloud, and they all passed through the sea, and in connection with the cloud and with the sea they all immersed themselves into Moses, also they all ate the same food from the Spirit, and they all drank the same drink from the Spirit—for they drank from a Spirit-sent Rock which followed them, and that Rock was the Messiah. (1 Cor. 10:1–4, CJB)

The rock, then, is created from the very beginning as an emblem of God's gracious and unlimited supply. Ultimately, the supply of water does not depend on Miriam, but on God's overflowing goodness. The people in their complaining and unbelief may be unworthy, but the Lord still intends to provide life-giving water. Moses needs only to speak to the rock and waters will come forth. Paul is reading the story well when he pictures the rock as Messiah, through whom God supplies the life-giving Spirit without measure even to the undeserving.

Through his subtle disobedience, however, Moses misrepresents God's gracious intentions toward Israel. Perhaps he is thinking of their entire history of complaint, and God's earlier acts of judgment against them. Perhaps Moses pictures waters gushing forth from the rock to sweep away the worst complainers, just as the Lord had earlier provided so much quail meat to those who complained about food that they choked upon it (Num. 11).

Here is a lesson for us. The Lord says to Moses, "Because you did not believe me, to hallow me in the eyes of the children of Israel, therefore you shall not bring this assembly into the land which I have given them." Certainly, Moses *believed* in the Lord, and *believed* his word. At this point, however, he could not *believe* his kindness toward his people. Where God intended mercy, Moses *believed* in judgment and wrath.

God says to Moses, "You did not make me holy in their sight." We might imagine holiness as a pure and uncompromising divine standard. But the Lord wanted to display his holiness by being kind to undeserving Israel. Let us beware of misrepresenting God, as Moses did, by making him the mouthpiece of our own self-righteousness.

For the journey: Self-righteousness is the pitfall of religious folk, which Yeshua spoke against constantly. We appoint ourselves the upholders of righteousness and truth, and enforce them at times with a harshness that far exceeds the Lord's. How can we embrace both God's righteousness and his grace at the same time?

THE MEEK AND THE MIGHTY
Parashat Balak, Numbers 22:2–25:9

Don't be so humble; you're not that great. (Golda Meir)

Now the man Moses was very humble, more than all men who were on the face of the earth. (Num. 12:3)

We sometimes joke about this verse declaring the humility of Moses, because Moses is the one who wrote it. He seems like the man who received the medal for humility, only to have it taken away because he wore it! But no, the humility of which Scripture speaks is not that sort of false modesty, which Golda Meir, the iron lady of Israeli politics in the early decades of the Jewish state, also lampooned. Rather, true humility means knowing who we are in relationship to the Almighty.

Moses displays such humility when he faces criticism from his own siblings, Aaron and Miriam. He says nothing when they issue their challenge, "Has the LORD indeed spoken only through Moses? Has He not spoken through us also?" (Num. 12:2). He does nothing to vindicate himself, but the Lord acts decisively, striking Miriam with leprosy because she has spoken against Moses. Moses continues to display humility by praying for Miriam until she is healed of the leprosy and restored to the camp of Israel.

Throughout the book of Numbers, Moses repeats this sort of behavior. Two chapters after the challenge from Miriam and Aaron, ten scouts return with an evil report after spying out the land of Canaan. After hearing this report, the Israelites rebel against Moses and Aaron and clamor for a new leader who will take them back to Egypt. Moses and Aaron refrain from defending themselves and instead fall on their faces before the Lord (Num. 14:5). The glory of the Lord appears to vindicate Moses and his leadership. In the end, Moses again prays for the very ones who have resisted his authority, asking God to forgive them.

Another two chapters pass and we come to the notorious rebellion under the leadership of Korach. During this incident, Moses again falls on his face three times, twice joined by Aaron. They know who they are before God, so their response to rebellion is to seek God in the posture of prayer and submission. This is the posture of humility, which reveals Moses as "very humble, more than all men who were on the face of the earth," and God again vindicates them.

Finally, when a new generation rises up to complain against Moses and Aaron, they again "fell on their faces" in the presence of the Lord (Num. 20:5). In this last incident, of course, Moses fails to follow through in his humility. Instead, he rises up in anger against his people and is punished severely: he will not be allowed to enter the Promised Land.

The word we are translating as "humble" is *anav*, referring to affliction and weakness, and also to the result of affliction, which is meekness. The same word appears in Psalm 37:11, repeated unforgettably by Yeshua in the Sermon on the Mount: "The meek shall inherit the earth." Just as Moses defers to God's power and wisdom and is vindicated by him, so shall the Lord vindicate those who fall on their faces before him and await his deliverance.

In the light of this clear teaching of the Torah, what are we to make of the behavior of Phinehas at the end of this week's parashah? The Israelites have just been blessed by the seer Balaam, whom the Midianites originally hired to curse them. Instead of moving on, the Israelites begin to worship the gods of their enemies and commit harlotry with their women. One of them even brings a foreign woman into his tent in the presence of the whole assembly.

> Now when Phinehas the son of Eleazar, the son of Aaron the priest, saw it, he rose from among the congregation and took a javelin in his hand; and he went after the man of Israel into the tent and thrust both of them through, the man of Israel, and the woman through her body. So the plague was stopped among the children of Israel. (Num. 25:7–8)

However we may define the word anav, this behavior seems its opposite. Yet this deed stops the plague of judgment among the Israelites, and Phinehas is highly praised for it, receiving for his family an everlasting priesthood "because he was zealous for his God" (Num. 25:13).

Phinehas is passionate for God, and Moses behaves at times like a man without passion. When people challenge him, he falls on his face before the Lord. What a disappointment to his foes! What satisfaction could they gain from fighting with a man who wouldn't fight back? Yet Moses reveals great passion when the reputation of God is at stake, praying for the fulfillment of God's plan. Indeed, it is precisely when Moses becomes passionate *on his own behalf*, and scolds the rebels to whom God desires to supply water, that he errs and is punished.

Phinehas, on the other hand, shows a passion that seems too intense, until we understand it in context:

> The rabbis were uncomfortable with Phinehas's act. Having slain a man impulsively, without either trial or prior warning, he took the law into his own hands, thereby creating a dangerous precedent. No wonder certain sages claim that Moses and the religious leaders would have excommunicated Phinehas were it not for the divine decree declaring that he had acted on God's behalf (*Jerusalem Talmud*, Sanhedrin 27b). However, Phinehas can be defended: He did not act on his own initiative but followed God's command.[14]

Phinehas follows God's command that the offenders should be impaled in his presence. Moses directed the judges of Israel to kill all those who "were joined to Baal of Peor" (Num. 25:4–5). He takes action when action is needed and receives a reward. As the Lord says, "he was zealous with My zeal" (Num. 25:11).

Both Moses the meek and Phinehas the mighty put all their passion into God's reputation and none into their own. Whenever the Israelites challenge Moses, he rushes, with one exception, to defend not himself, but the divine master plan. Likewise, Phinehas takes the great challenge to God's reputation personally. When Israel joins itself to the Baal of Peor, Phinehas does not hesitate to respond.

Yeshua, like Moses, described himself as humble: "Take My yoke upon you and learn from Me, for I am gentle and lowly in heart" (Matt. 11:29). And like Phinehas, he was consumed by zeal for God. When Yeshua drove the money-changers from the Temple courts, "His disciples remembered that it was written, 'Zeal for your house has eaten me up'" (John 2:17). Yeshua himself is the meek and the mighty, and an example for us to be so as well.

For the journey: Golda Meir reminds us that we don't need to be so humble, because we're not that great. But we can follow Moses, Phinehas, and Messiah in showing more concern for God's reputation than for our own. How would such a shift in emphasis change my outlook today?

A WORD FOR THE WISE
Parashat Pinchas, Numbers 25:10–30:1

Seven things distinguish a fool and seven things distinguish a wise person. The wise person does not speak in the presence of one who is wiser. The wise person does not interrupt when another is speaking. The wise person is not in a hurry to answer. The wise person asks according to the subject and answers according to the Law. The wise person speaks about the first matter first and the last matter last. If there is something the wise person has not heard, the wise person says, "I have never heard." The wise person acknowledges what is true. The opposite of all these qualities is found in a fool.[15]

Three times in the narrative of Torah, the Israelites encounter legal cases that the statues and ordinances they have received from God do not directly cover. The cases involve a blasphemer (Lev. 24:10–22), some men who were ritually unclean at the time of the Passover sacrifice (Num. 9:6–14), and a violator of Shabbat (Num. 15:32–36). Each time when the people ask Moses for a ruling, he must answer "I have never heard," until the Lord gives him additional instructions. Now, in *Parashat Pinchas*, a fourth case comes before Moses.

Zelophehad, of the tribe of Manasseh, has died leaving no heir—that is, leaving no son. His surviving daughters, however, appeal to Moses. As women, they cannot inherit land directly, and so they are concerned that their father's name and inheritance among the tribes will be lost to his family forever. Accordingly, they make their request: "Give us a possession among our father's brothers" (Num. 27:4). Moses seeks the Lord, who rules in favor of the daughters, and against the patriarchal assumption of the times, thus adding a new instruction to Torah: "If a man dies and has no son, then you shall cause his inheritance to pass to his daughter" (Num. 27:8).

Moses fulfills the description of the "wise person" in the quote above from *Pirke Avot*. When he does not know, he says "I do not know." The Midrash comments that Moses thereby provides an example for "the heads of the Sanhedrin of Israel that were destined to arise after him, that . . . they should not be embarrassed to ask for assistance in cases too difficult for them. For even Moses, who was Master of Israel, had to say, 'I have not understood.' Therefore Moses brought their cases before the Lord."[16]

The ability to admit "I have not heard; I do not know" is rare among leaders, especially in our day of spin and talking points. It seems to be an unspoken rule of politics that you don't admit mistakes, and you don't say "I don't know," even when you don't. How refreshing it would be to see those in power simply admit their mistakes and acknowledge the gaps in their knowledge!

The Psalmist says "The Torah of the LORD is perfect" (Ps. 19:7 [8]). A thousand years later, Paul writes, "All Scripture is given by inspiration of God, and is profitable for doctrine, for reproof, for correction, for instruction in righteousness, that the man of God may be complete, thoroughly equipped for every good work" (2 Tim. 3:16–17). But Scripture's perfection, its ability to make us complete and thoroughly equipped, does not mean that it spells out everything in detail. Sometimes it directs us back to the Lord for more instruction, or to another provision laid down toward the end of the Torah:

> If a matter arises which is too hard for you to judge . . . then you shall arise and go up to the place which the LORD your God chooses. And you shall come to the priests, the Levites, and to the judge there in those days, and inquire of them; they shall pronounce upon you the sentence of judgment. (Deut. 17:8–9)

Traditional Judaism often cites these verses as a basis for the Oral Torah, rabbinic teachings and interpretations not found in the written Torah, but seen as essential to properly applying it in the various times and places of the Jewish story. This tradition sees the Torah—written and oral—as given once for all, but discovered anew in every generation through discussion and friendly argument. Students in *yeshiva*, a Jewish school for Torah study, continue to study in this way today.

> To an outsider this method of study can appear chaotic. Each pair works at its own pace; everyone is talking out loud; boys are constantly jumping up to find books or consult with other

students; people come and go seemingly at random. But that's how yeshiva students have been learning for centuries.[17]

In the case of the daughters of Zelophehad, of course, the answer comes not through study and debate, but through an oracle of God. Nevertheless, their story establishes a truth that remains vital for us. God's word does not address every specific circumstance we will encounter in life, but it provides all the direction that we need. A wise student of Scripture must sometimes say "I have not heard; I do not know" and seek to learn more.

Thus, right after Paul tells Timothy that Scripture equips completely, he charges him, "Preach the word! Be ready in season and out of season. Convince, rebuke, exhort, with all longsuffering and teaching" (2 Tim. 4:2). Scripture itself ordains teaching, study, exhortation as the means of revealing all that it has to offer.

As we consider these general applications of the story, however, we should not overlook the specific ruling regarding daughters of Zelophehad, for it echoes the theme of Creation to completion that sounds throughout Torah.

The twelve tribes are about to enter the Promised Land, where each is to receive a divine allotment, and sin breaks into the story again. Zelophehad "died in his own sin," according to his daughters, leaving no heir (Num. 27:3). Thus, the division of the land is disrupted, and divine order is threatened. But God takes action to restore the wholeness of the land and people of Israel. What is most striking here is that he does so through the daughters, those who normally are marginalized. Women are generally subject to men in the Mosaic legislation, but God reveals that they are able to inherit, to bear the family name, and to preserve the legacy. God's ruling in this case reminds us that he originally created woman out of man, not to be subservient, but to be "a sustainer beside him" (Gen. 2:18 Alter). Here again the big story moves forward not on the strength of human custom or insight, but on the wisdom of God.

For the journey: How willing am I to say, "I have not heard; I do not know"? As we seek to learn Scripture more deeply, the traditional Jewish way of study through conversation and exploration remains a valid model for us. This sort of study does not mean always having the right answer, but having the wisdom to admit that we don't.

PATHWAY TO PROMISE
Parashat Mattot, Numbers 30:2–32:42

> May it be pleasing in your sight, O Lord our God and God of
> our fathers, that as I have fulfilled the commandment and
> dwelt in this sukkah, so may I merit next year to dwell in the
> sukkah of the skin of Leviathan. Next year in Jerusalem! (Fare-
> well to the sukkah, from the *Siddur*)

At the conclusion of Sukkot, the Feast of Tabernacles, Jewish tradition provides a prayer of farewell to the sukkah, the booth in which
we are commanded to dwell through the eight days of the festival.
But what in the world is the skin of Leviathan, and what does it
have to do with Sukkot?

Leviathan is the great sea-creature mentioned in Job 3:8 and
41:1 and Psalms 74 and 104. Isaiah sees Leviathan as an embodiment of anti-God forces of chaos that will be subdued in the Age to
Come: "In that day the Lord with his severe sword, great and
strong, will punish Leviathan the fleeing serpent, Leviathan that
twisted serpent; and he will slay the reptile that is in the sea" (Isa.
27:1). In the Talmud, Leviathan appears as a monstrous fish, vanquished in the Age to Come, when the Lord will make a banquet for
the righteous from its flesh, and a tabernacle for the righteous from
its skin.[18] With the slaying of Leviathan, the forces of disorder are finally subdued.

This project of vanquishing chaos began at Creation itself. The
second verse of Torah tells us that the newly-created earth was *tohu
vavohu,* "wild and waste."[19] Through the six days of Creation, God
orders and divides all the elements of heaven and earth, so that at
the end he can declare that it is very good. But the work of Creation
does not altogether end with the seventh day. When God creates
humankind, he assigns them to "subdue" the earth (Gen. 1:28).

Even before Adam and Eve fall into disobedience in the Garden of Eden, they have work to do. The primal state of humankind is not passive innocence, but active cooperation with God in bringing creation to its fulfillment. The human being as divine image-bearer has a share in the divine task of ordering Creation.

This same picture emerges in the second account of Creation, in Genesis 2. God places the newly-created Adam in the Garden of Eden "to tend and keep it" (Gen. 2:15) or more literally "to work and guard it." Eden is not the place of primal innocence, but of primal responsibility. The divine-human encounter there is not only one of intimate fellowship, but also one of shared effort. God has so designed Creation that it does not reach completion apart from the effort and diligence of humankind.

This truth is summed up in the phrase cited above from Genesis 1:28, "subdue the earth." Significantly, the same phrase appears twice in this week's parashah. Moses is speaking with the tribes of Gad and Reuben, who desire to settle east of the Jordan, outside of the land promised to the tribes of Israel. Moses tells them they cannot abandon the rest of the tribes, but must participate in the conquest of the land. Only later, when "the land is *subdued* before the LORD, then you may return and be blameless before the LORD and before Israel" (Num. 32:22, emphasis added). Moses then instructs Eleazar the priest, Joshua, and the chiefs of the rest of the tribes, "If the children of Gad and the children of Reuben cross over the Jordan with you, every man armed for battle before the LORD, and the land is *subdued* before you, then you shall give them the land of Gilead as a possession" (Num. 32:29, emphasis added).

"Subdued" in this passage is from the Hebrew root כבש *kavash*, the same verb commanded to Adam in Genesis 1. Significantly, it appears in Torah only in these two instances. Furthermore, "land" here is *aretz*, the same noun usually translated as "earth" in Genesis 1:28. Moses is repeating the phrase "subdue the earth" to apply to the conquest of the Promised Land. When the conquest is finally completed under Joshua, the phrase will appear again: "And the whole congregation of the children of Israel assembled together at Shiloh, and set up the tabernacle of the congregation there. And *the land was subdued* before them" (Josh. 18:1, emphasis added).

The conquest of the Promised Land is an extension of the foundational human task of subduing the earth, of bringing divine order to a Creation not yet perfected. The conquest of the land anticipates the reign of God over all the earth in the Age to Come. The tribes of Israel cannot fulfill their destiny in some quiet or hidden fashion, but only through struggle and perseverance.

Likewise, for us, the promise of God does not appear on a silver platter, but is reserved for the diligent and persevering. As Paul instructed his disciples, "We must through many tribulations enter the kingdom of God" (Acts 14:22). Tribulations are not simply obstacles to overcome on the way to the kingdom of God. Rather, they provide the essential pathway to the kingdom. There is no other route.

Accordingly, when Reuben and Gad request an inheritance east of the Jordan, outside the place of endurance and conquest, Moses says they can only have an inheritance if they have a share in the task of subduing. "Then afterward you may return and be blameless before the LORD and before Israel; and this land shall be your possession before the LORD" (Num. 32:22).

In the same way, Messiah Yeshua instructs us, "From the days of John the Baptist until now the kingdom of heaven suffers violence, and the violent take it by force" (Matt. 11:12), and "Enter by the narrow gate; for wide is the gate and broad is the way that leads to destruction, and there are many who go in by it. Because narrow is the gate and difficult is the way which leads to life, and there are few who find it" (Matt. 7:13–14).

The two gates not only address how many will enter the life of the kingdom of heaven. They also reveal the nature of the journey to life in the kingdom. It must at times be narrow and difficult, because narrowness and difficulty prepare us for God's fullness. Yeshua, who is the gate, reveals in his own death and resurrection the essential path to the promise of God.

For the journey: Sometimes the things that frustrate us the most are the most essential to our spiritual progress. What lies before me that I must *subdue* on my way to the kingdom of God?

COURAGE IS CONTAGIOUS
Parashat Masa'ei, Numbers 33:1–36:13

Perseverance and spirit have done wonders in all ages. (General George Washington)

The final parashah in Numbers opens with a recap of the history of the previous generation: "These are the journeys of the children of Israel, who went out of the land of Egypt by their armies under the hand of Moses and Aaron" (Num. 33:1). It concludes with the new generation encamped on the plains of Moab and ready to enter the Promised Land. "These are the commandments and the judgments which the LORD commanded the children of Israel by the hand of Moses in the plains of Moab by the Jordan, across from Jericho" (Num. 36:13).

Two generations with two very different destinies share the space of this final parashah. Our first reading, however, strikes us not with the contrast between the two, but with their similarities. Since the decade of the sixties, we've been accustomed to speak of a generation gap, the vast and sometimes irreconcilable differences between generations. In Numbers, however, instead of encountering a generation gap, we discover to our disappointment that the new generation repeats the sins of its parents' generation. They both complain against Moses and Aaron and mistrust their leadership, and ultimately the Lord himself. They even go so far as to protest their deliverance from Egypt!

The waters of Meribah highlight this similarity between generations. Just as the generation that "went out of the land of Egypt" complained about lack of water at this site in Exodus 17, so did the new generation in Numbers 20. It may have been shock at the unredeemed quality of the new generation that led Moses to transgress in his response to them, as we saw in *Parashat Hukkat*.

Nevertheless, despite such similarities, the new generation will enter the Promised Land, the very thing that the older generation failed to do. What is the difference between these generations? It may be summed up in one word: courage.

Courage, we are often told, is not the absence of fear. Rather, it is doing the right thing despite fear, inability, and uncertainty about the outcome. Such courage is contagious.

In the United States, we remember 1776 as the year of independence, but we forget that it was also a year of military defeat and near-disaster for the new republic. The British easily drove Washington and his troops out of New York City, which both sides saw as a strategic key to the entire war. The Continental Army fled across New Jersey, barely evading the far superior forces of the British army. Finally, it crossed the Delaware River into Pennsylvania for safety. Even then, the Continental Congress, meeting in nearby Philadelphia, felt so threatened that it fled to Baltimore. Finally, Washington saw an opportunity to turn things around. On Christmas night 1776, in the midst of a freezing storm, he led 2400 of his ill-clad, hungry, discouraged troops back across the Delaware, boatload by boatload, to attack the Hessian garrison at Trenton in the morning. It was the first clear victory for the Americans. A few days later, in response to a British counter-attack, Washington led his troops behind the front to attack Princeton. This led to a second American victory, but only after the field commander was killed and Washington took personal command. One of his officers describes the scene: "I shall never forget what I felt . . . when I saw him brave all the dangers of the field and his important life hanging as it were by a single hair with a thousand deaths flying around him. Believe me, I thought not of myself."[20]

Courage is contagious. Washington's display of courage inspired his officers and men to think not of themselves or the danger they faced, but only of the glorious cause.

Without courage there can be no obedience to God's word, no leadership of God's people. The first generation lacks the courage to enter the Promised Land; the new generation moves forward and enters in. When the twelve spies were sent to scout out the land, Moses instructed them, "*v'hit'chazaktem*" "and be of good courage" (from the root חזק or *hazak*). But only Joshua and Caleb had the courage to believe that they could actually take the land as God had commanded. Later, when Joshua is appointed to lead the people, God tells Moses, "*oto hazek*—encourage him, for he shall cause Israel to inherit it" (Deut. 1:38).

We have already seen that the wilderness is the place of both testing and blessing. Courage determines which will dominate. The same trials that wear down the fainthearted and lead them into sin motivate the courageous and lead them into new strength and dedication.

The Midrash captures both possibilities in its commentary on the opening words of our parashah, "These are the journeys. . . ." First, it says, "The Holy One Blessed Be He said to Moses: 'Write down the stages by which Israel journeyed in the wilderness, in order that they shall know what miracles I wrought for them.'"[21] Immediately after, it says, "The Holy One Blessed Be He said to Moses: 'Recount to them all the places where they provoked Me.'"[22]

The same locations can be places of miracle *and* scenes of provocation. Trials and difficulties inevitably come our way, but these are not what wear us down, for they also are occasions for miraculous intervention.

Courage is contagious, and so is its opposite, discouragement. Numbers teaches us that we lose courage, or become discouraged, when we respond in certain ways to our trials.

- We lose courage when we second-guess ourselves. Like our forebears, we contemplate a return to Egypt instead of preparing for the future into which God is leading us.

- We lose courage when we allow ourselves to complain and cast blame upon others instead of taking responsibility for our problems and seeking a solution.

- We lose courage when we listen to negativity and unbelief instead of remembering God's promise and all that he has already brought us through on the way to its fulfillment.

The first generation listened to words of discouragement and failed to enter the Promised Land. The next generation gradually learned to listen to and speak words of encouragement themselves, saying to Joshua: "All that you command us, we will do. . . . Only be strong and of good courage" (Josh. 1:16–18).

Courage is contagious. It is good to have models like Joshua or Washington, but the ultimate source of our courage is Messiah himself.

Let us, too, put aside every impediment—that is, the sin which easily hampers our forward movement—and keep running with endurance in the contest set before us, looking away to the Initiator and Completer of that trusting, Yeshua—who, in exchange for obtaining the joy set before him, endured execution on a stake as a criminal, scorning the shame, and has sat down at the right hand of the throne of God. Yes, think about him who endured such hostility against himself from sinners, so that you won't grow tired or become despondent. (Heb. 12:1b–3 CJB)

We can gain courage and we pass courage on to others through words of encouragement. Hence, as we conclude our reading of Numbers, as at the end of each book of the Torah, we repeat the traditional words: חֲזַק חֲזַק וְנִתְחַזֵּק—*Hazak! Hazak! V'nit'chazek!* Be strong! Be courageous! And let us encourage one another!

For the journey: Courage is contagious. It's not enough just to survive our trials and difficulties, for if we view them courageously they become the site of miracles. How can I encourage myself and those around me today?

דברים

THE BOOK OF DEUTERONOMY

Deuteronomy opens with the phrase "These are the words . . ." or *Eleh had'varim*, which yields the Hebrew title דברים (*D'varim*), or Words. The title is fitting because Deuteronomy consists almost entirely of Moses' extended discourse, which takes place on the eastern shore of the Jordan River. Only at the end does the narrative resume, with the account of Moses' death and burial by the hand of God.

Deuteronomy addresses the age-old challenge of continuity. Will a new generation carry on the legacy and fulfill the calling of the older generation? The generation that departed Egypt failed to enter the Promised Land; will the next generation do better? To encourage this new generation, Moses, leader of the old generation, will repeat the entire instruction of Torah in the book of Deuteronomy (which means "second law" in Greek).

The structure of these discourses is highly significant, because it reflects the structure of ancient Near Eastern covenant treaty documents which have been uncovered by modern archaeology.[1] These documents defined and protected the relationship between a mighty king and his vassals. In the same way, Deuteronomy defines to a new generation the terms of their relationship with God, and the destiny that this implies. The entire book then, is a covenant renewal document, which corresponds in structure to ancient covenant treaties. Here we see the normal components of an ancient covenant, and the corresponding sections of Deuteronomy:

1.	Preamble which identifies the covenant grantor	1:1–5
2.	Historical prologue	1:6–4:49
3.	Covenant obligations: a. The great commandment, dedication to God b. Detailed commandments	5:1–26:19 5:1–11:32 12:1–26:19
4.	Blessings and curses, with invocation of witnesses	27:1–30:20
5.	Covenant continuity, including stipulations for copies (see Exodus 25:16, 21; Deut. 10:1–2)	31:1–34:12

In Deuteronomy, God is the mighty king, who has made a covenant with the descendants of Abraham that he will be their God and they will be his people. Therefore, covenant fidelity or love, termed *hesed* in Hebrew, becomes a dominant theme throughout Deuteronomy. Hesed is the basis for the great commandment of Deuteronomy, as stated in the *Shema*, Israel's declaration of allegiance to the Lord: שמע ישראל יהוה אלהינו יהוה אחד (*Sh'ma Yisrael Adonai Elohenu Adonai Echad*), "Hear, O Israel! The LORD is our God, the LORD alone. You shall love the LORD your God with all your heart and with all your soul and with all your might" (Deut. 6:4–5 NJPS).

The detailed stipulations that follow this great commandment simply define and apply that love within the various situations and conditions that Israel will encounter, especially as it takes possession of the Promised Land. God's requirements are simple but demanding, and Israel will fall short. In Deuteronomy, Moses testifies "regarding them, telling them what the future would bring in exile, as well as the future redemption which would come after total despair."[2]

Deuteronomy prepares Israel, from the inside out, for the next great stage in their journey, the conquest of Canaan. This victory will clear the way for a theocratic realm displaying the covenant faithfulness of God to future generations of Israelites, and to the surrounding nations as well. Moses predicts, however, that this realm will fail and end in exile, but he also pictures the day of restoration, which Jews and Christians still await in hope.

> When all these things befall you—the blessing and the curse that I have set before you—and you take them to heart amidst the various nations to which the LORD your God has banished you, and you return to the LORD your God, and you and your children heed His command with all your heart and soul, just as I enjoin upon you this day, then the LORD your God will restore your fortunes and take you back in love. (Deut. 30:1–3a, NJPS)

The message of the last of the Five Books of Moses is that the way from Creation to completion, introduced in the first of the Five Books, is found through love of God. And even if human love fails, God's love will ensure the way.

GOD CARRIES ISRAEL
Parashat D'varim, Deuteronomy 1:1–3:22

Rabbi Judah said: Come and see the meekness of God. Among human beings, when a man has a young child he carries him on his shoulders, but if the child angers him he at once throws him down. But, if one may say so, with God it is not so; Israel were in the wilderness forty years and they provoked Him to anger and yet He bore them.[3]

Deuteronomy will reiterate the statues and ordinances laid down in the rest of Torah, along with warnings against disobedience and its outcome, which is exile. But before Moses speaks of these things, he reminds the Israelites of a more basic truth:

In the wilderness . . . you saw how the LORD your God carried you, as a man carries his son, in all the way that you went until you came to this place. Yet, for all that, you did not believe the LORD your God, who went in the way before you to search out a place for you to pitch your tents, to show you the way you should go, in the fire by night and in the cloud by day. (Deut. 1:31–33)

When my sons still lived at home, I took them backpacking in the wilderness every summer. Especially in their younger years, I had to make sure they packed the right clothes and equipment, and I planned the ultra-light meals that we had to carry. When we were actually hiking, I'd keep an eye on the time to make sure that we started early enough to look for a place to pitch our tent. My boys could probably have found the right place themselves, but I saw it as my fatherly role to choose the spot that would be dry, safe, and comfortable through the night.

In Israel's wanderings, future as well as past, the Lord carries Israel, sustaining, protecting, and going before his people to show the way. This truth is all the more striking because Moses has already reminded the people, using the same Hebrew verb, that *he* cannot carry them. "And I spoke to you at that time, saying: 'I alone am not able to bear you'" (Deut. 1:9). The burden is too great for any human being, but God himself will take it up. Like a father watching out for his children, God will go before Israel to find a good campsite that is safe and sheltered.

The story above emphasizes God's faithfulness, but there is another old story about a child carried on his father's shoulders. This child cannot see the father who is bearing him and begins to ask every passerby, "Where is my father?" He does not believe them when they tell him that his father is carrying him, but keeps wondering where his father can be. Finally, the father becomes exasperated with his unbelieving son and puts him down—none too gently—to walk on his own two feet, where he is soon attacked by a dog and bitten.

This story illustrates Israel's distrust of God, and the exile that results, an exile in which Israel is indeed attacked by many dogs. It reminds us that we too are often slow to recognize God's presence in our lives, even though he sustains us every step of the way.

Throughout Torah, beginning with Abraham, the people of Israel are on a journey with God, and so is each individual Israelite. Indeed, the only generations in Torah that do not journey are those that dwell in Egypt as slaves. Deuteronomy reminds us that God is with us on this journey, both in its toughest stretches and in its moments of glory. And since God is with us, he will bring us to journey's end, the land of promise, the place of rest. With this destination assured, there is no room in our lives for anxiety and distrust.

Important as this personal reminder is, however, the primary concern of Deuteronomy is not the individual spiritual journey, but the destiny of Israel. Moses reminds Israel that this destiny will be fulfilled through God's faithfulness, if not through theirs.

In the synagogue, we normally read *Parashat D'varim* just before *Tish'ah B'Av*, the ninth day of the month of Av, a date that commemorates the greatest tragedies in Jewish history. On this date, both the first and second Temples were destroyed and the exile of the people of Israel from their land began. Throughout the centuries of exile, on this same day, a number of other disasters befell the Jewish people, most notably the expulsion from Spain in 1492, which ended a golden age of Jewish history.

Moses reminds us that the Lord has been present with his people throughout all these disasters. Exile does not end Israel's covenant relationship with the Lord. Rather, it is a journey of discipline that leads to Israel's final restoration. The God of Israel is working out his own purpose throughout history, sometimes with human cooperation, and more often without it. His purpose is to reveal his own love and faithfulness to all humankind, and to restore the original purpose of blessing established at the Creation.

It would be a mistake, however, to think of Israel as simply a means to this end, as if the Lord had to find someone through whom to demonstrate his goodness, and arbitrarily chose Israel. Instead, the image of God carrying Israel as a father carries his son, and going before Israel throughout their wanderings, speaks of the Lord's intimate involvement in Israel's story. "For the LORD your God has blessed you in all the work of your hand. He knows your trudging through this great wilderness. These forty years the LORD your God has been with you; you have lacked nothing" (Deut. 2:7).

God carries Israel because he loves him as a father loves his children. He carries Israel throughout its entire journey of glory, exile, and restoration.

Deuteronomy echoes the promise established here in *Parashat D'varim* throughout. The B'rit Hadashah applies this promise to all who follow Yeshua. "He Himself has said, 'I will never leave you nor forsake you.' So we may boldly say: 'The LORD is my helper; I will not fear. What can man do to me?'" (Heb. 13:5–6; see Deut. 31:6, 8).

Surely, God intends such faithfulness to be not only an encouragement, but also an example to us. We too have made commitments that we must honor through good times and bad. We demonstrate our wholeness as human beings by our ability to remain faithful to other human beings, who can be just as flawed and unlovable as we are.

In the past, Christian theology often pictured the election of Israel as only a means to an end, a vehicle to bring about the Messiah and his redemption. Now that Messiah has come, in such thinking, God can replace the vehicle. Surely, however, such a view dishonors God as much as Israel, and erodes our sense of God's faithfulness. Instead, God faithfully carries Israel even through times of discipline. In the end, this same faithfulness will carry Israel to its redemption, as Moses sings:

> Happy are you, O Israel!
> Who is like you, a people saved by the LORD,
> The shield of your help
> And the sword of your majesty! (Deut. 33:29a)

For the journey: In Messiah, God says, "I will never leave you nor forsake you," a promise that both encourages us and provides an example. God has been faithful to us—how faithful have we been to our children, our loved ones, and all those whom God has placed in our lives?

THE GREAT COMMANDMENT
Parashat Va'etchanan, Deuteronomy 3:23–7:11

One of the Torah-teachers came up and heard them engaged in this discussion. Seeing that Yeshua answered them well, he asked him, "Which is the most important mitzvah of them all?" Yeshua answered, "The most important is,

> *'Sh'ma Yisra'el, ADONAI Eloheinu, ADONAI echad* [Hear, O Israel, the LORD our God, the LORD is one], and you are to love ADONAI your God with all your heart, with all your soul, with all your understanding and with all your strength.'

The second is this:

> 'You are to love your neighbor as yourself.'

There is no other mitzvah greater than these." (Mark 12:28–31, CJB)

Deuteronomy is a document that renews the covenant between God and Israel. This covenant is lengthy and detailed, but at its heart is a simple requirement, captured in the great commandment known in Judaism as the Shema, or "Hear!" from the first word of Deuteronomy 6:4. This verse is among the most important in the entire Torah, and like that other vitally important verse, Genesis 1:1, its exact meaning has been debated for centuries.

The most familiar approach to translation would be the one reflected above; "Hear, O Israel, the LORD our God, the LORD is one." An alternative version is, "Hear, O Israel! The LORD is our God, the LORD alone" (NJPS). This reading is less familiar (although it does go all the way back to the medieval Jewish commentator Ibn Ezra), but it may reflect the context of Deuteronomy better than the older interpretation, "the Lord is one."

> The first, older translation, which makes a statement about the unity and indivisibility of God, does not do full justice to this

175

text. . . . The verse makes not a quantitative argument (about the number of deities) but a qualitative one, about the nature of the relationship between God and Israel.[4]

When Moses addresses the children of Israel who are about to enter the Promised Land, he is not concerned with defining the nature of God—"the Lord is one" —but with calling them to loyalty to God, to "the Lord alone." Hence, he goes on to say, "You shall love the LORD your God with all your heart, with all your soul, and with all your strength" (Deut. 6:5).

The towering Jewish intellectual figure of the middle ages, Rambam, cites the Shema to answer a question not of theology, but of devotion:

> What is the way that we should love God? We should love Him with an overwhelming and unlimited live, until our soul becomes permanently bound in the love of God, like one who is love-sick and cannot take his mind off the woman he loves, but always thinks of her—when lying down or rising up, when eating or drinking. Even greater than this should be the love of God in the hearts of those who love Him, thinking about Him constantly, as He commanded us, "And thou shalt love the Lord thy God with all thine heart and with all thy soul."[5]

The prophet Zechariah reflects this understanding of the Shema as a declaration of covenant love when he quotes it to describe the conditions of the Age to Come:

> And the LORD shall be King over all the earth.
> In that day it shall be—"The LORD is one,"
> And His name one. (Zech. 14:9)

Surely, Zechariah is not quoting the Shema as a statement about the *nature* of God, because God's nature will not change "in that day." Rather, it is a statement about our relationship with God, for "in that day," we will worship him alone, and his name alone will be recognized in all the earth.

Thus, as Yeshua teaches, the Shema is a commandment, "the first and great commandment" (Matt. 22:38). It is not a statement of God's absolute and indivisible unity, as one approach to translation assumes, but a statement of our undivided loyalty to God. When the Shema tells us to worship God "with all your heart, with all your soul, and with all your strength," it is not dividing us into different compartments, but speaking of the whole person as one.

> All of man's strivings should be directed toward the Creator, blessed be He. A man should have no other purpose in whatever he does, be it great or small, than to draw nigh to God and to break down all separating walls . . . between himself and his Master, so that he may be drawn to God as iron to a magnet.[6]

Jewish law or halakhah directs the worshiper to recite the Shema (in its entirety, comprising Deuteronomy 6:4–9, 11:13–21, and Numbers 15:37–41) twice every day, "when you lie down, and when you rise up," thereby accepting "the yoke of the Kingdom of heaven."[7] By reciting the Shema, the worshiper binds himself to the God of Israel as sovereign king.

> Modern readers regard the Shema as an assertion of monotheism, a view that is anachronistic. In the context of ancient Israelite religion, it served as a public proclamation of exclusive loyalty to Hashem as the sole Lord of Israel. [By reciting the Shema], the worshipper . . . reenters, twice daily, the original covenant ratification ceremony that, in Deuteronomy, took place on the plains of Moab.[8]

The Shema is not the great *description*, but the great *commandment*, which we can fulfill only by loving God with all our hearts, souls, and might.

> The Torah-teacher said to him, "Well said, Rabbi; you speak the truth when you say that he is one, and that there is no other besides him; and that loving him with all one's heart, understanding and strength, and loving one's neighbor as oneself, mean more than all the burnt offerings and sacrifices." When Yeshua saw that he responded sensibly, he said to him, "You are not far from the Kingdom of God." (Mark 12:32–34, CJB)

The Kingdom of God is another term for Creation completed, the goal of the entire age in which we are living. When we love God with all our hearts and understanding and strength, we are "not far" from that glorious destination.

For the journey: What is the way that we should love God? Love for God should resemble the longing of one who is love-sick for a man or woman. How do I cultivate such an all-consuming love for God? What are the lesser loves that divide my heart?

THE REWARD OF RIGHTEOUSNESS
Parashat 'Ekev, Deuteronomy 7:12–11:25

> With thousands feared drowned in what could be America's deadliest natural disaster in a century, New Orleans' leaders all but surrendered the streets to floodwaters and began turning out the lights on the ruined city—perhaps for months.
>
> [Mayor] Nagin called for an all-out evacuation of the city's remaining residents. Asked how many people died, he said: "Minimum, hundreds. Most likely, thousands." [9]

In the final days of August 2005, Hurricane Katrina pounded the Gulf Coast of Louisiana, Mississippi, and Alabama. New Orleans was evacuated and the entire city became flooded after the hurricane passed. Television screens around the world were filled with images of people who did not, or could not because of poverty or disability, leave when the evacuation order came. Some were wading chest-deep through filthy water in what had been their neighborhoods. Others were trapped in apartments and on rooftops waiting for days to be rescued. Those who had finally escaped the flood waters found refuge on the bare concrete expanse of interstate highways waiting again for help. Others were transported to huge shelters where they'd be warehoused for days until someone could figure out the next step.

These images remind us of the question, is there justice in this world? Is disaster a punishment for wrongdoing? Conversely, is there a reward for doing right instead of wrong? This week's parashah opens with a promise of reward for those who do right, but later portrays the limitations of reward.

> Then it shall come to pass, because you listen to these judgments, and keep and do them, that the LORD your God will keep with you the covenant and the mercy which He swore to your fathers. And He will love you and bless you and multiply you; He

will also bless the fruit of your womb and the fruit of your land, your grain and your new wine and your oil, the increase of your cattle and the offspring of your flock, in the land of which He swore to your fathers to give you. You shall be blessed above all peoples (7:12–14b).

There may be a reward for doing right, as this passage states, but one of the early sages, Antigonos of Socho, downplays its importance: "Don't be like those who would serve a master on the condition that they would receive a reward. Rather, be like those who would serve without that condition. Even so, let the fear of Heaven be upon you."[10]

Antigonos's distrust of reward may arise out of the historical setting in which he lived, as hinted at by his name. He is the first of the rabbinic figures to have a Greek name, and lived in the era when the land of Israel was ruled by the Hellenistic empire established by Alexander the Great. Many Jews lived in Israel in those days, but it was hardly the scene of reward as promised in Deuteronomy. Under the imperial occupation, as during the New Orleans flood, the lesson is that even if reward is slow in coming, one must still remain faithful.

Centuries later, under a different foreign occupation, Yeshua likewise instructs his disciples not to serve on the condition of receiving a reward. "So likewise you, when you have done all those things which you are commanded, say, 'We are unprofitable servants. We have done what was our duty to do'" (Luke 17:10). At the same time, he does promise a reward to his followers, both in this age and the Age to Come:

Assuredly, I say to you, there is no one who has left house or brothers or sisters or father or mother or wife or children or lands, for My sake and the gospel's, who shall not receive a hundredfold now in this time—houses and brothers and sisters and mothers and children and lands, with persecutions— and in the age to come, eternal life. (Mark 10:29–30)

Of course, this promise is a bit different from the promise in *Parashat 'Ekev*, because it comes "with persecutions." But the Torah also reminds us that rewards have their problems.

> When you have eaten and are full, then you shall bless the LORD your God for the good land which He has given you. *Beware that you do not forget the LORD your God by not keeping His commandments, His judgments, and His statutes which I command you today, lest . . . you say in your heart, "My power and the might of my hand have gained me this wealth."* (8:10–17, emphasis added)

The reward should lead us to be wary, because prosperity can make us forget God. In the contemporary world, the nations that are the most prosperous are filled with secularism, unbelief, and depravity, falling under the deception that "My power and the might of my hand have gained me this wealth." Surely, in the midst of the materialism and consumerism of our modern world, we need to be on guard. The practical instructions of Torah about care for the poor may provide a safeguard for us.

> If there is among you a poor man of your brethren, within any of the gates in your land which the LORD your God is giving you, you shall not harden your heart nor shut your hand from your poor brother, but you shall open your hand wide to him and willingly lend him sufficient for his need, whatever he needs. (Deut. 15:7–8)

I once encountered a man who appeared a bit deranged begging on a street corner, crying out, "I just need $2.89 for a plate of spaghetti at Tommy's [a local restaurant]!" I walked right by him, but had hardly gotten across the street when I felt compelled, as if from above, to go back and give the man $5.00 so could buy lunch. When I walked away, I thought, "But who knows if he really even *needs* the money?" Again, I felt a divine intervention, this time saying, "Right, who knows if *he* needs the money, but *you* need to give it to him."

We may never have an answer in this world to the questions about justice raised by the New Orleans flood and other natural calamities. As we keep our hearts and hands open to the poor among us, however, we guard ourselves from the deceptiveness of prosperity—even prosperity that we might consider a reward from God. And we will always have poor among us, "[f]or the poor will never cease from the land" (Deut. 15:11). Or as Yeshua reminded us, "For you have the poor with you always, and whenever you wish you may do them good" (Mark 14:7).

The poor, of course, have many needs, but we who have much also need them.

For the journey: The Torah says to "beware" when we are well fed, that we don't forget God. Surely, this warning must be in full force for us in the West today! When we encounter those who are not so prosperous, whether on a local street corner, or in the world news, how does their presence help us to beware?

THE GODS OF OTHERS
Parashat Re'eh, Deuteronomy 11:26–16:17

Professing to be wise, they became fools, and changed the glory of the incorruptible God into an image made like corruptible man—and birds and four-footed animals and creeping things. Therefore God also gave them up to uncleanness, in the lusts of their hearts, to dishonor their bodies among themselves, who exchanged the truth of God for the lie, and worshiped and served the creature rather than the Creator, who is blessed forever. Amen. (Rom. 1:22–25)

Nowhere is the Jewishness of Paul more evident than in his response to idolatry. In his letter to the Romans, Paul, like the Hebrew prophets before him, portrays idolatry as the source of all sin and rejection of God. A thousand years later, Rambam or Maimonides likewise sees the prohibition of idolatry as the root of all the other laws of Torah:

> For the foundation of the whole of our Law and the pivot around which it turns, consists in the effacement of these idolatrous opinions from the minds and of these monuments from existence. . . . For the sages say: *Herefrom you may learn that everyone who professes idolatry, disbelieves in the Torah in its entirety; whereas he who disbelieves in idolatry, professes the Torah in its entirety.*[11]

The prohibition against idolatry appears as the first of the Ten Commandments: "I am the LORD your God, who brought you out of the land of Egypt, out of the house of bondage. You shall have no other gods before Me" (Exod. 20:2–3).

"Other gods" here is *Elohim acherim,* but Rashi finds this reading problematic. How can the Torah warn us against serving other gods, when there *are* no other gods? Hence, he reads the phrase as *Elohey acherim,* "the gods of others."

This means that they are not divine, but others made them gods over them. It is impossible to explain the term as "other gods," that is, "gods other than Myself," for it is an affront to-ward Him Who is above to call them "gods" alongside Him.[12]

The reading "the gods of others" took deep root in traditional Judaism, countering not only idolatry, but all worship that reflected the ways of the surrounding nations. This tradition helps to explain the resistance to Yeshua still encountered in the Jewish world today. As long as Yeshua appears to be the God of the Gentiles, that is, "a god of others," most Jewish people will not even consider him as the Messiah. Moses' warning against false prophecy in *Parashat Re'eh* reinforces this reaction.

> Whatever I command you, be careful to observe it; you shall not add to it nor take away from it. If there arises among you a prophet or a dreamer of dreams, and he gives you a sign or a wonder, and the sign or the wonder comes to pass, of which he spoke to you, saying, "Let us go after other gods [or the god of others]"—which you have not known—"and let us serve them," you shall not listen to the words of that prophet or that dreamer of dreams, for the LORD your God is testing you to know whether you love the LORD your God with all your heart and with all your soul. (Deut. 12:32–13:3 [1–4])

How would we know if a powerful prophet is leading us astray from the God of Israel? He will "add to" or "take away from" the God-given instructions. If Yeshua taught a way "which you have not known," he is not to be followed. Even the signs and wonders that he performed, including the great sign of the resurrection, cannot override this prohibition in the minds of traditionally oriented Jew-ish people.

If Yeshua had come to destroy the Torah, God forbid, he could not be the Messiah of Israel, or the savior of the nations. But of course, the idea that Yeshua supplants Torah can only arise from a gross misinterpretation. Yeshua himself made it clear. "Don't think that I have come to abolish the Torah or the Prophets. I have come not to abolish but to complete. Yes indeed! I tell you that until heaven and earth pass away, not so much as a *yud* [the smallest Hebrew letter] or a stroke will pass from the Torah—not until every-thing that must happen has happened" (Matt. 5:17–18, CJB).

For the Messianic Jewish community, this issue underlines our imperative to restore Yeshua to his place *within* Israel, rather than to call Jews out of Israel to follow him.

The same issue calls the wider body of Messiah to realize that it serves the God of *Israel*, not a god of others, which leads to a new and deeper respect for the teachings of the Torah. Gentile believers do not relate to all the details of Torah in the same way that Jews do, but they should read Torah as foundational to the rest of Scripture, including the New Testament or B'rit Hadashah.

Only a false reading of the B'rit Hadashah would make one think that Yeshua led people away from Torah. He not only affirms Torah, but he becomes the source of Torah, divine instruction, to the nations, fulfilling the ancient Jewish hope founded in the words of Isaiah:

> Now it shall come to pass in the latter days . . .
> Many people shall come and say,
> "Come, and let us go up to the mountain of the LORD,
> To the house of the God of Jacob;
> He will teach us His ways,
> And we shall walk in His paths."
> For out of Zion shall go forth the Torah,
> And the word of the LORD from Jerusalem. (Isa. 2:2–3)

Followers of Yeshua have not always acknowledged Zion as their spiritual homeland, or Torah as the word of God sent out from there. Such followers may have separated themselves from Torah, but Yeshua never did. Instead, he has brought multitudes from all nations to the God of Israel and his ways, even as the prophets foretold.

For the journey: We live in a day of reconciliation, as more and more Christians realize that in Messiah they do not serve the god of others, but the God of Israel, and Torah, the unique heritage of the Jewish people, becomes a source of guidance to all believers. How do I play a part in this reconciliation?

THE PROPHET LIKE MOSES
Parashat Shof'tim, Deuteronomy 16:18–21:9

> The Rock, perfect in all his deeds; who can say to him, 'What do you do?' The One who says and does, do undeserved grace upon us, and in the merit of him who was bound like a lamb, hear and act. (From the traditional Jewish burial service of the *Siddur*)

One of the age-old controversies between Judaism and Christianity concerns the need for a mediator between God and man. The rabbinic writings often assert that Israel needs no intermediary with God, but can approach him directly. Thus, Sforno comments on the first of the Ten Commandments: "I am *Hashem*, the LORD your God" (Exod. 20:2):

> I alone am *Hashem* who grants existence; the Prime Cause known to you through tradition and proof; and I confirm that you have accepted upon yourself My sovereignty, to be your God, with no need for a mediator. Therefore, to Me alone shall you pray, and Me alone shall you serve without any mediator.

Likewise, Rambam says that this commandment and the one following—"You shall have no other gods before Me"—"reached [Israel] just as they reached Moses our Master and that it was not Moses our Master who communicated them to them."[13] All Israel stood before the Lord at Sinai and received His revelation directly with no mediator.

Yet, as the prayer above attests, another strain of Jewish thought calls out for a mediator, for one whose merit will benefit all Israel, as Isaac's is believed to have done. This ambivalence about a mediator reflects a tension within the biblical text itself. For example, it is true that God appeared directly to all Israel at Mount Sinai, but it is also true that Moses serves as an intermediary through much of that encounter. Only by ignoring this major element of the story could one say that Israel needs no mediator with God.

Thus, just before Rambam claims that the first two commandments came to Israel with no mediator, he writes,

> It is clear to me that at the Gathering at Mount Sinai, not everything that reached Moses also reached all Israel. Speech was addressed to Moses alone . . . and he, peace be on him, went to the foot of the mountain and communicated to the people what he had heard. The text of the Torah reads: *I stood between the Lord and you at that time, to declare unto you the word of the Lord.* (Deut. 5:5)[14]

At Mount Sinai, Israel encounters the Lord "face to face," according to Deuteronomy 5:4, but in the next verse Moses "stands between" the Lord and Israel to mediate the divine word. Indeed, this seems to be Moses' unique place within the story of the Jewish people. He alone communicates with the Lord "face to face" and brings the report of this communication back to the people.

> It was after they had heard that first voice that they were terrified of the thing and felt a great fear, and they said: *And ye said, Behold the Lord hath shown us,* and so on. *Now therefore why should we die,* and so on. *Go thou near and hear,* and so on. Thereupon he, who was greater than anyone born of man, went forward a second time, received the rest of the commandments one after the other, descended to the foot of the mountain, and made them hear these commandments in the midst of that great gathering.[15]

Moses, then, indeed serves as mediator between God and Israel. In this week's parashah, he is contemplating the end of his life, which means the end of his mediatory work. Was this mediation only necessary for the first generation, for those who received the Torah at Mount Sinai? Can Israel now meet with God face to face with no one to stand between them and him? No, as Moses says that when he is gone,

> The LORD your God will raise up for you a Prophet like me from your midst, from your brethren. Him you shall hear, according to all you desired of the LORD your God in Horeb in the day of the assembly, saying, "Let me not hear again the voice of the LORD my God, nor let me see this great fire anymore, lest I die." (Deut. 18:15–16)

This prophet will be a mediator in the same way that Moses was a mediator. Like Moses, he will hear the voice of the Lord and see the fire of God's presence, and then he will speak to the people. Through him, God will reveal himself to Israel. "And it shall be that whoever will not hear My words, which He speaks in My name, I will require it of him" (Deut. 18:19).

The Torah will conclude at the end of Deuteronomy with a statement that the prophet like Moses had not yet appeared. "But since then there has not arisen in Israel a prophet like Moses, whom the LORD knew face to face" (34:10). For Messianic Jews, of course, this Prophet arose many centuries later, in the person of Yeshua.

Based on our text, Peter urges the Jews of Jerusalem to heed the message of Yeshua.

> But this is how God fulfilled what he had announced in advance, when he spoke through all the prophets, namely, that his Messiah was to die. Therefore, repent and turn to God, so that your sins may be erased; so that times of refreshing may come from the Lord's presence; and he may send the Messiah appointed in advance for you, that is, Yeshua. . . . For Moshe himself said, "*ADONAI* will raise up for you a prophet like me from among your brothers. You are to listen to everything he tells you." (Acts 3:18–20, 22 CJB)

Judaism then, like Christianity, recognizes the need for a mediator. His identity remains an all-important question, and we are confident that it is resolved in Yeshua the Messiah. But we cannot neglect another question, one implied by the ambivalence within the text. *Why* do we need a mediator at all? All Israel stood before God at Mount Sinai. All Israel has a share in his Torah, and a claim on the riches of Jewish heritage. These things are not the province of a priestly caste, but of all the people.

Why do we need a mediator? Our sins distance us from God, but even more relevant is the ineffable holiness of God. He reaches out to us in mercy, yet his purity and splendor are so great that a vast gulf remains between him and us. God's inapproachability may not jibe with our modern, consumer-centered expectation that we should all enjoy a divine connection 24/7, but the picture is clear. Between the holy God of Israel and humankind, even the best of humankind, is a vast gulf. Thank God that he has sent a Prophet like Moses to bridge that gulf.

For the journey: My need for a mediator is a comment on the holiness of God. It means that *in myself* I am never worthy to approach him at all. How does this realization change the way that I pray, worship, and serve God and those around me?

REMEMBER AMALEK
Parashat Ki Tetse, Deuteronomy 21:10–25:19

> The task of requesting deliverance is too formidable for an individual alone, no matter how great the individual is. Even Moses himself could not approach Hashem on his own to ask Him to rescue the Jewish nation from Amalek; Moses needed two others to demonstrate that his entreaty represented the will of the whole nation.[16]

Twentieth-century rabbi Joseph Soloveitchik relates this story about the battle against Amalek to the *Kol Nidrey* prayer that opens the services for Yom Kippur, or the Day of Atonement. The battle with Amalek begins when they attack the Israelites shortly after Israel left Egypt.

> So Joshua . . . fought with Amalek. And Moses, Aaron, and Hur went up to the top of the hill. And so it was, when Moses held up his hand, that Israel prevailed; and when he let down his hand, Amalek prevailed. But Moses' hands became heavy; so they took a stone and put it under him, and he sat on it. And Aaron and Hur supported his hands, one on one side, and the other on the other side; and his hands were steady until the going down of the sun. So Joshua defeated Amalek and his people with the edge of the sword. (Exod. 17:10–13)

At the end of the battle, the Lord declared that he would have war on Amalek through all generations. Now, in *Parashat Ki Tetse*, Moses commands a new generation to "[r]emember what Amalek did to you on the way as you were coming out of Egypt" (Deut. 25:17), and to blot out the memory of Amalek from under heaven, because "he met you on the way and attacked your rear ranks, all the stragglers at your rear, when you were tired and weary; and he did not fear God" (Deut. 25:18).

The Kol Nidrey, literally "All Vows," prayer is chanted to a beautiful melody at the opening of Yom Kippur. It is an ancient appeal to God to forgive any vows made to him that are impossible to fulfill, thus preparing the worshiper to meet him on this holiest of Jewish holidays.[17] As the cantor chants the prayer, it is customary for two people to stand on either side of him or her, just as Aaron and Hur stood on either side of Moses during the battle against Amalek.

What is the connection between Amalek and the opening prayer of Yom Kippur? Throughout the Days of Awe from Rosh HaShanah through Yom Kippur, we pray for God to establish his sovereignty in our midst, and that we would be fit subjects of his reign. Rabbi Soloveitchik notes, however, that "Hashem's sovereignty is not absolute as long as Amalek continues to exist."[18] He goes on to ask, "Who then is Amalek, whose presence somehow inhibits Hashem's sovereignty?"[19]

In a remarkable insight, Rabbi Soloveitchik places Amalek in the context of the Creation story, when "Hashem created the earth from tohu vavohu, chaos and void" (Genesis 1:2). At the Creation, the Lord did not completely eliminate chaos, but allowed some to remain. "Amalek represents this leftover chaos, identified with sin, which remained behind so man himself can actively play a role in destroying it."[20]

God's ultimate design for humankind, as we have seen throughout this book, is not simply a return to the Garden of Eden and its innocence. Even in the Garden, human beings had a work to accomplish, and God's purposes will not be fulfilled without human participation. As we have heard repeatedly in the big story of Torah, when God rested on the seventh day after creating all things, the Creation was good and holy, but it had not yet reached its consummation. That would take human cooperation. From the beginning, human beings were representatives of God, assigned the task of multiplying, filling the earth, and subduing it. This task was, and is, no mere charade. The stakes are real. God has permitted a measure of chaos to remain in his Creation and man is responsible to deal with it in God's strength.

Israel saw chaos defeated in Egypt and ultimately at the splitting of the Red Sea, when Pharaoh's armies were drowned in its waters. In the attack of Amalek, the Israelites were put on notice that chaos and evil were still at play, ready to break into their world again. Now in *Parashat Ki Tetse*, as they are about to enter the

Promised Land, they are reminded of the same truth. The Torah has come full circle. The themes established at the beginning are still at play: God created all things from nothing, and established order in the midst of the chaos of the primordial Creation. But this order is not absolute. It is threatened by chaos, and humanity itself, even though created in the image of God, often succumbs to the chaos. Israel is chosen to overcome the chaos, to fulfill the human calling as the image of God. It must remember Amalek, especially as it stands on the threshold of the Promised Land.

Rabbi Soloveitchik provides an additional insight into the battle against Amalek, which adds a new dimension to our reading of the grand narrative of Torah. The essential struggle takes place within.

> The Jew must eternally battle with this insidious enemy, the tohu vavohu which resides within each of us. . . . Amalek exists within everyone, and through our attempt at his destruction we at the same time endeavor to crown Hashem.[21]

The true battle is not with the other, with the enemy outside, but within ourselves. Indeed, we sometimes seek external enemies to avoid the real battle we must wage with our inner chaos and disorder. Religious believers seem particularly adept at finding enemies without and engaging in holy war rather than facing their own inner turmoil. Perhaps this is why the letter to the Hebrews tells us, "Follow peace with all men, and holiness, without which no man shall see the Lord" (Heb. 12:14).

Whether the battle is without or within, however, we do not fight it alone. Moses had Aaron and Hur standing on either side, for as Rabbi Soloveitchik says, "the task of requesting deliverance is too formidable for an individual alone." Likewise, the B'rit Hadashah instructs us to "work out your own salvation with fear and trembling; for it is God who works in you both to will and to do for His good pleasure" (Phil. 2:12b–13).

The rabbis ask concerning the original battle against Amalek: "Did the hands of Moses control the course of war? No! The text teaches that as long as the Israelites set their sights on High and subjected themselves to their Father in Heaven, they prevailed; otherwise they failed."[22] The battle against Amalek is the essential human struggle, sharing in the divine work of bringing order out of chaos. Yet even in this struggle, the Lord gives us the strength to prevail.

For the journey: There is an Amalek without and an Amalek within. We need to address the inner chaos before we will have success against the outer. We have a divine ally in this struggle. How do we draw upon God's help as Moses did in the original battle against Amalek?

ALL THINGS NEW
Parashat Ki Tavo, Deuteronomy 26:1–29:8

> No matter how much we travel throughout the creation, no matter how many pictures we take of its flowers and mountains, no matter how much knowledge we acquire, if we fail to cultivate wonder we risk missing the very heart of what is going on.[23]

The Promised Land is "a land flowing with milk and honey." This phrase reminds us of the Garden of Eden, where "the LORD God made every tree grow that is pleasant to the sight and good for food" (Gen. 2:9). The Promised Land *flows* with milk and honey—its goodness arises on its own, unlike the post-Eden world, where man must toil and eat in the sweat of his brow (Gen 3:17–19). In the Land, God restores the abundant goodness of the Garden.

> For the land which you go to possess is not like the land of Egypt from which you have come, where you sowed your seed and watered it by foot, as a vegetable garden; but the land which you cross over to possess is a land of hills and valleys, which drinks water from the rain of heaven, a land for which the LORD your God cares; the eyes of the LORD your God are always on it, from the beginning of the year to the very end of the year. (Deut. 11:10–12)

The Torah reinforces the connection between the Promised Land and the Garden by repeating the phrase "land of milk and honey"—three times in this week's parashah, and fifteen times throughout the Torah, in every case but one describing the Promised Land. The exception comes in Numbers 16:13, where Dathan and Abiram challenge Moses, "Is it a small thing that you have brought us up out of a land flowing with milk and honey, to kill us in the wilderness?" Here the land flowing with milk and honey is

Egypt! The rebels reveal their perversity by describing the place that is the very opposite of the Promised Land.

This exception is the eighth appearance of the phrase "land of milk and honey." Seven times—the number of Creation—it describes the Promised Land. One time it is used to describe the opposite, the land of bondage. Then seven more times it describes the Promised Land. The lesson is that the entry to the Promised Land reflects the fullness of God's creative purpose, and the opposite of sin and bondage. It is an essential stage on the journey from Creation to completion, launched in the beginning of all things. Sin may postpone the journey, but it cannot keep the journey from reaching its goal in the end.

If Israel's entry into the Land of Canaan is a reversal of the exile from the Garden, then it must also reverse the disobedience of Adam and Eve. Through Israel, humankind gains another opportunity to obey God and participate in his work of cosmic renewal. Hence, obedience becomes a dominant theme of Deuteronomy, the final series of teachings that prepare Israel to enter the Promised Land. Moses repeatedly instructs the Israelites to obey, as in this parashah: "This day the LORD your God commands you to observe these statutes and judgments; therefore you shall be careful to observe them with all your heart and with all your soul" (Deut. 26:16).

The *Sefat Emet* speaks of this call to obedience in terms not unlike Peterson's call to wonder cited above. It emphasizes the phrase "This day" that opens Deuteronomy 26:16.

> The Midrash and Rashi both say: "Each day these commands should be like new in your eyes." Why "like new"? . . . The renewal is there within everything, since God "renews each day, continually, the work of Creation." . . . Nothing exists without the divine life-force, and the point in each thing that comes from Him never grows old, since His words are constantly alive and flowing.[24]

God's word is alive "this day" and every day. We respond to it through obedience. But Moses goes on to warn Israel that they will not obey, and again, as at the beginning, the result will be exile. If Israel stumbles, the Lord warns, he will not break His covenant with them, but will impose the ultimate consequence of covenant disobedience, exile.

Against the background of Israel's exile throughout history, and especially its horrifying climax in the twentieth century, Moses' warning is haunting:

> Then the LORD will scatter you among all peoples, from one end of the earth to the other, and there you shall serve other gods, which neither you nor your fathers have known—wood and stone. And among those nations you shall find no rest, nor shall the sole of your foot have a resting place; but there the LORD will give you a trembling heart, failing eyes, and anguish of soul. Your life shall hang in doubt before you. (Deut. 28:64–66)

In exile, Israel's very survival hangs in doubt, but exile is not the final word:

> If any of you are driven out to the farthest parts under heaven, from there the LORD your God will gather you, and from there He will bring you. Then the LORD your God will bring you to the land which your fathers possessed, and you shall possess it. He will prosper you and multiply you more than your fathers. And the LORD your God will circumcise your heart and the heart of your descendants, to love the LORD your God with all your heart and with all your soul, that you may live." (Deut. 30:4–6)

In the same way, the final word of the drama of exile in modern times is not the Holocaust. Rather, a great ingathering to the Land of Israel continues in our day. If expulsion from the Garden foreshadows the expulsion from the land of Israel, might the restoration to the land of Israel foreshadow restoration to the Garden? Such restoration, of course, will require a return to God, renewed obedience, and renewed wonder as well.

In the restoration of all things, this renewal will shape everything: "Then He who sat on the throne said, 'Behold I make all things new'" (Rev. 21:5). We partake of this renewal even in our own troubled times as we let God's word shape our lives.

For the journey: In our own minds, we might not link obedience with renewal and wonder, but Scripture seems to do so. Yeshua says, "If you love Me, keep My commandments" (John 14:15). How does obedience to God's word help me to see the Creation, and my everyday life, in a new way?

TWO RETURNEES
Parashat Nitzavim, Deuteronomy 29:9–30:20

> And how does one repent? A sinner should abandon his sinfulness, drive it from his thoughts and conclude in his heart that he will never do it again, as it says, "Let the wicked man abandon his way (Isaiah 55:7).... Additionally, he should regret the past, as it says: "For after I repented, I regretted (Jeremiah 31:18).... And let the sinner call to Him who knows all hidden things to witness that he will never return to sin that sin again. (From *The Laws of Repentance* by Rambam[25])

The name of this parashah, *Nitzavim*, means "you are standing," as if Moses says to Israel, "After all my warnings of exile and cursing in the preceding chapter, you are still standing. God still has a promise of mercy for you."

This promise of mercy will be fulfilled when Israel returns to God, or makes *teshuvah* (from the Hebrew root cua *shuv*, meaning turn, or return). In ten verses of *Parashat Nitzavim*, Moses describes this teshuvah by employing the root shuv seven times:

> And it shall come to pass when all these things come upon you ... and you shall *return* your heart ... and *return* to *Adonai* and heed his voice ... that *Adonai* will *return* your captivity ... and *return* and gather you from all the nations where Adonai your God has scattered you. ... And you shall *return* and heed the voice of *Adonai* ... and *Adonai* will *return* to rejoicing over you ... if you *return* to *Adonai* your God with all your heart and with all your soul. (Deut. 30:1–10, author's translation)

In this passage, the verb shuv has two subjects; Israel must return to the Lord, of course, but the Lord also returns to Israel. In the drama of repentance there are two returnees, God and humankind. "'Return to Me and I will return to you', says the Lord of Hosts" (Mal. 3:7).

So how are we to return to God? As Rambam noted eight hundred years ago, teshuvah involves distinct phases or components. We may summarize these as *recognition* of sin, *regret*, *restitution*, and *resolve*.

The first of the seven "returns" in *Parashat Nitzavim* speaks of recognition: "[A]nd you shall return your heart," or more literally, "you shall return *to* your heart," meaning "come to your senses," or "take to heart" what has happened to you. Without this inner awakening, there can be no return to God. Rambam compares this dramatic recognition to the wake-up call of the shofar at Rosh HaShanah:

> The blowing of the shofar on Rosh Hashanah is an explicit decree of Scripture [Lev. 23:24; Num. 29:1], and it is also a symbol, as if to say, Awake, O you sleepers, awake from your sleep! O you slumberers, awake from your slumber! Search your deeds and turn in teshuvah. Remember your Creator, O you who forget the truth in the vanities of time and go astray all the year after vanity and folly that neither profit nor save. Look to your souls, and better your ways and actions. Let every one of you abandon his evil way and his wicked thoughts, which are not good.[26]

This wake up call leads to *regret*. Modern people often see regret itself as the problem, rather than as an indicator that something else is a problem. Instead of denying such feelings, however, we are to let them drive us to genuine moral change, which will be expressed in *restitution*, doing all we can to reverse the effect of our sin. Restitution often includes confession of sin.

> And he must also confess with his lips and declare those things that he has concluded in his heart. If one confesses verbally but does not resolve in his heart to abandon his sinful ways, he is like one who immerses himself in the ritual bath while holding an impure creature.[27]

Restitution may also mean paying back a debt, returning to the one that we have offended and offering to do whatever it takes to make things right.

Regret and restitution lead us to a fourth stage of teshuvah mentioned above—*resolve* to turn away from sin and back to God and his ways. Resolve means changing our direction from wrongdoing and back to God and his ways. "You shall return to *Adonai* your God with all your heart and with all your soul."

We can see these four stages of teshuvah—recognition, regret, restitution, and resolve—in a story that Messiah once told, about a man and his two sons (Luke 15:11–32).

One day the younger son said to his father,

> "Father, give me the portion of goods that falls to me." So he divided to them his livelihood. And not many days after, the younger son gathered all together, journeyed to a far country, and there wasted his possessions with prodigal living. But when he had spent all, there arose a severe famine in that land and he began to be in want. Then he went and joined himself to a citizen of that country, and he sent him into his fields to feed swine. And he would gladly have filled his stomach with the pods that the swine ate, and no one gave him anything. But when he came to himself. . .

Here we see the first phase of teshuvah, recognition. The son came to himself, or returned to his heart, as our parashah would state it. He woke up and realized that he was standing among the pigs, and longing for their food! And so, when he recognized his condition,

> He said, "How many of my father's hired servants have bread enough and to spare, and I perish with hunger! I will arise and go to my father, and will say to him, 'Father, I have sinned against heaven and before you, and I am no longer worthy to be called your son. Make me like one of your hired servants.'" And he arose and came to his father.

The son displays regret for his sin and is ready to make restitution by returning to his father, confessing his sins, and offering to live with him like a hired servant. Finally, he resolves to return, changing his whole life direction from a journey away from home to a journey back.

The most remarkable element in Yeshua's story, however, is the response of the father. It reveals a fifth stage in teshuvah, which is *restoration*. The son comes to his senses and returns to his father; the father has been ready to return to the son all along.

> But when he was still a great way off, his father saw him and had compassion, and ran and fell on his neck and kissed him. And the son said to him, "Father, I have sinned against heaven and in your sight, and am no longer worthy to be called your son." But the father said to his servants, "Bring out the best robe and put it on him, and put a ring on his hand and sandals on his feet. And bring the fatted calf here and kill it, and let us eat and be merry; for this my son was dead and is alive again; he was lost and is found." And they began to be merry.

Thus, the father embodies the words of the prophet, "Return to me and I will return to you." But the story doesn't end here. Messiah told the story because "[t]he tax collectors and sinners were all drawing near to hear him. And the Pharisees and the scribes murmured, saying, 'This man receives sinners and eats with them'" (Luke 15:1–2). Messiah welcomed the younger son—the sinner—and, with equal love, appealed to the older son—the religious expert.

> Now his older son was in the field. And as he came and drew near to the house, he heard music and dancing. So he called one of the servants and asked what these things meant. And he said to him, "Your brother has come, and because he has received him safe and sound, your father has killed the fatted calf." But he was angry and would not go in. Therefore his father came out and pleaded with him. So he answered and said to his father, "Lo, these many years I have been serving you; I never transgressed your commandment at any time; and yet you never gave me a young goat, that I might make merry with my friends. But as soon as this son of yours came, who has devoured your livelihood with harlots, you killed the fatted calf for him." And he said to him, "Son, you are always with me, and all that I have is yours. It was right that we should make merry

and be glad, for your brother was dead and is alive again, and was lost and is found."

Yeshua doesn't tell us the end of the story, because the end is up to us. So, whichever son *you* are, the invitation from the Father stands: "Return to me and I will return to you."

For the journey: We need to practice teshuvah, continually turning back to God and his ways. We also need to rejoice as others make teshuvah, and not begrudge the bounties of God's forgiveness to anyone. Am I ready to return to God—and to welcome those who return as well?

THE HIDDEN GOD
Parashat Vayelekh, Deuteronomy 31

> Where is Esther indicated in the Torah? — In the verse, And I
> will surely hide [*asteer*] my face.[28]

The sages of the Talmud look for a reference to Esther in the Torah
and find it among the warnings of exile in *Parashat Vayelekh*: "And I
will hide, yes hide my face" (Deut. 31:18). In Hebrew this phrase
reads, *anochi haster asteer panai. Asteer*—"hide"—sounds like the
name Esther, and the phrase "hide the face" describes the conditions of Israel's long exile, which dominate her story.

    Purim, the holiday based on the story of Esther, comes a month
before Passover in the Jewish calendar. Passover, the holiday of freedom, leads to Israel's inheritance of the Promised Land. Purim, in
contrast, is the holiday of exile. At Passover, God revealed himself
openly both to Israel and to Egypt by a mighty hand and an outstretched arm. At Purim, God hid his face, and the story of deliverance is filled with irony and paradox. Mordecai, the hero, advises
Esther to hide her Jewish identity to marry an impetuous and fool-
ish Gentile king. Haman, the villain, is a bungler who habitually
shows up at the wrong time and becomes trapped in his own evil
schemes. The Passover story is majestic; Purim is farcical. Yet both
holidays celebrate a miraculous deliverance by God and are insti-
tuted as days of remembrance forever.

    Purim helps us to understand God's warning that he will hide
his face and understand Israel's subsequent history, which the final
chapters of Deuteronomy describe. As the festival of exile, it also
provides a perspective on our own day.

    The God who works to make himself known throughout Torah
hides his face in the book of Esther. Thus, as numerous commentators have noted, the name of God appears not even once in the
story. In contrast, the Passover story begins with the Lord revealing
himself visibly to Moses in the Burning Bush. Its goal is that "you

shall know that I am HASHEM your God" (Exod. 6:7), and that "the Egyptians will know that I am HASHEM" (Exod. 7:5).

Paradoxically, one contemporary rabbi, Isaac Greenberg, says of the comparison between Passover and Purim that "the holiday of Purim represents a great step forward in the history of revelation."[29] Why does he see Purim as a step forward? Rabbinic Judaism emphasizes free will, and the responsibility to preserve Torah through all difficulties, even when divine help is not at all evident. In this view, Purim is a step forward because human responsibility is more evident than divine intervention.

Passover initiated an entire age of Jewish history that finally ended with the destruction of the Temple and the crushing of Jewish sovereignty by the Romans in the first and second centuries of our era. Purim originated before the destruction of the Temple, but it symbolizes the age inaugurated by that horrendous event. The first age began with a crisis of redemption, Passover; the second age, symbolized by Purim, began with a crisis of destruction.

In modern times we have witnessed a re-enactment of these two crises, but in reverse order; first the destruction of European Jewry under the Nazis, and then redemption—the restoration of Jewish sovereignty over the land of Israel. These events, especially coming at the same moment of history, seem nearly as significant as the events described in Scripture. Greenberg argues that these events mirror Purim more than Passover, that God's face remains hidden, even though redemption is evident.

> Purim is the holiday for the post-Holocaust world; it is the model for the experience of redemption in the rebirth of Israel. In this era, too, the redemption is flawed—by the narrow escape, by the great loss of life, by the officially "irreligious" nature of the leadership, by the mixed motives and characters of those who carried it out, by the human suffering it brought in its wake, and by the less-than-perfect society of Israel.[30]

In the post-Holocaust world, God's face may remain hidden, but there has been a resurgence of the most traditional, God-centered branches of Judaism, and the rise of a viable Messianic Jewish community. For Messianic Jews, and many traditional Jews as well, the restoration of Israel, even with all its problems, is not so much a flawed redemption as an open intervention of the divine, a modern replay of the Exodus from Egypt.

Parashat Vayelekh warns that God will hide his face because of our sins, but it sounds a note of hope as well. After Moses records its warnings, he inaugurates Joshua as Israel's new leader with words from the Lord: "Be strong and of good courage; for you shall bring the children of Israel into the land of which I swore to them, and I will be with you" (Deut. 31:23).

Our times are filled with hiddenness and with hope. Purim and Passover converge. God intervenes in our affairs, but in ways that seem obscure. Israel has been restored, yet we remain in exile. Human beings seem to be in charge, but evidence of God's redemptive purposes abounds to those who look for it. In this era, God speaks through paradox, perhaps even the great paradox of a Jewish Messiah ignored by the Jewish world for twenty centuries.

> He will not quarrel nor cry out,
> Nor will anyone hear His voice in the streets.
> A bruised reed He will not break,
> And smoking flax He will not quench,
> Till He sends forth justice to victory;
> And in His name Gentiles will trust. (Matt. 12:19–21)

Matthew quotes this prophecy of Isaiah to portray a hidden Messiah who will reveal himself to those looking for him in this age and beyond. Indeed, in this Messiah, God's face is hidden no longer: "For it is the God who once said, 'Let light shine out of darkness,' who has made his light shine in our hearts, the light of the knowledge of God's glory shining in the face of the Messiah Yeshua" (2 Cor. 4:6, CJB).

For the journey: Esther and Mordecai lived in a time when God hid his face, yet they were agents of God's purpose for the whole Jewish people. Is it possible that God is doing the same thing today—working among us when we cannot even see him? How do we cooperate with God's purposes in such conditions?

TORAH AND SPIRIT
Parashat Ha'azinu, Deuteronomy 32

> Levi [a young Hasidic rabbi] doesn't teach Torah in any structured way to the addicts he works with, but he brings Judaism into every counseling session by talking about the value of life and what that person can contribute. "I explain to them that they're not nothing. . . . I tell them, 'God created this world as an imperfect place. He implanted a piece of Himself in each one of us, and there's one part of this world that will not be perfect until you make it so. It's out there waiting for you.'"[31]

As Moses completes the writing of the Torah, he knows that his death is near, so he writes a song warning Israel of their future sins and that "evil will befall you in the latter days" (Deut. 31:29). Songs in the Torah, say the rabbis, transcend time, and look into the past, present, and future. Thus, Moses' song, which peers into the future, also looks back to the very beginning, thus providing a framework for the entire Torah.

Where does the song refer to the beginning? Two verses contain a clue:

> He found him in the wilderness land,
> in the *waste* of the howling desert.
> He encircled him, gave mind to him,
> watched him like the apple of His eye.
> Like an eagle who rouses his nest,
> over his fledglings he *hovers*,
> He spread His wings, He took him,
> He bore him on His pinion. (Deut. 32:10–11, Alter;
> emphasis added)

Two Hebrew words appear only in these verses and one other place in the entire Torah, Genesis 1:2, highlighting again the big story of Creation to completion.

The first of the two special words in this verse is *tohu*, translated as "waste." As we have seen, Genesis 1:2 opens, "And the earth was tohu vavohu—chaos and void," or "wild and waste" (Fox). This rarely used word describes the chaos of Creation in its primitive state, out of which God will form the beauty and goodness of heaven and earth.

The *Midrash* also notices the unusual word "waste" in this passage.

> Consider the verse, *He found him in a desert land . . .* for the world was a desert before Israel came out of Egypt. *And in the waste, a howling wilderness*; waste and howling was the world before Israel came out of Egypt and before they received the Torah. He did not tarry, but as soon as Israel departed from Egypt and received the Torah, what does Scripture say? *He compassed him about, He gave him understanding, He kept him as the apple of His eye. 'He compassed him about'* [or 'he encircled him' as above] means that He set clouds of glory around them.[32]

Just as tohu or "waste" describes the unformed state of the heavens and earth at the beginning of Creation, so it describes the unformed state of the world before the revelation at Mount Sinai. As we have seen, the redemption from Egypt is a new Creation that begins to restore the order of the original Creation.

Not only Israel, but ultimately all followers of Messiah fit into this vast scheme of cosmic restoration. As Levi the Torah teacher says, "There's one part of this world that will not be perfect until you make it so. It's out there waiting for you."

But how are we able to find this part, and join with the Creator in his work of renewal?

The Midrash above detects a remez, or hint, that will help answer this question when it says "He set clouds of glory around" Israel. Where does it get this idea?

This question brings us to our second repeated word, "hovers" or *yirachef*—"over his fledglings he hovers." The same verb appears in slightly different form in Genesis 1:2: "The spirit of God hovered (*m'rachefet*) over the face of the deep." Genesis portrays this spirit as the creative, life-giving breath of God, about to bring forth life and order from the great deep. This same Spirit of God, present at Creation to bring order out of chaos, is present in the glory-cloud that accompanies the Israelites during the Exodus from Egypt. As Isaiah writes:

> Then he remembered the days of old, Moses and his people, saying:
> "Where is He who brought them up out of the sea
> With the shepherd of His flock?
> Where is He who put His Holy Spirit within [or among] them?
> (Isa. 63:11, 14)

The same idea appears in the book of Nehemiah:

> Yet in Your manifold mercies You did not forsake them in the wilderness.
> The pillar of the cloud did not depart from them by day,
> To lead them on the road;
> Nor the pillar of fire by night,
> To show them light,
> And the way they should go.
> You also gave Your good Spirit to instruct them. (Neh. 9:19–20a)

The Spirit of God, which appears at the very beginning as the divine creative force bringing order out of tohu vavohu (the wild and waste of the primordial chaos), accompanies Israel in the pillar of cloud. This divine presence not only guides Israel in its wanderings, but also dwells in the tabernacle in the midst of the camp of Israel. The connection is clear: the work begun at Creation continues in Israel as the chosen people. God redeems the seed of Abraham from the bondage of Egypt to establish his creative and renewing presence among them. He will lead Israel by his Spirit, and dwell in the midst of the camp of Israel in a cloud of glory. Thus, the call of Israel is an essential stage in the journey from Creation to completion.

Whether we are Jewish or Gentile, as we seek to find our part in this journey, there is a clear message for us as well. The same creative, life-giving spirit dwells among the community of those united with Messiah Yeshua. "For it was by one Spirit that we were all immersed into one body, whether Jews or Gentiles, slaves or free; and we were all given the one Spirit to drink (1 Cor. 12:13).

> For you are the temple of the living God. As God has said:
>> I will dwell in them
>> And walk among them.
>> I will be their God,
>> And they shall be My people. (2 Cor. 6:16)

The Spirit of God dwells in the midst of those who follow Messiah. Through his power, we find and fulfill our part on the way to Creation fulfilled.

For the journey: Levi, the young rabbi, says "There's one part of this world that will not be perfect until you make it so. It's out there waiting for you." May I be on the watch for this part of the world today.

"THIS IS THE BLESSING . . ."
Parashat V'zot HaBrachah, Deuteronomy 33:1–34:12

> Favor them, Oh Lord, with happiness and peace.
> Oh, hear our Sabbath prayer. Amen.[33]

Just as the six days of Creation conclude with the blessing of Shabbat, so the Torah itself, the story of Creation to completion, concludes with a blessing. Moses stands before the tribes of Israel, who are about to enter the land of promise without him, and pronounces blessings upon them, as the final act of his public life.

We might consider all of chapter 33 to be the blessing, beginning with Moses' words over the first of the twelve tribes, "Let Reuben live, and not die." (Deut. 33:6) Sforno, however, in his comments on this chapter, claims that the blessing does not begin until verse 25. In the preceding verses, Moses prays for each of the tribes, one by one, but, says Sforno, "words of blessing are always said when speaking directly to the one who is being blessed." Therefore, he believes that the blessing begins as Moses addresses Israel directly, concluding with the words,

> Happy are you, O Israel!
> Who is like you, a people saved by the LORD,
> The shield of your help
> And the sword of your majesty!
> Your enemies shall submit to you,
> And you shall tread down their high places. (Deut. 33:29)

Before this passage, Moses speaks *of* the tribes; now he speaks *to* the tribes. Before, he speaks almost entirely in the third person, calling each tribe "he." Now, he speaks in the second person, addressing the tribes directly as "you." If we accept Sforno's conclusion that the blessing begins at verse 25, we notice another significant shift in emphasis. Before this verse, Moses speaks to each tribe separately; now he speaks to the all the tribes at once.

Here is a theme that plays throughout Scripture: Unity brings blessing. Moses can pray for the tribes separately, but blessing will rest upon them collectively, when they dwell together as one. This interpretation is borne out by verse 5:

> And He was King in Jeshurun,
> When the leaders of the people were gathered,
> All the tribes of Israel together.

Jeshurun, or more accurately Yeshurun, is the name of Israel as the ideal people of God, based on the root rah *yashar*, meaning upright, pleasing, or straight.[34] When Israel gathers as one, they become Yeshurun, the upright people whose king is the Lord himself. As Rashi comments (on Deut. 33:5), "When they are gathered together in a single group and there is peace among them, He is their king, but not when there is discord among them."

A recent biography of Benjamin Franklin notes that he advocated unity among the British colonies in North America long before he advocated their independence. As a pragmatist, Franklin saw that the colonies could accomplish far more together than they could separately. When the colonies were threatened by French military successes in the Ohio River Valley in 1754—twenty-two years before the Declaration of Independence—Franklin printed "the first and most famous editorial cartoon in American history: a snake cut into pieces, labeled with the names of the colonies, with the caption, 'Join, or Die.'"[35]

Likewise, the tribes of Israel struggled for centuries to unite for military defense and improved commerce, from the time of the Judges until the rise of Saul and David. Beyond the pragmatic considerations of defense and trade, however, is the blessing that comes upon unity. Moses might well have said to the tribes, "Join, or Die . . . without the full blessing that God intends." The blessing that God imparts through Moses is far more powerful than Israel's united military strength. With the blessing, they will become a people under the divine shelter and sustained by the arms of the eternal One, "a people saved by the LORD."

V'zot HaBrachah is the parashah read in the synagogue on the festival of *Simchat Torah*, or "Rejoicing in Torah." On this day, just after Sukkot, we reach the end of the annual cycle of readings at Deuteronomy 34, and start over again at Genesis 1. Thus, we express a value that has unified Israel through its history, and may bring unity today as well. In *V'zot HaBrachah*, Moses reminds Israel of God's revelation at Mount Sinai a generation before. There,

> Moses commanded Torah for us,
> A heritage of the congregation of Jacob. (Deut. 33: 4)

This heritage is the Scriptures, beginning with the Five Books of Moses and becoming the complete canon, which for believers in Yeshua includes the writings of the B'rit Hadashah. In Messiah, it becomes the heritage of all nations as well as of the Jewish people.

The community of Yeshua's followers encompasses diverse streams and traditions, but we have a potent source of unity: the Scriptures themselves, the source of the life-changing story of Creation fulfilled. We may read these Scriptures differently, but we are united in seeing them as divine revelation, and we are united in seeing that this revelation reaches its culmination in Yeshua the Messiah, the Living Torah. This affirmation of the whole body of Scripture that rests on the foundation of Torah, and of Yeshua as Lord and Messiah, is a unique and precious legacy. May we not abandon the blessing of unity carelessly, but instead build upon this legacy.

The Torah concludes with a blessing to remind us that it began with a blessing. When God created man and woman in his image, before they had done anything to merit it, he blessed them. Now, as Israel is about to enter the Promised Land, before they have fulfilled God's purpose, he imparts a blessing again. As Yeshua's friend Peter wrote, "[K]now that you were called to this, that you may inherit a blessing" (1 Pet. 3:9).

For the journey: Torah concludes with a blessing, and so do all the Scriptures that arise from it. May we who read and study these words inherit a blessing as well: "Blessed is he who keeps the words of the prophecy of this book. Blessed are those who do His commandments, that they may have the right to the tree of life, and may enter through the gates into the city" (Rev. 22:7, 14).

EPILOGUE

"Turn it, and turn it, for everything is in it. Reflect on it and grow old and gray with it. Don't turn from it, for nothing is better than it." (Pirke Avot 5.22)

When an author finishes a book, I imagine he or she hopes to have included everything that is relevant to the subject at hand, and to have left nothing out. In my case, however, the opposite is true. I could go through the entire cycle of Torah readings again and discover endless material that has been left out of this book. God gave us his Torah to be our life-long text of learning and growth, and it rewards multiple readings.

As we saw in Parashat Masa'ei, when we finish a book of the Torah, we encourage each other with the words *Hazak! Hazak! v'nit'chazek!* Be strong! Be strong! And let us be strengthened! [to carry out the instructions we have just read]. That's why on Simchat Torah, the festival when we rejoice at having received this book of instruction, we immediately read Genesis 1, after concluding Deuteronomy 34. We start learning again.

This is my encouragement to you as well. Keep journeying by studying the Scriptures, seeking within them not only inspiration and truth, but also instruction for life. A life that is guided by the age-old wisdom of Scripture will be fruitful and fulfilling.

The instruction above to "Turn it, and turn it" supports the tradition of reading through the entire Torah each year. Whether or not you follow this specific tradition, however, I encourage you to practice daily study of God's Word.

Another old saying tells us to work as if it all depends on us, and pray as if it all depends on God. We know that it all really does depend on God, but our efforts are significant, as well. Indeed, the theme of Creation to Completion is that God has designed things from the beginning to involve human beings like you and me in his redemptive purposes for the world.

These two old sayings come together in this: We have a vital role to play during our days on earth, and it is in continual engagement with Scripture that we discover our part, and find the power to fulfill it.

Thank you for letting me have input into your life-long journey. May the Lord bless you and keep you.

NOTES

1. Alter translation.

Introduction

1. Fried 93.
2. Kravitz and Olitzky, *Pirke Avot* 1:2.
3. Fox 910.
4. Chavel 169.
5. Freedman and Simon, Genesis xxviii.
6. Ibid. Numbers 13:15–16.
7. Kravitz and Olitzky, *Pirke Avot* 2:16.

Genesis

1. Alter 14.
2. Scherman.
3. *Chavel, Genesis,* 23.
4. Freedman 6.
5. Freedman and Simon, Genesis 19:9.
6. *Soncino Talmud,* Sotah 14a.
7. *Zohar,* 73a.
8. Buber 111.
9. Goldin 132.
10. Fox translation.
11. Freedman and Simon, Genesis 39.9.
12. Ibid. Genesis 56:3.
13. Friedlander 31.
14. Kravitz and Olitzky, *Pirke Avot* 1.2.
15. Fox, Gen. 23:1–2.
16. Freedman and Simon, Genesis 18:3.
17. Ibid. Genesis 8:13.
18. *Soncino Talmud,* Sotah 14a.

19. "There Is a River." Words and Music by Max and David Sapp, 1969.
20. Chavel, Genesis 169.
21. *Soncino Talmud,* Shabbath 21b.
22. Neusner, *Sukkah* 4:5.
23. Ibid. *Sukkah* 5:1.
24. Freedman and Simon, Genesis 70:8.
25. Chavel, Deuteronomy 28.
26. Ten Boom, Sherrill, and Sherrill 99.
27. Wyschogrod 180, emphasis added.
28. Ibid. 184–185.
29. Ibid. 186.
30. Freedman and Simon, Deuteronomy 2:12.
31. Ibid. Genesis 93:6.

Exodus

1. Fox 241.
2. Peterson 167.
3. Maimonides 154.
4. Pelcovitz, Exod. 6:6.
5. Dylan, "Gotta Serve Somebody," from *Slow Train Coming.*
6. Kravitz and Olitzky, *Pirke Avot* 3:15.
7. Buxbaum 149.
8. *Soncino Talmud*, Sotah 30b.
9. Freedman and Simon, Exodus 6:4.
10. Ginzberg, vol. III, 92.
11. Tolkien 282.
12. Bialik, and Rawnitzki 459.
13. *Soncino Talmud*, Shabbath 70a and 97b.
14. Sarna, *Exploring Exodus*, 213.
15. Ibid. 214.
16. Hashem, or HaShem, meaning "The Name," is a term used for God in Jewish writings. See glossary.
17. Arthur Green, trans. *The Language of Truth: The Torah Commentary of the Sefat Emet.* (Philadelphia: Jewish Publication Society, 1998) p. 132.
18. Freedman 44–45.

19. Adapted from Encyclopedia Judaica.
21. *Freedman and Simon,* Exodus 40:2.
22. Ibid. Genesis 2:4.
23. Ibid. Exodus 40:4.
24. Friedman xii.
25. Green 140.

Leviticus

1. Alter 541–542.
2. *Israel Today,* December 15, 2005.
3. Herczeg, Leviticus 2.
4. *Scherman* 544, emphasis added.
5. Buber, Vol. II, 59.
6. Alter 564.
7. Wiesel 11.
8. Hilberg 262–266.
9. "Letter Placed by Pope John Paul II at the Western Wall."
10. Green 167.
11. Ibid.
12. Sarna, *JPS Torah Commentary, Exodus,* 125.
13. *Soncino Talmud,* Sanhedrin 98b.
14. Ibid. Sanhedrin 98a.
15. Ibid. Yoma 67b.
16. Weinberg 168.
17. Chavel, Leviticus, 220.
18. Ibid.
19. Hertz 484.
20. Robinson 98.
21. Ibid. 49.
22. Ibid. 98.
23. *Behind the Scenes with the Left Behind Series.*
24. *Soncino Talmud,* Tamid 33b.
25. Dylan, "Forever Young," from *Planet Waves.*
26. *Soncino Talmud,* Tamid 33b.
27. Telushkin 147.
28. Pelcovitz 614.
29. Kravitz and Olitzky, *Pirke Avot* 2:7.

Numbers

1. Vermes 9.
2. Silverman 20.
3. *Chavel*, Numbers 54–55. Note the use of "G-d" in place of "God" here, a traditional way to avoid any possible transgression of the commandment, "You shall not take the name of the Lord your God in vain" (Exod. 20:7).
4. *JPS Hebrew-English Tanakh*.
5. Molloy
6. Milgrom 343.
7. Ibid.
8. Ibid. 344.
9. Ibid. 345.
10. Ibid. 346.
11. Lewis 707.
12. Pelcovitz, Numbers 16:14.
13. *Soncino Talmud*, Pesachim 54a.
14. Milgrom 410.
15. Kravitz and Olitzky, *Pirke Avot* 5:9.
16. Milgrom 182.
17. Fishkoff 61.
18. *Soncino Talmud*, Bava Batra 75a.
19. Fox, Gen. 1:2.
20. McCullough 289.
21. Freedman and Simon, Numbers 23:1.
22. Ibid. 23:3.

Deuteronomy

1. Tigay xiv–xv.
2. Pelcovitz 828.
3. *Freedman and Simon*, Deuteronomy 7:12.
4. Berlin and Brettler.
5. Buxbaum 5.
6. Luzatto 18.
7. Nulman 294.
8. Berlin and Brettler.
9. "New Orleans mayor orders looting crackdown."
10. Kravitz and Olitzky, *Pirke Avot* 1:3.

11. Maimonides 521–522.
12. Herczeg, Exodus, 235.
13. Maimonides 364.
14. Ibid. 363–364.
15. Ibid. 365.
16. Lustiger 76.
17. Nulman 202–204.
18. Lustiger 77
19. Ibid 78.
20. Ibid.
21. Ibid.
22. Sarna, *JPS Torah Commentary, Exodus*, 70.
23. Peterson 122.
24. Green 323–324.
25. *Yom Kippur* 61.
26. *Rosh Hashanah* 59.
27. *Yom Kippur* 61.
28. *Soncino Talmud*, Chullin 139b.
29. Greenberg 1.
30. Ibid. 2.
31. Fishkoff 308.
32. *Freedman and Simon*, Numbers 2:6.
33. "Sabbath Prayer" from *Fiddler on the Roof*. Words by Sheldon Harnick, 1971.
34. See *Parashat Vayishlach*, and note 25 in Genesis.
35. Isaacson 159.

GLOSSARY

Adonai. Hebrew for "Lord." In many instances it serves as a substitute for the ineffable name of God, spelled with the four Hebrew letters יהוה or YHVH.

Aggadah. From the verb "to tell." Stories, legends, anecdotes, and sayings in the Talmud, *Midrash*, and other rabbinic literature, often based on the narrative of the Torah, that illustrate biblical truths.

Amidah. From the Hebrew for "standing," this is a series of blessings recited daily in traditional prayer services.

B'rit Hadashah. Hebrew for "New Covenant," used as an alternate name for the New Testament.

Cohen. A priest, a member of the tribe of Levi and the family of Aaron, who performed essential rituals in the tabernacle and temple. Jewish tradition has retained special roles for *cohanim* (plural of cohen) until this day.

G'milut hasadim. Deeds of loving kindness, such as visiting the sick, burying the dead, or attending a wedding, which Jewish thought considers foundational to a righteous life.

Gematria. The study of the numerical values of Hebrew letters and words.

Halakhah. From the verb "to go," Halakhah refers to the body of rulings derived from Torah that have shaped the Jewish "walk" or way of life since the earliest times.

Hashem. Literally "the name." This is a circumlocution for the unpronounceable name of God, spelled יהוה or YHVH.

Hoshana Rabbah. "The great Hosanna." The final day of Sukkot or Tabernacles, which concludes the festival with great rejoicing.

Huppah. The canopy under which the bride and groom stand to exchange vows in the traditional Jewish wedding.

Ibn Ezra, Abraham. Born in Tudela, Spain, in 1089, he spent his later years wandering throughout the Mediterranean world and died in 1164. A poet and thinker as well as Torah scholar, his commentary was second only to Rashi's in popularity, but today much of it has been lost.

Ketubah. A marriage contract signed by the bride and groom in the traditional Jewish wedding ceremony.

Levi. A Levite or member of the tribe of Levi, which was charged with the care and performance of tabernacle and temple ritual.

Midrash. An interpretation of the text of Scripture, often highly imaginative, seeking to bring out meaning beyond the plain sense. Midrash employs word play, verbal echoes, context, and other literary qualities in creative ways. The plural is midrashim.

Midrash Rabbah. A collection of midrashim on the five books of Moses and the five *megillot* or scrolls (Esther, Ruth, Lamentations, Song of Songs, and *Kohelet* [Eccelesiastes]), which was compiled beginning in the early fifth century CE, but contains older material as well.

Mishnah. A collection of Jewish laws and legal discussions compiled in about 200 CE by Rabbi Judah the Prince. Later commentaries on the Mishnah are comprised in *Gemara.* Mishnah plus Gemara form the Talmud.

Mitzvot. Hebrew for "commandments" given by God.

Parashah. One of the 54 weekly portions of the Torah, which together constitute the weekly reading cycle. Each parashah has a title, usually based on one of the first words in that section. When the term parashah is combined with the specific name of the section, its form changes slightly according to the rules of Hebrew grammar. Hence, we say *Parashat B'resheet* ("In the beginning"), not *Parashah B'resheet.* The plural form is parashiyot.

Pesach. Known in English as Passover, the holiday that celebrates the Exodus from Egypt.

Rambam. Acronym for Rabbi Moshe ben Maimon, or Maimonides, the premier Jewish figure of the Middle Ages. He was born in Cordoba, Spain, in 1135, but spent most of his adult life in Egypt, where he served as a physician, adviser to the sultan, and Jewish community leader, as well as writing extensively on Scripture, Jewish law, and philosophy. He died in 1204.

Ramban. Acronym for Rabbi Moses ben Nachman, or Nachmanides, born in Spain in 1195. Ramban wrote extensively in many fields, including Torah. He participated in the most famous of the disputations that the Catholic Church forced upon medieval rabbis, the Barcelona disputation of 1263, after which   he found it prudent to leave Spain for Israel, where he died   in 1270.

Rosh HaShanah. Hebrew for "Head of the Year." The traditional Jewish New Year, which is the beginning of a ten-day period of repentance leading up to Yom Kippur (Lev. 23:23–24).

Rashi. Acronym for Rabbi Shlomo ben Isaac, born in Troyes, France in 1040. His Torah commentary brings together the best of earlier commentaries and remains definitive to this day. He also produced a definitive commentary on the Talmud, even as he made his living tending several vineyards that he owned. He lived through a period of mounting anti-Jewish persecution in France and Germany, especially in his later years, and died in 1105.

Shechinah. From the verb "to dwell." This post-biblical rabbinic term refers to the glorious presence of God, especially as it appears on an earthly plane.

Seder. Hebrew for "order." Refers to the order of the ritual meal eaten at Passover to remember the Exodus from Egypt.

Sefat Emet. "The language of truth," a nineteenth-century rabbinic commentary on the Torah by Rabbi Yehudah Leib Alter of Ger, in Poland.

Septuagint. The ancient Greek translation of the Hebrew Scriptures widely used during Yeshua's time, it is the source of many of the quotations from the Tanakh (Old Testament) that appear in the B'rit Hadashah (New Testament).

Sforno. Obadiah ben Jacob Sforno, born in Cesena, Italy, around 1470. He studied philosophy, mathematics, philology, and medicine in Rome, and became a physician. He is best known for his commentary on the Torah.

Shabbat. Hebrew for "[day of] rest; Sabbath." Shabbat is the seventh day of the week, lasting from Friday sunset to Saturday sunset. God commanded Israel to cease from work on this day and to assemble for worship (Exod. 20:8–11; Lev. 23:3).

Shavuot. The Feast of Weeks, falling forty-nine days, or a "week of weeks" after Passover. It celebrates the grain harvest, which takes place in the late Spring or early Summer in the land of Israel (Lev. 23:15–21). According to tradition, it also marks the giving of the Torah on Mount Sinai. It was during Shavuot that the Holy Spirit was poured out after the resurrection of Messiah (Acts 2).

Shofar. The trumpet made of a ram's horn that appears throughout Scripture as an instrument of alarm, proclamation, and praise. It is used to this day in Jewish worship, particularly on Rosh HaShanah, the Jewish New Year.

Siddur. The traditional Jewish prayer book. References from the Siddur are the author's translation, compared with traditional sources.

Sukkot. The Feast of Booths, or Tabernacles, commemorating Israel's forty years in the desert before entering the Promised Land. During this period, Israel was vulnerable to the elements and fully dependent on God, a reality symbolized by their dwelling in sukkot (Lev. 23:33–43; Deut. 8).

Talmud. The vast collection of discussions of Torah and its laws, which was committed to writing, first in the Land of Israel in the fifth century, and then in Babylon a century later. The Talmud contains both Halakhah, which comprises discussions of legal requirements based on the text of Scripture, and Aggadah, which comprises stories, legends, anecdotes, and sayings that expand and illustrate biblical principles.

Talmid, talmidim (pl.). The Hebrew term for disciples, based on the root *lmd*, meaning to learn or teach.

Tanakh. An acronym for the Hebrew Scriptures comprising Torah, Nevi'im or Prophets, and Ketuvim or Holy Writings. These books are the same as in the Christian Old Testament, although in a different order. Messianic Jews and other students of Scripture tend to avoid the term Old Testament because it implies antiquation or obsolescence.

Tish'ah B'Av. The ninth day of the month of Av, a date that commemorates the greatest tragedies in Jewish history, including the destruction of the first and second temples in Jerusalem.

Tikkun Olam, or simply *Tikkun.* A Hebrew phrase meaning "repair" or "restoration of the world." This refers to various practices and activities that reverse the cycle of sin and corruption in the created order, and contribute to the fulfillment of God's purposes for Creation.

Torah. From a Hebrew root meaning "instruction." Torah refers primarily to the Five Books of Moses, Genesis through Deuteronomy, but is sometimes used to apply to the entire body of Scripture, or to the body of rabbinic commentary and writing that arose out of discussions on the Five Books of Moses. Torah is best understood not as law, but as an extended instruction that includes poetic and historic narratives, detailed ordinances for all aspects of the life of Israel, and broad ethical principles as well.

Yeshiva. The traditional Jewish study hall, in which students learn Torah, Talmud and other rabbinic literature in an informal, highly interactive, and intensive fashion.

Yeshua. Hebrew for "Adonai (the Lord) saves." Yeshua is Jesus' Hebrew name.

Yom HaShoah. Holocaust Remembrance Day, which occurs in the Spring, shortly after Passover.

Yom Kippur. Hebrew for "Day of Atonement." The holiest day of the Jewish calendar; a fast day, the culmination of a ten-day period of repentance and prayer for the forgiveness of sin (Lev. 16; 23:26–32).

BIBLIOGRAPHY

Alter, Robert. *The Five Books of Moses: A Translation with Commentary.* New York: W. W. Norton & Company, 2004.

Behind the Scenes with the Left Behind Series (Part 1). http://www.leftbehind.com.

Berlin, Adele, and Marc Zvi Brettler, eds. *The Jewish Study Bible.* New York: Oxford University Press, 2004.

Bialik, Hayyim Nahman, and Yehoshua Hana Rawnitzki, eds. *The Book of Legends—Sefer Ha-Aggadah: Legends from the Talmud and Midrash.* Translated by William G. Braude. New York: Schocken Books, 1992.

Buber, Martin. *Tales of the Hasidim.* New York: Schocken Books, 1991.

Buxbaum, Yitzhak. *Jewish Spiritual Practices.* Northvale, NJ: Jason Aronson, 1990.

Chavel, Charles B., trans. *Ramban: Commentary on the Torah.* New York: Shilo Publishing House, 1971.

Dylan, Bob. *Planet Waves.* Columbia Records, 1974.

Dylan, Bob. *Slow Train Coming.* Columbia Records, 1979.

Encyclopedia Judaica. Jerusalem: Judaica Multimedia, Ltd.

Fishkoff, Sue. *The Rebbe's Army: Inside the World of Chabad-Lubavitch.* New York: Schocken Books, 2003.

Fox, Everett. *The Five Books of Moses.* New York: Schocken Books, 1995.

Freedman, David Noel. *The Nine Commandments: Uncovering the Hidden Pattern of Crime and Punishment in the Hebrew Bible.* New York: Doubleday, 2000.

Freedman, H., and Simon Maurice, eds. and trans. *Midrash Rabbah.* London, New York: Soncino Press, 1983.

Fried, Stephen. *The New Rabbi: A Congregation Searches for Its Leader.* New York: Bantam Books, 2002.

Friedlander, Gerald, trans. *Pirke de Rabbi Eliezer, Scholar PDF Edition.* Skokie, IL: Varda Books, 2004.

Friedman, Dayle A., ed. *Jewish Pastoral Care: A Practical Handbook from Traditional and Contemporary Sources.* Woodstock, VT: Jewish Lights Publishing, 2001.

Ginzberg, Louis. *The Legends of the Jews.* Philadelphia: Jewish Publication Society, 1987.

Goldin, Judah, trans. *The Fathers According to Rabbi Nathan.* New Haven: Yale University Press, 1955.

Green, Arthur, trans. *The Language of Truth: The Torah Commentary of the Sefat Emet.* Philadelphia: Jewish Publication Society, 1998.

Greenberg, Isaac. "A New Stage of Revelation," excerpted from *The Jewish Way: Living the Holidays* (New York: Touchstone, 1988) at http://www.beliefnet.com/story/15/story_1511 _1.html.

Herczeg, Yisrael Isser Zvi, trans. *The Torah: With Rashi's Commentary.* Brooklyn: Mesorah Publications, 1997.

Hertz, J. H., ed. *The Pentateuch and Haftorahs.* London: Soncino Press, 1971.

Hilberg, Raul. *Perpetrators, Victims, Bystanders.* New York: Harper Collins, 1992.

Isaacson, Walter. *Benjamin Franklin: An American Life.* New York: Simon & Schuster, 2003.

JPS Hebrew-English Tanakh: The Traditional Hebrew Text and the New JPS Translation, Scholar PDF Edition [NJPS]. Skokie, IL: Varda Books, 2001.

Kravitz, Leonard, and Kerry M. Olitzky, eds. and trans. *Pirke Avot: A Modern Commentary on Jewish Ethics.* New York: UAHC Press, 1993.

"Letter Placed by Pope John Paul II at the Western Wall." Israeli Ministry of Foreign Affairs, 26 March 2000, http://www.mfa .gov.il/mfa/go.asp?MFAH0ho60.

Lewis, C.S. *The Chronicles of Narnia*, The Last Battle. New York: HarperCollins, 1994.

Linetsky, Michael, trans. *Rabbi Abraham Ibn Ezra's Commentary on the Creation.* Northvale, NJ: Jason Aronson, 1998.

The Lord of the Rings: The Two Towers. DVD, 179 min. New Line Productions, Inc., 2002.

Lustiger, Arnold, ed. *Before Hashem You Shall Be Purified: Rabbi Joseph B. Soloveitchik on the Days of Awe.* Edison, NJ: Ohr Publishing, 1998.

Luzatto, Chaim Moshe. *The Path of the Upright: Mesillat Yesharim.* Translated by Mordecai M. Kaplan. Northvale, NJ: Jason Aronson, 1995.

Maimonides, Moses. *The Guide of the Perplexed.* Translated by Shlomo Pines. Chicago: The University of Chicago Press, 1963.

McCullough, David. *1776.* New York: Simon & Schuster, 2005.

Milgrom, Jacob. *The JPS Torah Commentary, Numbers. Scholar PDF Edition.* Skokie, IL: Varda Books, 2004.

Molloy, John T. *The New Dress for Success.* New York: Warner Books, 1988.

Neusner, Jacob, trans. *The Mishnah: A New Translation.* New Haven and London: Yale University Press, 1988.

"New Orleans mayor orders looting crackdown." www.msnbc.msn .com, Sept. 1, 2005.

Nulman, Macy. *The Encyclopedia of Jewish Prayer.* Northvale, NJ: Jason Aronson, 1993.

Pelcovitz, Raphael, trans. *Sforno: Commentary on the Torah.* Brooklyn: Mesorah Publications, 2001.

Peterson, Eugene H. *Christ Plays in Ten Thousand Places: A Conversa-*

OTHER RELATED BOOKS FROM
MESSIANIC JEWISH PUBLISHERS

Complete Jewish Bible

Presenting the Word of God as a unified Jewish book, here is an English translation for Jews and non-Jews alike. Names and key terms are presented in easy-to-understand transliterated Hebrew, enabling the reader to pronounce them the way Yeshua (Jesus) did! 1,697 pages

Available in Hardback, Paperback, and Blue Bonded Leather

They Loved the Torah

What Yeshua's First Followers Really Thought About the Law
Did Yeshua observe the law? Did Paul teach congregations to abandon the Torah? Is there a place for the "Old" Testament in churches today? Most Christians are disconnected from their Jewish roots. Reading this book will reconnect them. 144 pages

The Voice of the Lord

Messianic Jewish Daily Devotional
Here are words of encouragement that offer insight into the Jewish Scriptures–both Old and New Testaments. Twenty-two prominent contributors provide practical ways to apply biblical truth. 416 pages

Kingdom Relationships

God's Laws for the Community of Faith
Focuses on the teaching of the Torah (the five books of Moses), tapping into truths that help modern-day members of the Body. Paul had the Torah in mind when he wrote "all Scripture is valuable for teaching the truth, convicting of sin, correcting faults, and training in right living." 64 pages

More resources continued on next page

God's Appointed Times

A Practical Guide for Understanding and Celebrating the Biblical Holidays
How can the biblical holy days such as Passover/Unleavened Bread and Tabernacles be observed? What do they mean for Christians today? Discusses historical background, traditional Jewish observance, New Testament relevance, and prophetic significance. 155 pages

God's Appointed Customs

A Messianic Jewish Guide to the Biblical Lifecycle and Lifestyle
Explains how biblical customs(like circumcision and the wedding) impact both Jews and Christians. Two sections: "Biblical Lifecycle" and "Biblical Lifestyle." Each chapter offers historical background, traditional Jewish observance, and relevance to the New Testament. 170 pages

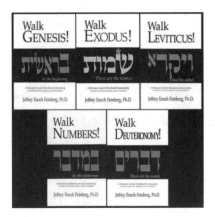

Five-book Walk! Series
Messianic Jewish Devotional Commentaries
Each section includes a brief Hebrew lesson for the beginner, key biblical concepts, and practical applications. A devotional and Bible study tool. Each book is over 200 pages and is available individually.